# Methodology of Uniform Contract Law

Maren Heidemann

# Methodology of Uniform Contract Law

## The UNIDROIT Principles in International Legal Doctrine and Practice

Springer

Dr. Maren Heidemann
19F Penzance Street
London W11 4QX
United Kingdom
mheidera@aol.com

Library of Congress Control Number: 2006938274

ISBN 978-3-540-44461-9 Springer Berlin Heidelberg New York



Springer is part of Springer Science+Business Media

springer.com



Production: LE-TEX Jelonek, Schmidt & Vöckler GbR, Leipzig
Cover-design: Erich Kirchner, Heidelberg

SPIN 11861867 64/3100YL - 5 4 3 2 1 0 Printed on acid-free paper

# Foreword

## By Professor Mads Andenas*

Maren Heidemann has written an important book on the relationship between national law and international principles in the field of international commercial law. This is a practically important field which is also well suited for theoretical analysis. The book explores the barriers to the use of uniform contract law and the focus is on what Dr Heidemann refers to as 'legal methodology'. She identifies and analyses the barriers found in national legal systems and the ways in which these can be overcome. She proposes an international contract law methodology and provides us with the outline for such a methodology.

Dr Heidemann raises matters of method which go far beyond commercial law and contributes to the understanding of law and the legal process at a more general level. Her own method in approaching this is new. It deserves attention from both scholars and practitioners.

Dr Heidemann organises the obstacles to the application of uniform contract law in two main categories. In Part 1 of this book she discusses barriers erected by the traditional theory of contract law. In Part 2 she analyses the approaches by national lawyers in applying uniform law. She explores how their attitudes are formed, why they provide an obstacle to the success of such law, and how they could be changed.

The main question is how national legal systems react and adapt to the strong internationalisation in a field such as international commercial law. The answer Dr Heidemann gives us is that they do so rather badly. In her analysis of the different actors (legislators, courts, legal academic scholarship), she shows how national contract law becomes an obstacle to finding rational solutions.

National legal scholarship is a pocket of particularly strong resistance. Dr Heidemann's book should cause particular concern for legal scholars. Her criticism requires to be taken seriously by the legal academic community at large. The mainstream of contract scholarship is plainly not providing adequate contributions

---

* PhD (Cambridge), MA, DPhil (Oxford). Professor of Law, University of Leicester; Senior Fellow, Institute of European and Comparative Law, University of Oxford; Honorary Fellow, and former Director, of the British Institute of International and Comparative Law; former Director of the Centre of Euopean Law, King's College, University of London.

to the legal developments that legislators and courts are recognising. Dr Heidemann is critical of national legislators and courts, as they too are resistant to the application of international sources. But her criticism is particularly powerful against legal scholarship, which should have a particular role in facilitating the inevitable change and reorientation. The prevailing view in the two countries that Dr Heidemann studies (England and Germany) maintains the theory of unity of law and state, and it does not see the necessity and potential of a unity of law. This applies also where the business activity is not limited by national jurisdictional borders, and where the typical transaction is one involving more than one national jurisdiction. The national discipline of contract law, and in particular the national contract law doctrine, becomes an obstacle to a necessary development and holds that development back. In this process, the mainstream scholars turn the discipline into a less helpful one, and their writing and themselves into something gradually approaching irrelevant relics. We are still dominated by a generation of national contract law scholarship which is much outdated and which (and who) as a consequence will be rapidly overtaken and most happily forgotten. Dr Heidemann's book makes this a very clear conclusion.

The first part of the title of Dr Heidemann's book is 'Methodology of uniform contract law'. The second part or sub-title is 'The UNIDROIT principles in international legal doctrine and practice'. Much of her focus, however, is on the national reception. Here she has chosen the English and German law on international construction contracts. The national reception of international sources is notoriously difficult as a topic or as an approach. One has to have a good command of the international sources and of the different national systems that are included in the study. Comparative methodology remains at such an early stage of development that the scholar who ventures into a specialist topic as Dr Heidemann here does has to devote much care and attention to the methodological issues. She does so, and she has a good command of the general topic and of the legal systems she focuses on. Very few scholars should attempt this kind of demanding project, which Dr Heidemann here has undertaken so well.

Many of the issues that Dr Heidemann addresses have much in common with the issues of national implementation in European Union law. Her conclusions are helpful in those contexts. Her focus is on the UNIDROIT principles which fall in the so-called 'soft law' category. They contribute to what is often described as 'transnational', or 'a-national', uniform contract law. This subject has an established role in legal education and has been the subject of recommendations by scholars at numerous international conferences. The prevailing views of legislators, courts and scholars do not give sufficient weight to the UNIDROIT principles or to the underlying theories. Focus remains on internal markets and participants within the home territory. The limited application of transnational uniform contract law is not without consequences. Dr Heidemann points out the negative fall-out from the subsequent shortfall in the international law of trade.

Dr Heidemann's discussion in the book's Part 3, on the position of uniform law in the context of the conflict of laws, provides new perspectives on the discipline of conflicts of laws and its gateway function in the integration of uniform law into domestic legal systems. She gives particular attention to international arbitration proceedings and how uniform contract law can be applied within a domestic law context as *lex contractus*. Conflict of laws is a discipline based on national law, and on the nationally limited transaction as the typical transaction. Where the business activity in a sector is not limited by national jurisdictional borders, and where the typical transaction is one involving more than one national jurisdiction, the conflict of laws model is not any longer appropriate. Dr Heidemann is critical of the treatment of the UNIDROIT principles in the conflict of laws. The conservative attitude in legal doctrine and legislation hinders its application and creates insecurity as to whether decisions relying on transnational uniform law will be upheld and enforceable.

Dr Heidemann then turns to the ways of overcoming the obstacles in national legal systems to the application of transnational uniform contract law. Here she makes use of the English and German law relating to international construction contracts. The obstacles in current legal theory of contract law as it is developed in legal doctrine require a review of the traditional positions. Dr Heidemann argues one cannot any longer claim universal acceptance for the unity of law and state. This is not necessarily followed in a modern doctrine of international contract law. She presents a strong argument to the effect that the assertions about the lack of legitimacy of transnational law rules, which are used against transnational uniform law, are unfounded. A pluralistic concept of legislative power in contract law is emerging as an accepted contemporary standard, while the doctrine of unity of law and state is increasingly outdated and unduly limits understanding of nation state and national law. Linking territoriality and state sovereignty with law and legislation is not appropriate in the area of private law, especially contract law. Her argument is that modern pluralistic democracies have to review the underlying concepts of modern contract law on this new basis. The openness of contract doctrine gives room for developing it to accommodate uniform contract law, and the UNIDROIT principles, as a legitimate form of contract law.

Dr Heidemann argues that uniform contract law provides uniformity of sources covering areas where there is a need for it. This need promotes and maintains the standard and the degree of such uniformity, not a central political power. The development of the law here is driven by arbitrators, merchants, lawyers and the national courts. Uniform law derives its justification from the need for uniformity of contract law in international trade. This would not need to conflict with values like predictability and uniformity of results, which are used by advocates for the national system, but on the other hand do not find their primary justification in those values. Dr Heidemann provides the foundation for a modern methodology of international contract law by reviewing established concepts that are often used uncritically to create barriers against modern developments in international trade law. She points out that the assumptions about adverse effects and difficulties in existing domestic contract law are often unfounded.

Dr Heidemann's analysis of substantive legal rules and concepts in Part 2 of the book provides further support for the need for scholarship that can challenge the assumptions in the use of doctrinal concepts. She shows how concepts are often superficially understood and how little effort is made to integrate them into domestic law. She shows how the common law concept of specific performance is no general obstacle to integrating the UNIDROIT principles into English law. She argues that the individual rule regulating payment obligations in the UNIDROIT principles (Art 7.2.1), if appropriately applied, does not lead to any rigid right to performance.

Dr Heidemann shows how different aspects of the reception in English and in German law provide solutions. She finds that in English law the approach taken by the courts is providing a partial reception. Under German law, the UNIDROIT principles can be applied to international commercial contracts under the doctrine of *lex specialis* regulating specialised issues and superseding the national contract rule. The UNIDROIT principles have also served as a model for law reform of the existing law of construction contracts. Dr Heidemann explores the established methods of using international uniform law in the conflict of laws, and she shows how they can be successfully employed. She highlights how they are often seen as conflict rules in the context of the theory of gaps and the complementary use of domestic law. She argues that it is important to use an autonomous method of interpretation and reconsider the theory of gaps. The assumption of a general superiority of national contract law is no longer tenable. If the consequences of this insight are drawn, the established methods of applying uniform law can be successfully applied. This will respect the international character of the norms and their subject matter, international commercial contracts.

Dr Heidemann calls for legal scholarship in collaboration with the national courts to develop a consistent theory of uniform contract law. Inspiration can be drawn from English and German case law where arbitration awards based on uniform law are generally upheld. The new doctrine and method of uniform international contract law has to work out a definition of international commercial contract. The new doctrine has to move away from the static concepts of contract doctrine. It can no longer give unqualified priority to national contract law as it is not designed for, or suitable for, regulating international transactions. This new doctrine of international contract law will be based on an autonomous method of application of rules of transnational uniform contract law, drawing upon concepts and doctrines in general contract law. The UNIDROIT principles will here take their place as a source of law *sui generis* and can also be chosen as governing law of international commercial contracts. They apply as *lex specialis* in relation to domestic contract law, and national contract law will apply as a complementary law where the uniform law leaves gaps. The gaps arise on the level of substantive uniform law and do not amount to further choice of law effects like a conflict of law rule.

Dr Heidemann argues that this method also has to be applied to international conventions such as CISG and other Model Laws, and also to international Treaties affecting private law, such as Double Taxation Treaties and certain EU legislation.

This is a very powerful argument. I am sure it will attract much attention. There will be differing views. But the broad argument must be right. I can only recommend this book to the reader.

# Preface

Uniform contract law is undergoing rapid development and there is an inspiring scholarly discourse. It is a great pleasure to be able to contribute to the discussion of some of the core problems in this area of law by publishing this book. My arguments will reach an international forum and become accessible to a wider audience.

My position is an unequivocal one. I believe that the growing attention being paid to the subject will have the effect of encouraging a review of the traditional positions in national legal research, legislation and practice. The traditional positions have limited the use of uniform law in international contract law. New scholarship and policy discussion will increasingly expose the legal professions to uniform contract law and other international norms. My belief is that a better acquaintance with these international norms will lead to an appreciation of the possibilities.

The sections on German contract law reflect the transitional period which is still governing some areas of law even four years after the reform of the civil code. Uniform international law can help to point to new directions, on both a national and an international level.

This work also addresses established views on the antagonism between the conflict of laws approach, as opposed to uniform law solutions, by recommending a specifically contract law based viewpoint.

This book is based on my doctoral thesis, which was accepted by the University of Nottingham in October 2005. New relevant literature has been included up to July 2006, considering current developments and the latest views in legal research.

Maren Heidemann

London, July 2006

# Acknowledgements

First I would like to thank the University of Nottingham and my supervisor Prof Dr Mads Andenas, in his capacity as Director of The British Institute of International and Comparative Law (BIICL), in London, for their support which made this thesis possible. I am grateful in particular to the following people without whom the thesis would not have been undertaken and who enriched the course of this research:

At the University of Nottingham:

Prof Michael Bridge, Prof D J Harris and Mr Patrick Twomey for helping to lay the foundations of this work; Prof Paul Torremans as internal supervisor for coordinating various international views on the subject and advising on style; Prof Robert McCorquodale and Mrs Sandra Mienczakowski for allowing the project to continue under external supervision; and Prof Sue Arrowsmith and Ms Maureen Welch for mastering all sorts of ensuing administrative problems.

At the BIICL:

Prof Dr Mads Andenas for essential supervision sessions and heading the uniquely fruitful environment for research at the BIICL; Miss Liane Hoogland for managing a busy schedule; Mr Michael Anderson for organising and chairing many inspiring meetings and receptions; and Prof Jonathan Rickford for providing fascinating talks and discussions.

Elsewhere:

Prof Dr Gunther Teubner, University of Frankfurt, for highly appreciated encouraging comments on drafts; Dr Astrid Grieger, Schwäbisch Gmünd, for many critical discussions on methodology and continuous encouragement; Mrs Intan Murnira Ramli, LL M and Mr Sufian Jusoh, LL M, Kuala Lumpur/ Canterbury, for fruitful conversations about English law and international practice, for proof-reading, strong moral support and sharing research on style; Mr Kamran Arif, Peshawar, for firm moral support and knowledgeable input; and Dr Michael Barlow and Mrs Alison Barlow, MSc, Nottingham, for many years of friendship and sharing views about anything from astro-physics to the presentation of a thesis.

# Contents – Summary

# Contents – Outline

# List of Abbreviations

| | |
|---|---|
| alt | Alternative (relates to the wording of a rule) |
| AmJCompL | American Journal of Comparative Law |
| M/ Bearbeiter | *Münchener Kommentar* (Munich Commentary) / author of section, commentator |
| BGH | *Bundesgerichtshof / Entscheidungen des Bundesgerichtshofs* |
| BGHZ | *Entscheidungen des BGH in Zivilsachen* (Decisions of the Federal Court in civil matters) |
| BT-Drs | *Bundestagsdrucksache* |
| BR-Drs | *Bundesratsdrucksache* |
| BVerfG | *BundesVerfassungsgericht / Entscheidungssammlung des Bundesverfassungsgerichts* |
| Cambr LJ | Cambridge Law Journal |
| CJS | *Corpus Juris Secundum* |
| Comm | *Commentary* contained in UNIDROIT Publication of the Principles (see bibliography) |
| Einl v | *Einleitung vor* (Introduction to) |
| ECJ | European Court of Justice |
| FAZ | *Frankfurter Allegemeine Zeitung* |
| FRG | Federal Republic of Germany |
| GB | Great Britain |
| GG | *Grundgesetz der Bundesrepublik Deutschland* |
| ICC | International Chamber of Commerce |
| ICLQ | International and Comparative Law Quarterly |
| KG | *Kammergericht* (supreme court of the Land of Berlin) |
| LM | *Lindenmaier-Möhring* (dictionary of the BGH) |
| MüKo | *Münchener Kommentar /Bearbeiter* (name of commentator) |
| OGH | *Oberster Gerichtshof für die Britische Zone* |
| OGHZ | *Entscheidungssammlung* (law reports) *des Obersten Gerichtshofs für die Britische Zone in Zivilsachen* |
| OLG-NL | *Oberlandesgerichte Neue Länder* (*Entscheidungssammlung*, reports) |
| OLGZ | *Entscheidungen der Oberlandesgerichte in Zivilsachen* |
| OR | *Bundesgesetz über das Obligationenrecht* (Swiss Civil Code) |
| ROHG | *Reichsoberhandelsgericht* (German Imperial Commercial Court, collection of decisions) |
| S | *Satz* (sentence in a written rule) |
| UCC | Uniform Commercial Code |

| | |
|---|---|
| Vorb v | *Vorbemerkung vor* (Introductory remarks to) |
| ZPO | *Zivilprozeßordnung* (German Code of Civil Procedure) |

# Table of Cases

*Alfred C Toepfer* v *Peter Cremer* [1975] 1 Lloyd's Rep 406 (CA)
*Amalgamated Investment and Property Co Ltd* v *Jon Walker & Sons Ltd* [1976] 3 All ER 509
*American Trading & Production Corp* v *Shell International Marine* [1972] 453, F 2d 939 (2d Cir 1972)
*André Cie SA* v *Tradax Export SA* [1981] 2 Lloyd's Rep 355
*Avery* v *Bowden* [1855] 5 E & B 714
*Banque Financiére de la Cité SA* v *Westgate Insurance Co Ltd* [1987] 2 All ER 923; [1989] 2 All ER 952 (CA); [1992] 2 All ER 947 (HL)
*Beswick* v *Beswick* [1967] 2 All ER 1197
*Bomberger* v *McKelvey* 220 P 2d 729 (Cal) [1959]
*BP Exploration* v *Hunt (No 2)* [1982] 1 All ER 125
*Bremer Handelsgesellschaft mbH* v *Vanden Avenne-Izegem PVBA* [1978] 2 Lloyd's Rep 109
*Brook* v *Brook* [1858] 3 Sm and G 481
*Brown Paper Mill Co* v *Irvin* [1944] 146 F2d 232 (8th Cir)
*Carter* v *Adler* [1955] 291 P2d 111
*Chandler* v *Webster* [1904] 1 KB 493
*Charnikow* v *Roth Schmidt & Co* [1922] 2 KB 478
*Cheni* v *Cheni* [1965] P85
*Clark* v *Marsiglia* [1845] 1 Denio 317, 43 Am Dec 670 (NY)
*Clea Shipping Corporation* v *Bulk Oil International, The Alaskan Trader* [1984] 1 All ER 129
*Co-operative Insurance Society Ltd* v *Argyll Stores* [1997] WLR 895 (HL)
*Cricklewood Property and Investment Trust* v *Leighton's Investment Trust Ltd* [1945] AC 221
*Deutsche Schachtbau- und Tiefbohrgesellschaft mbH* v *R' As al-Khaimah National Oil Co* [1987] 3 WLR 1023
*Earth & General Contractors* v *Manchester Corp* [1958] 108 LJ 665
*European Grain & Shipping Co* v *JH Rayner & Co* [1970] 2 Lloyd's Rep 239 (CA)
*Eurotunnel* v *Balfour Beatty* [1992] 2 Lloyd's Rep 7 (CA); [1993] 1 Lloyd's Rep 291 (HL)
*Felton* v *Wharrie* [1906] HBC ($4^{th}$ ed) Vol 2 398 (CA)
*Finelli* v *Dee et al* [1968] 67 DLR (2d)

*Foster* v *Briscoll* [1929] KB 470
*Glenn* v *Leith* [1853] 1 Comm Law Rep 569
*Greenshields* v *Johnston* [1981] 119 DLR (3d) 714
*Hoechster* v *De la Tour* [1853] (QB) Eng Rep 922
*The Hollandia* [1982] QB 872
*Hounslow London Borough Council* v *Twickenham Garden Developments Ltd* [1971] Ch 234
*Hyundai Heavy Industries Co Ltd* v *Papadopoulos* [1980] 1 WLR 1129
*Ingram* v *Little* [1961] 1 QB 31 (AC)
*Interfoto Picture Library Ltd* v *Stiletto Visual Programmes Ltd* [1989] QB 433
*Krell* v *Henry* [1903] 2 KB 740
*National Carriers* v *Panalpina (Northern)* [1981] 1 All ER 161
*Nissho Iwai Petroleum Co Inc* v *Cargill International SA* [1993] 1 Lloyd's Rep 80
*O'Reilley* v *Mackman* [1983] 2 AC 237
*Paradine* v *Jane* [1647] Aleyn 26; Eng Rep (KB) 897
*Parsons Bros* v *Shea* [1965] 53 DLR (2d) 86
*Phelps* v *Hero* [1957] 215 Md 223,137 A 2nd 159
*Philips Electronique Grand Public* v *British Sky Broadcasting Ltd; Philips International BV* v *British Satellite Broadcasting Ltd* [1994] (unreported, Lexis transcript)
*R Pagnan & Fratelli* v *NGJ Schouten NV (The Filipinas I)* [1973] 1 Lloyd's Rep 349
*Regazzoni* v *Sethia* [1958] AC 301
*Richco International Ltd* v *Alfred C Toepfer International BmbH (The Bonde)* [1991] 1 Lloyd's Rep 136
*Richco International* v *Bunge (The New Prosper)* [1991] 2 Lloyd's Rep 92
*Scott* v *Liverpool Corp* [1858] 28 LJ Ch 230
*Slade's case* [1602] 76 Eng Rep 1074 (KB 1602)
*Taylor* v *Caldwell* [1863] 3 B&S 826, 122 Eng Rep 309 KB
*Taylor* v *Johnston* [1975] 15 Cal 3d 130, 539 P 2d 425
*Tito* v *Waddell (No 2)* [1977] Ch 106
*The Torni* [1932] P 78, 84
*Tradax Export SA* v *André Cie SA* [1975] 2 Lloyd's Rep 118
*Tradax Export SA* v *André Cie SA* [1976] 1 Lloyd's Rep 416
*Varley* v *Whipp* [1900] 1 QB 513, 517
*Vita Food Products* v *Unus Shipping Company* [1939] AC 277
*Vitol SA* v *Esso Australia* [1988] The Times 1 February 1988
*Webb* v *Emo Air Cargo* [1995] 1 WLR 1454
*White & Carter (Councils)* v *McGregor* [1962] AC 413
*Wilson* v *Western Alliance Corp* [1986] 715 P 2d 1344, 1346 (Or Ct App)

# Table of German Cases

BGHZ 11, 1
BGHZ 54, 236
BGHZ 40, 42
RGZ 155, 148
BGHZ 11, 83
OGHZ 1, 279
RGZ 112, 329
BGHZ 45, 372
OLGZ 90, 341
BGHZ 31, 224
RGZ 150, 232
BGHZ 47, 184
RGZ 57, 363
BGHZ 9, 94
BGHZ 1, 31
BGHZ 5, 189
RGZ 66, 291
RGZ 232, 249
[1917] RGZ 90, 268 ('*Altmetallfall*')
BGH NJW 1982, 2553
BGH NJW 1993, 1972
BGH LM No 12
BGH BB 1962, 497
BGH WM 1968, 847
BGH LM No 83
BGH NJW 1967, 721
BGH LM No 21
BGH JZ 1977, 177
BGH WM 1984, 1375
BGH NJW 1961, 31
BGH NJW-RR 1986, 569
BGH NJW 1978, 695
BGH NJW-RR 1995, 1360
BGH [1972] NJW 1972, 820
BGH NJW 1997, 1231
BGH NJW 1973, 1190

BGH NJW-RR 1989, 1248 [1989]
BGH WM , 1025. [1972]
BGHZ 31, 224. [1959]
BGHZ 59, 163 = NJW 1972, 1799. [1972]
BGHZ 60, 98.
BGHZ 74, 48.
*Börsenkursfälle (stocks price case)* RGZ 97, 138; 101, 51; 116, 15
LG Düsseldorf [1996] NJW-RR 96,1419
LG Frankfurt/Main MDR 1971, 841
LG Munich NJW-RR 1990, 1406
LG Waldshut [1987] EWiR 105
OLG Celle [1960] MDR 1961, 318
OLG Cologne ZIP 90, 433
OLG Karlsruhe ZR 174 / 70
*Rubelfall (rubel case)* RGZ 94, 65
*Silberfall (silver case)* RGZ 101, 107
346 BGHZ 13

# Introduction

## 1 Modern developments

The remarkable pace at which the global exchange of goods, services and information develops, leads to new challenges for those who deal with contract law, both on a national and international level. More specifically, the law relating to commercial contracts is an area of growing interest.

Both the formal, and the so-called 'soft law', legislation relating to cross-border trade have attracted great interest in the past ten years in legal scholarship and practice. This area of law has become more accessible through publication of the UNIDROIT Principles of International Commercial Contracts (by the UNIDROIT Institute in Rome, 1994 and 2004) and through other publications on the 'New *Lex Mercatoria*', which collectively provide lists and overviews of current laws and model laws and similar.[1] The term which describes the thereby highlighted type of law is often 'transnational', or 'a-national', uniform contract law. The subject has also been successfully integrated into legal education, following recommendations by scholars at numerous international conferences throughout the last ten years. Despite this, the prevailing views of jurisprudence, judiciary and legislative organs in most European states do not agree with the underlying theories. Instead, national legislators tend to remain focused on internal markets and participants within the home territory.

As a result, transnational uniform contract law is not used as widely as it could be, and this therefore, leads to a shortfall in the potential of international trade law as a whole.

## 2 Research questions and structure of the book

This book explores the questions concerning barriers to the use of uniform contract law – in the area of legal methodology – which exist in modern nation states, the ways in which these can be overcome, and whether it is thereby possible to create a specific methodology of international contract law. In answering those

---

[1] See for instance K P Berger, *The Creeping Codification of the Lex Mercatoria* (1999).

questions, three obstacles to the application of uniform contract law are to be distinguished and analysed.

The study is therefore organised into three parts; each one exploring one of the methodological obstacles and providing answers to the question of how they can be overcome. Part 1 discusses barriers erected by the traditional theory of contract law. Part 2 analyses the attitude taken by national lawyers when applying uniform law and asks how this attitude is formed, why it provides an obstacle to the success of such law, and how it could be changed. Part 3 deals with the position of uniform law in the context of the conflict of laws, which has a gateway function in relation to the integration of uniform law into domestic legal systems, especially in international arbitration proceedings. This section also asks how seemingly opposite positions from the modern and traditional theories of private international law can be reconciled and how uniform contract law can be applied within a domestic law context as *lex contractus*.

The second and third sections of the book deal with the arising questions of international legal methodology through examples, namely, the application of rules of the UPICC within domestic legal systems, and more specifically, English and German law relating to international construction contracts.

This choice was made with a view to answering the arising questions in a specific rather than general way in order to facilitate more concrete results. This choice also intended to balance the extensive treatment which matters of international sales law have received in the past, due to the existence of the Vienna Sales Convention and preceding uniform sales law sets. It responds to the wider scope of the UPICC which cover commercial contracts rather than just sales contracts.

Within European legal systems, the German and the English legal systems differ most from each other. English law shows the Anglo-American approach to social and commercial matters in its purest and original form, while German law displays the opposite end of the most distinguished historic polarities among the world's established legal systems. Together with Austria and Switzerland, Germany has a continental legal tradition preserving some extremely scholastic features. One could say it represents the heart of Europe's legal tradition in an undiluted way. Reference to German and English law therefore provides interesting examples for highlighting typical problems arising from cross-border commercial activities.

This study therefore focuses on aspects of international contract law which although analysed under English and German domestic laws are nevertheless significant beyond those systems. This allows the presentation of results of a universal character by carrying out a very detailed analysis of individual questions.

## 3 The subject matter: Transnational uniform contract law

Legislation regulating international commercial contracts takes at least three different forms; that of domestic law dealing with international matters, that of international law constituted by interstate negotiation such as bilateral treaties and finally, uniform law rules which provide a common textual basis for application in several states such as the Vienna Sales Convention (CISG), or the UNIDROIT Principles of International Commercial Contracts.[2] The latter type is subject to analysis in this study, particularly the method of applying such rules of law.

One of the institutions that contribute to the foundations of the legal framework of international trade and especially uniform law is the UNIDROIT Institute (International Institute for the Unification of Private Law) in Rome. This institute is an independent international organisation with its seat in Rome. It was founded in 1926 as part of the institutions of the League of Nations. In 1940, it was reconstituted by a multilateral convention which is now the charter of UNIDROIT. As of 1996, there are 58 state members of UNIDROIT. Although funded by its member states, it is not a political body. It can therefore operate according to scientific rather than political standards. Its task is to assess the possibility of harmonisation and coordination of private law originating from different sources, and also to gradually provide and prepare (draft), uniform private law rules for adoption by its member states and other interested parties.

UNIDROIT has drafted about seventy studies and drafts concerning areas of law such as sales, credit arrangements, transportation, liability, as well as the law relating to procedure and travel. Some of its model laws and draft conventions have been accepted on international diplomatic conferences and have subsequently been implemented into domestic law. Others exist as model laws for reference of all kinds, such as law reform projects or arbitration.

Examples of conventions based on UNIDROIT's work are:

- The 1964 Hague Convention on Uniform Sales Contracts and the Sales Convention
- The 1970 Brussels Convention on Travel Contracts
- The 1983 Geneva Convention on Agency, (Sales of Movables)
- The 1988 Ottawa International Leasing Convention
- The 1988 Ottawa Factoring Convention

Some other international organisations, such as the 1980 Vienna Sales Convention (CISG), issued by UNCITRAL and the United Nations' trade law commission, have also based their drafts on UNIDROIT suggestions. The platform that UNIDROIT provides is not a political one, but predominantly a purely scientific one. This is seen as a guarantee for a special quality of the outcome of its work.

The UNIDROIT Principles for International Commercial Contracts[3] are one of several sets of international uniform private law rules. Although not formally law,

2 Hereinafter referred to as UPICC. For comprehensive listings of other uniform private law instruments see K P Berger, *The Creeping Codification of the Lex Mercatoria* (1999); W J H Wiggers, International Commercial Law – Source Materials (2001); S R Goode, H Kronke, and E McKendrick, *Transnational Commercial Law: International Instruments and Commentary* (2004).

3 Hereinafter UPICC. Published by UNIDROIT 1994 and 2004. The black letter rules can also be obtained from the internet (UNIDROIT homepage <www.unidroit.org>/

they are a source of law of a certain quality.[4] In this study, they serve to exemplify the application of transnational law in a national law setting.

The UPICC were first published in 1994, and were supplemented by five new chapters in April 2004; they were the outcome of research which had been carried out over many years. They provide rules for international contracts of all kind, not just for sales contracts, as for example, the CISG or the Hague conventions do.

In the 2004 edition, the UPICC consisted of ten chapters: General Provisions, Formation, Validity, Interpretation, Content, Performance, Non-Performance, Set-Off, Assignment, and Limitation Periods. The UPICC are intended to serve as a reference for many purposes. They have proved to be useful to lawyers in contract drafting, as well as in international arbitration where they serve as 'general principles of law' often referred to in international contracts.[5]

The UPICC do not have the force of law in any country since they have never been accepted on any diplomatic conference or otherwise been implemented into national law. They have, however, already served as a model for the creation of law reform projects such as the new Dutch Civil Code, and for rebuilding civil law in some Eastern Countries after the end of the Cold War (eg, Hungary, Russia, Lithuania, Estonia, but also China and some African countries)[6]. UNIDROIT provide regular updates and briefings on the status quo of the principles by way of a database,[7] conferences and its quarterly publication, 'Uniform Law Review'.

---

UNIDROIT Principles Main Page); the complete version (including the comments which are meant to be an integral part of it), can be obtained in print from UNIDROIT, 28 Via Panisperna. 00184 Rome, Italy; e-mail: unidroit.rome@unidroit.org (ISBN 88-86449-00-3).

4 Compare *infra* Part 3 (Chapters 6, 7 and 8).

5 Cf, for example *Eurotunnel* v *Balfour Beatty* [1992] 2 Lloyd's Rep 7 (CA); [1993] 1 Lloyd's Rep 291 (HL).

6 See M.J. Bonell, 'UNIDROIT Principles 2004 – The New Edition of the Principles of International Commercial Contracts adopted by the Institute for the Unfication of Private Law' Uniform Law Review 1 (2004) 5 at 7-8.

7 <http://www.unilex.info>.

# Part 1 General aspects of uniform private law: Jurisprudential categories and purpose

Part 1 identifies the impeding effect of traditional general doctrines of contract and conflict law within nation states on the application of uniform contract law. Chapter 1 asks what these concepts are, and questions the position of uniform contract law in this context. Chapter 2 asks why uniformity of law is needed, and considers the extent to which, and how, uniform contract law can be defined. Thereby, the first part examines the generic quality and definition of the phenomenon of uniform contract law on a general doctrinal level, as it is a relatively new term in legal theory and is still not subject to intense or systematic cross-border analysis. Part 1 therefore questions how barriers against the use of transnational law arising from traditional legal theory can be overcome, by suggesting a modern and novel approach to existing concepts which will allow the accommodation of a doctrine of transnational uniform contract law.

The concepts of harmonisation and unification are more than just instantaneous policies in the current political body of the EU, but rather, are reflections of the values of societies in their time. The transformation of these phenomena from concepts of arts, music and philosophy, deeply rooted in Western culture, into suitable tools in legal science and practice is not normally reflected very well in the literature. It involves an analysis of the use of terminology in the legal sciences in general. The development and use of scientific terminology is a discipline in its own right which plays a decisive role in the development of a modern branch of legal science;[1] dealing with private law rules on an international level, and thereby

---

[1] H Brinckmann, *Juristische Fachsprache als Wissenschaftssprache?*, 70-71; D Busse, 'Juristische Semantik: Grundfragen der juristischen Interpretationstheorie in sprachwissenschaftlicher Sicht' Vol 157, 1993; G Frege, *Conceptual Notation and related articles* (1972); C S Haight, 'Babel Afloat: Some Reflections on Uniformity in Maritime Law' Journal of Maritime Law and Commerce 28.2 (1997) 189-205; K Hyland, 'Scientific Claims and Community Values: Articulation in an Academic Culture' Language & Communication – an Interdisciplinary Journal 17 (1997) 13-31; B S Jackson, 'Making Sense in Jurisprudence' Vol 5, 1996; B S Jackson, 'Making Sense in Law' Vol 4, 1995; B S Jackson, *Semiotics and Legal Theory* (1985); M Jefferson, 'Comparing the proper law and the law applicable' Student Law Review 9, sum (1993) 16-19; M Kramm, *Rechtsnorm und semantische Eindeutigkeit*, Doctoral thesis, Erlangen-Nürnberg, 1970; U Ladnar, and C V Plettnitz, eds, *Fachsprache der Justiz* (1977); S Levinson, *Law as Literature* 155-173; S Levinson and S Mailloux, eds, *Interpreting Law and Literature: a Hermeneutic Reader* (1988); D Mellinkoff, *The Language of the Law* (1963); Paulsen, 'An Historical Overview of the Development of Uniformity in International Maritime

forming the legal basis for cross-border commercial activity. An evaluation of this use of language through a review of relevant literature in this field[2] provides two insights: firstly, it reveals very vague usage of the expressions, harmonisation and unification of laws, a use of language which is not normally employed in law and legal science. Secondly, the expression harmonisation serves to disguise the process of uniformisation, reference to which is avoided due to its political relevance.[3] The idea of unity plays a profound role in western history of thought, history, philosophy, and subsequently, politics. Nevertheless legal science does not assign a high priority to explaining its meaning and potential. The significance of unity and creating uniformity in the law needs to be understood in a wider context than that of the immediate background which is typically seen when used in current trade law or European Union institutional law. Harmonisation is a euphemism and means uniformisation. This is the meaning I am attaching to it in this study.

Another insight is that the notion of diversity of laws, which is presupposed by harmonisation efforts, remains unquestioned. Without also analysing this notion, legal processes cannot arrive at suitable conclusions. Unity and diversity are naturally opposites and create tension when occurring simultaneously, as with the phenomenon of transnational law facing domestic legal systems or vice versa. Therefore, this study highlights the transition between the two spheres and suggests ways of reconciling unity and diversity in the law.

Law' Tulane Law Review 57 (1983) 1065 et seq; A Podlech, *Die juristische Fachsprache und die Umgangssprache*; H Weinrich, *Sprache und Wissenschaft.*

2 A range of publications prepared in the course of the Twenty-Fifth Annual Workshop on Commercial and Consumer Law, 'Harmonisation and Change', Faculty of Law, University of Toronto may serve as a useful starting point, together with a selection of other general publications on this question: M Boodman, 'The Myth of Harmonisation of Laws' AmJCompL (1991) 699; G Frege, *Conceptual Notation and related articles* (1972); H P Glenn, 'Harmonisation of Law, Foreign Law and Private International Law' European Review of Private International Law 1 (1993) 47-66; H P Glenn, *Unification of Law, Harmonisation of Law and Private International Law*, 783 et seq; J Ziegel, ed, D W Leebron, 'Lying down with Procrustes: an analysis of harmonisation claims' 1995, 1-61; S Levinson, and S Mailloux, eds, *Interpreting Law and Literature: a Hermeneutic Reader* (1988); A Rosett, 'Unification, Harmonisation, Restatement, Codification and Reform in International Commercial Law' AmJCompL 40 (1992) 683.

3 It implies assuming a centralised power at the expense of sovereignty of other political entities.

# 1 Diversity in the law

From our point of view the illusion is not the international unification of the law. On the contrary, it is the refusal to contemplate unification and the desire to preserve law as strictly an instrument of state power and thus divided among the states...[1]

Chapter 1 investigates the concept of diversity of laws between nation states as a logical pre-requisite for unity of laws[2] by contrasting traditional legal theory with modern concepts.

Three aspects are discussed in this chapter; the role of the state ascertaining sovereignty in the area of private law (1.1), the role of the substantive contract law itself (1.2), and the role of the individual contracting party (1.3). The chapter thereby analyses the current position of uniform law in general contract law doctrine and in the conflict of laws, namely, considering the role of party autonomy when it comes to choosing transnational law rules as the law governing the contract.

## 1.1 Sovereignty of states and the role of private law

This section examines the relationship between the notion of sovereignty of nation states and private law in general within current legal doctrine. It asks whether transnational (non-state) contract law can be a legitimate source of law within a sovereign nation state. It asks what the role of the state is when dealing with such law rules, of which the UFICC are an example; and whether sovereignty as a defining aspect of nation states is necessarily an argument against a source of law function of transnational law.

In the following section, three different aspects are discussed; instances where states demonstrate their sovereignty directly by acts affecting international trade (1.1.1), instances where they do so towards individuals in private dealings (1.1.2), and thirdly the question of whether law and state necessarily form an alliance and cannot be separated from each other: the doctrine of unity of law and state, with the state as the sole source of law (1.1.3).

This analysis serves to answer the question of the correct definition of contract law compared with other national law according to its specific nature, history and function. The role and nature of transnational law within contract law can be de-

1 R David, 'The Methods of Unification', Am J Comp L 16 (1968) 13, 14.
2 To be examined in Chapter 2 below.

termined by this analysis too, because – and to the extent which – it is also contract law. The majority of the literature on harmonisation and unification of laws introduce an image of laws as separate entities which can be unified or harmonised, in order to create a whole new entity, or a bundle of entities.[3] It makes sense to stay with this picture and continue using this game of metaphors. Traditional legal doctrine upholds the opinion that laws are such entities and that these are formed exclusively by state power. According to this view, the border lines between the laws coincide with the political borders between the states. The quoted opinion of the comparative lawyer (above) disagrees with this view and calls it an illusion. The image of laws as individual entities implies that there are clear border lines or distinctions between them. However, the image loses its persuasive force when considering the extent to which domestic legal borders are effectively crossed and the dividing lines between laws blurred.

In the area of contract law, states express and define the distinctiveness of their legal systems in relation to those of other states by two main factors; the approach towards the application of foreign law (1.2) and the extent of party autonomy (1.3) embodied in a choice of law rules.

Traditional legal doctrines of the sources of law in both the English and the German jurisdictions,[4] representing typical common law and continental jurisdictions, presuppose that the force of law flowing from or equalling state power is an expression of the sovereignty of states.

This forms a great impediment for the development of legal doctrine towards the integration of transnational law as an important tool in international commercial dispute settlement. It is this restrictive understanding governing current legislation which is governing choice of law and commercial arbitration in both countries. Modern legislation has still not incorporated a clear admission of transnational legal regimes into domestic law.[5] Transnational legal rules are disputed as to their nature as sources of law both in a formal and substantive sense. [6]

The agreed terminology in choice of law matters is 'law' including transnational law rules and 'rules of law' referring exclusively to state law.[7] This distinction determines whether or not a regime such as the UPICC can be stipulated governing law (*kollisionsrechtliche Verweisung*) by contracting parties, or merely as contractual clauses (*materiellrechtliche Verweisung*).

Due to the nature of contract law regulating the legal relationships between private individuals, the strict combination of state power (sovereignty) and legitimacy of law rules is particularly questionable in this area of law.

This section describes the role of the state in private law and points out aspects of legitimacy which are relevant for establishing a revised understanding of the

---

3 Compare B Fauvarque-Cosson, 'Comparative Law and Conflict of Laws: Allies or Enemies? New Perspectives on an Old Couple' Am J Comp L 49 (2001) 407, eg, 416.

4 Although their viewpoints are not genuinely the same due to historic reasons.

5 See Part 3 for further discussion.

6 Compare Chapters 6 and 7.

7 Eg, the UNCITRAL Model Law on International Commercial Arbitration, in Art 28 EGBGB or the Contracts (Applicable Law) Act 1989 (see 7.1.2).

prospective role of transnational law rules in national contract law, conflict of laws, and the law governing commercial arbitration. A detailed account of the current law governing these matters in relation to the application of the UPICC is provided in Part 3.

The focus of this study is not to exhaustively deal with all issues of legal theory to be brought up in the course of this chapter, but to rather, to present and discuss relevant matters forming a pragmatic approach to integrating transnational law into domestic contract law, on both the doctrinal,[8] and the practical,[9] level of application. This process of recollecting and revisiting is a formative element of a suggested novel doctrine of international uniform private law.[10]

### 1.1.1 Assertion of sovereignty in international trade

The most prominent and rigid methods for a state exercising power in areas of private law are by regulatory acts directly affecting contractual agreements. This is done through rules of competition law, anti-dumping legislation, taxes and tariffs, and also at times, through embargoes. An example is provided by the 'Russian Pipeline Case', referred to by Maier [11] Here, the United States government relied on judicial measures to balance their national interest against that of another state (the USSR) – a situation which could have been (and eventually was) – resolved by way of diplomacy. Here the US asserted a claim of authority over (both US and foreign) private individuals, and trading activities by issuing a ban of certain goods manufactured in the US.[12] This affected the trading activities and interest of non US companies involved in the same deal and also banned equipment produced by foreign subsidiaries of US companies, as well as their licensees.[13] Thus, US jurisdiction was exercised internationally outside their territory. European states protested against these measures and encouraged firms to comply with contractual agreements regardless of the governmental and presidential orders. This illustrates the role sovereignty can play in private law and shows how states can directly exercise authority over individuals interfering with private activities. However, the prevailing interest of the international political and trading community is to guarantee 'a system that would lend support to the reliability of transnational contracts and reaffirm the authority and responsibility of sovereign states to plot their own economic and political destinies', rather than, 'to create … the expectation that a single nation … could legitimately pressure foreign business entities to act con-

---

[8] Chapter 1.

[9] Chapter 2.

[10] Compare Part 2 at 3.2.

[11] H G Maier, 'Interest Balancing and Extraterritorial Jurisdiction' Am J Comp L 31 (1983), 579. See also P Hay, *'Zur extraterritorialen Anwendung US-amerikanischen Rechts.' Rabels Zeitschrift für ausländisches und internationales Privatrecht* 60 (1996) 303.

[12] US government decision of 29 December 1981.

[13] Decision by President Reagan of 18 June 1982, acting under Export Administration Act 1979, Pub L No 96-72, 93 Stat 503 (1979). See Maier, op cit, n 3.

trary to the perceived interests of their host or national states'.[14] This view was supported at the time by a number of public statements and comments in newspapers from all countries involved. 'The possibility of an adverse impact on the reliability of contracts was a common criticism of the sanctions on both sides of the Atlantic ...' [15] The example illustrates the power of the idea of private law.

### 1.1.2 Assertion of sovereignty towards the private individual

In a domestic context a state's sovereignty materialises as a supreme power subordinating the private individual (*hoheitliches Handeln*). This is reflected by the concept of 'hierarchy of norms' within the domestic legal system,[16] as well as, specifically in German legal theory, the further distinction between private and public law. According to the latter, a rule forms part of public law if and when it concerns a legal relationship between parties, one of whom is subordinate to the other. This subordination is seen as a typical feature created by the state's authority towards the private individual. Private law, as opposed to that, exists on a level of equality between the individuals involved.[17] Rules of administrative, procedural, criminal, and public international law qualify as public and often embody the state's function in the field of enforcement by sanctions, penalties, punishment etc. However, if and when a state acts privately, state and individual are on equal terms, eg, concluding building or sales contracts when private law rules are binding to state parties.[18] Nevertheless, imposing duties unilaterally on the individual, backed by fines and measures of enforcement which go beyond the legal capacities of private individuals,[19] is considered one of the characteristic ways of state

[14] Maier, op cit, 586. This statement emphasises the need of independence in international trade as well as its significance within international law. It does not see the international merchant as a 'state-free', 'a-national' actor.

[15] See Maier, op cit, n 26.

[16] Compare also G Teubner, 'Breaking Frames: Economic Globalisation and the Emergence of the *Lex Mercatoria*', European Journal of Social Theory 5.2 (2002) 199 at 199, 206. This concept does, however, perhaps not apply to the same extent in every state, namely to a lesser extent in common law countries, see also below.

[17] For details see *Münchener Kommentar, 'Einleitung'*, No 3. The theory of subordination is applied by the Federal Court: BGHZ 14, 222, 227 = NJW 1954, 1486; BGHZ 27, 283; 66, 229, 233 et seq; 67, 81, 84; 97, 312, 314; 102, 280, 283 and by its predecessor, the Imperial Court (*Reichsgericht*) in RGZ 167, 284.

[18] This distinction has received 'formal recognition' in England in 1982 in *O'Reilley* v. *Mackman* [1983] 2 AC 237. A similar view was expressed in the Australian High Court (1988) 165 CLR 30 (the *Spycatcher* case): equitable duties qualified public law since they had been generated by the relationship between the British Government and (ex-agent) Peter Wright. The distinction public-private law proved vital in deciding the question whether the British Government's legal position was enforceable in Australia. In Germany, the nature of the public legal rule rather than any specific legal effect resulting there-from is subject to intense scholarly discussion. See Chapter 7 for discussion of contracts with state parties in commercial arbitration.

[19] Such as taxation rules.

acting. Its nature is fundamentally different from private acting so that state involvement in contract law often involves specialised procedures and rules.[20] How 'private', ie, how autonomous, can private law be, given that due to the territorial distribution of the earth, all private acting necessarily takes place in a state?

### 1.1.3 Unity of law and state: The state as the sole source of law?

The notion of unity of law and state can be perceived as the identity of law and territory. It can also mean the state being the sole source of law. The latter concept is closely related to that of positivism.

#### *1.1.3.1 Territorial matters and the paradox of contract law*

If a state's legal sphere of influence regarding private law is deemed congruent with its territory it follows that its geographical boundaries define the dividing line between domestic law and foreign law:

> Boundaries evidence the extent of State sovereignty and form the limits of the operations of the domestic legal system. They demarcate the territorial framework within which jurisdiction is established and exercised. [21]

The principle *uti possidetis iuris* stems from land law, ie, private law and has Roman origins. '... it operated as an interdict of the *Praetor* by which the disturbance of the existing state of possession of immovables as between two individuals was forbidden. *Uti possidetis ita possideatis.*'[22] The territory of a state can thus be conceived as the whole of its 'immovable property' in relation to other 'individuals' (sovereign states). Ownership of the territory then forms the state rather than the more abstract social and political entity commonly understood to form a 'nation'. Legislative power, which is understood to be directly and exclusively derived from the state, is thus also confined to its territory.

This land related concept has for long been supported by the fact that a single person such as a king, duke or emperor, was the sovereign who owned the territory. As long as states are regarded to be sovereign and distinct, their laws can thereby be regarded to be distinct in the same way, meaning that the borders of the legal systems run along the geographical borders of the states. Contemporary private law in western states, however, has developed in close association with the

---

[20] See Chapter 7 for further discussion; another example is public procurement procedures regulating state involvement in contractual relationships. For an overview over modern developments in international procurement law see S Arrowsmith, 'Public Procurement: An Appraisal of the UNCITRAL Model Law as a Global Standard' ICLQ 53 (2004) 17.

[21] M N Shaw, 'The Heritage of States: the Principle of *Uti Possidetis Juris* Today' The British Yearbook of International Law 67 (1996) 75, 77.

[22] Shaw, ibid, 99.

formation of the nation state as a historic process.[23] The direct link between the sovereignty of states and the distinctiveness of laws could thus be seen by the fact that the legitimacy of law is created separately and individually by political communities in each state. In a modern pluralistic state the feudalistic conception of legislation lacks an equivalent in that legislative power is exercised on the basis of majority decisions and impersonal institutions. The 'sovereign will' is not clearly recognisable anymore as the will of a single person. The state, representing a 'unit' (for the purposes of the metaphoric game in this section[24]) will give law from a single source coinciding with a now rather abstract central power. This understanding however, even in states where sovereignty is attributed to 'the people' rather than to a monarch, still seems to presuppose a conception or image of a sovereign in the traditional sense. In practice, law is often presented as originating from the personal work of a person (minister) or a small body of people, conceived as an entity (party, law commission).[25] It is an attempt to give the source of law a face and to re-personalise it. Apparently the idea of 'unity' of source has a strong attraction even in a pluralistic society, preserving the concept of unity of law and state and that of the hierarchy of norms like a centre of gravitation.

In the area of private law, this nevertheless deserves further consideration since private law is addressed to private individuals who tend to go beyond territory boundaries in modern times marked by 'globalization'. Individuals make use of (state guaranteed) party autonomy, and they are also more and more seen as subjects in international relations and law. There are more instances where they can acquire personal individual rights to claim under international conventions before international courts, and individuals are often seen as the 'generator of political power and actions': '... international relations and law are generated by the people, or more specifically, the individuals and groups which constitute states'.[26]

This simultaneous occurrence of the doctrine of unity of law and state on the one hand, and an increasingly autonomous international legal practice[27] created by individuals exercising party autonomy on the other, presents contract law in a paradoxical situation.

---

[23] R Hayder, '*Privatrechtsvereinheitlichung durch die Europäische Gemeinschaft - Kommentar zum Vortrag von Hans Claudius Taschner*' in P C Müller-Graff (ed), *Gemeinsames Privatrecht in der Europäischen Gemeinschaft* (Baden-Baden: Nomos, 1993), 167-170.

[24] Compare 1.1.

[25] U W Saxer, '*Die Zukunft des Nationalstaates*' Vol 6 (1994) 14-15.

[26] B F Fitzgerald, 'An Emerging Liberal Theory of International Law and the Non-Enforcement of Foreign Public Laws' Australian Yearbook of International Law 16 (1995), 311.

[27] Eg, carried out by international arbitration courts, trade associations or other agencies providing legal services. See Chapters 7 and 8 for further discussion. Compare also G Teubner: 'Breaking Frames: Economic Globalisation and the Emergence of the *lex mercatoria*' European Journal of Social Theory 5.2 (2002) 199, 206 with further references: 'Technical standardisation and professional self-regulation have developed tendencies toward world-wide coordination with minimal intervention of official international politics'.

Therefore, the traditional concept of the relationship between law and state seems to fit particularly badly for contract law. The paradox occurs in three respects: first, regarding the simultaneous occurrence of subordination typical for state acting and the equal relationship typical for private law. Second, in the contradiction between the confined space of the state territory defining the scope of the contract law rules, and the commercial space used by the protagonists of international commercial contract law which does not coincide with the domestic legal space. Third, the doctrine of unity of law and state leads to the paradox of law and non-law presented by the *lex mercatoria*; at least some of its components are recognised as sources of law even under the traditional doctrine,[28] but they are still positively excluded from being law in the formal sense on the level of current conflict of laws and arbitration legislation.[29]

Several suggestions have been made to resolve this paradox; besides accepting the oscillating nature of certain types of law rules, and working out strategies to operate them in the practical context,[30] one promising approach is to 'reframe' the traditional doctrine of sources of law. This is done by 'shifting' the centre point of political legislator as the sole source of law away to the 'periphery' and allowing private law making as additional sources of law.[31] This creates legal pluralism between several types of sources of law (as opposed to the alleged diversity between separate and uniform state laws). Together with appropriate methods of integrating specialised transnational contract law into domestic practice this can resolve the paradoxical situation of current international contract law. It can also be done by drawing on truly traditional concepts of European legal history[32] rather than insisting on limiting ideas from the era of nation-state and positivism.

#### 1.1.3.2 Sovereignty and legitimacy of private law

The prevailing traditional understanding, however, is that law, especially contract law, is still necessarily related to the state as legislator. The state with its institutions including courts is the only possible instance to give law, to provide for legitimacy. Therefore, although there are recognised areas in which law can be created by private individuals independently and self-governing, the sovereign nation state is regarded as the sole source of law in prevailing legal doctrine.

It is doubtful, however, whether this concept can claim to reflect a universal understanding of legitimacy.[33] Private individuals, persons or corporations, moving around internationally, acting globally in many different states at a time might have different standards which make them believe in domestic and transnational

---

28 See also Chapter 6 for further discussion.

29 In both England and Germany. See also Part 3 for further discussion.

30 As done by some game theorists such as M v d Kerchove, and F Ost, *Le droit ou les paradoxes du jeu* (1992).

31 Compare Teubner, op cit, 207.

32 Compare, eg, 1.2.1.1.

33 Compare for some considerations on legitimacy Teubner, op cit, 207-208.

private law rules. This belief does in fact contribute to the formation of law without a state by way of custom and usage.[34]

In a substantive sense, individuals recognise voluntarily the state privilege to provide the law; states provide the necessary framework for legal procedure and enforcement of law. Despite the judicial bodies of most states being independent (of the legislative and administrative bodies) they are still derived from the political sovereign, the political 'unit', which provides for their identification and grants the power they need to give effect to law rules.[35] As far as private parties seeking the assistance of courts to pursue their rights within a jurisdiction they recognise the given underlying 'legal instruments' which the courts will use in order to decide the issue. The interrelation of courts, law and territoriality thus seems to confirm the identity between law and state as if it were part of the very nature of law. And yet, a number of connecting factors may lie outside the territory and jurisdiction such as, the place of performance, the place where a crime or tort is committed, or nationality or domicile of a deceased, and which thereby brings foreign law into the domestic sphere.[36]

One archaic model of source of law is that of 'divine law', gods as legal sources and ultimate authority.[37] Examples are mythic codifications often given by gods to men such as Yahweh giving the law to Moses, or as Apollo ruling through the Delphi oracle. Various religious traditions as well as Greek and Roman mythology show that legislation and justice are themes which the human mind is deeply concerned with and that the ultimate origin of the law is conceived as somehow beyond the human sphere and rather of a transcendental nature and origin. In the course of western history, military leaders and emperors such as Napoleon, Frederic the Great and Justinian made use of their worldly power as sovereigns, often referring to divine powers to enact codes. These carried the names of their 'spiritual fathers', who had acted as initiators or mentors to certain codes, and this added to the authority of the law. It illustrates the above mentioned[38] attraction of the personalised single source of law.

This procedure might, however, still lack a substantive source of law quality in the sense that people believe in this law more than in law without a personal reference to the legislator. Alan Watson, however, emphasises that the main source of authority in those cases was the law itself; the ease of its application - its persuasive force, was decisive for its enactment and adoption. The emperor's role really was to, 'end discussion, controversy and doubt'.[39] This shows that the worldly power attached to the state function is confined to the decision-making rather than to the creation of the law itself. The law carries its source of law function within

[34] Compare also Chapter 7.

[35] It may be noted that historically, the jurisdiction of the courts in Europe sometimes stretched beyond political entities. Jurisdictions of German courts did not necessarily coincide with the geographical borders of the German states (kingdoms, duchies and counties).

[36] 1.3.1.1.

[37] A Watson, *Legal Transplants* (1974) 88.

[38] 1.1.3.1.

[39] Watson, op cit, 89, n 10.

itself as a self-referring quality and is therefore, outside the sphere of state regulation regarding its substantive side.[40]

Today, theories of the legitimacy of law in modern states explain states as being both sources of power and complex human societies drawing on more than one scientific discipline, such as legal science, philosophy, ethnology and sociology. The evolution from aristocratic systems towards the democratic and pluralistic (civil) state concept involves a complex component in the concept of legitimacy; how can a society simultaneously be the source and the subject of the law? Theories of legitimacy in legal theory were put to a real life test in Germany after the reunification. The law of the 'old' federal republic acquired the force of law within the territory of the 'old' democratic republic. The inhabitants of the former communist state which ceased to exist were confronted with a complete legal system which they experienced as new and uncanny. Questions of legitimacy appeared in every day life, not only in academia. 'We wanted justice – we got the rule of law', as Bärbel Bohley, who fought for civil liberties in the GDR, phrased it.[41] This phrase which stood for the deep concerns of a large faction of the new citizens of the reunified Germany, expresses scepticism and confusion towards the legal system. 'Justice' is used here as different from, and perhaps even opposed to, 'rule of law', and thus stirs up fundamental concerns of legitimacy. One substantive aspect of the legitimacy of law is that generally every legal system tries to achieve 'justice'. The rule of law is to serve this aim. But not in the colloquial sense,[42] in which it is used in the above quoted phrase by Mrs Bohley, but rather in a more complicated way. Canaris explains the relevance of the two categories of consensus and procedure in this context. He explains that after reunification a majority of people in the GDR had formally and legally accepted the social, economic and legal system of the Western German state. The consensus arose from the establishment of a government created out of free and equally held elections and who negotiated the Treaty. This was ratified by the parliament of the GDR which had been formed by democratic elections before. This consensus, nevertheless, cannot be regarded as a mere majority decision. The fact that a minority of citizens disagreed with the reunification and the accession to the FRG shows that an explanation has to be made as to how this new legal status could be called legitimate. Many citizens of the larger German state felt estranged and confused re-

---

[40] Compare Chapters 6 and 7.

[41] This phrase of hers is quoted here after C-W Canaris: '*Konsens und Verfahren als Grundelemente der Rechtsordnung – Gedanken vor dem Hintergrund der 'Eumeniden' des Aischylos*'. *Juristische Schulung* (1996) 7, 573, 574, who emphasises that there are several literal forms in which she is said to have put it but in all of which they suggest the same spirit.

[42] This is an almost religious conception of the notion of justice. See below in this section for another example. This study does not undertake to discuss the notion of justice and its treatment in philosophy and jurisprudence in depth but wants to contribute to the understanding of legitimacy of law by giving selected examples of understanding in the contemporary political and commercial sphere. Compare Chapter 2 at 2.2.1.

garding the legal rules which they were confronted with.[43] Are these rules therefore illegitimate in relation to these individuals?

The problem of a dissenting minority, or part of a population within a legal system, is looked at in the context of the Eumenides-myth by Canaris: as the Erinyes were appeased by the granting of land and worship in the city of Athens, the losing party of a legal action has to be respected on a general basis of equal rights. 'The general acceptance of the legal system as a whole is of utmost importance.'[44] Otherwise, the losing party may become an enemy of the law.

Another way of explaining consensus is by the 'theory of recognition' (*Anerkennungstheorie*). Rules acquire the force of law through the acceptance and recognition of the individuals to be subjected to the law rules.[45] Whether this recognition concerns each and every individual law rule and its specific application in the courtroom, or whether this is just a basic rule, has been subject to extensive discussion among scholars.[46] This basic rule contains both the substantive claim that law shall exist, as well as the formal aspect of recognising an authority as competent to issue that law.

One of the basic substantive objectives of the 'rule of law' and therefore of 'justice' and the existence of law itself, is to replace archaic forms of pursuing one's own rights and interests; e.g. by means of violence such as blood feud. Thus, the enforcement of legal claims, by private individuals against each other, has to be generally prevented and instead, entrusted to a judiciary dealing with conflicts and representing the ban of violence corresponding to the 'monopoly of violence' of the state.[47] In the mythology referred to by Canaris, the Erinyes represent this essential feature of law: the threat of violence as a means of enforcement of law.

The legitimacy of rules that establish this order in a social context, confined to a specific state or nation, is to a great extent established by way of procedure. The notion of procedural legitimacy has become popular recently, but is only one aspect of the ratio of the force of law.[48] Canaris explains in his article the meaning and role of the tale of the Eumenides, as reported by Aeschylus, within legal theory. He shows how the recognition of law as such, results in a discourse (between Athena and the Erinyes) which creates the force of law by procedure (the decision by the *areopag*). But in addition to this procedure the myth reports that Athena gave reasons for her vote in favour of Orestes. Here, the legitimacy is created by reasoning. Canaris emphasises that in this ancient myth legitimacy is said not only to consist of the pure element of procedure, but also, of that of reasoning and thus,

---

[43] As concerns contract law: eg, when people entered into insurance contracts or investment agreements on the doorstep being unaware of the implications of such deals in a way which was fundamental and scattered their confidence in 'the state' and 'the system'. These are original instances of legitimacy issues: people did not 'accept' the law as their law.

[44] C-W Canaris, '*Konsens und Verfahren als Grundelemente der Rechtsordnung - Gedanken vor dem Hintergrund der 'Eumeniden' des Aischylos*' J S 7 (1996) 573, 577.

[45] Ibid, 578.

[46] See references in Canaris, ibid, 575, n 2.

[47] See German constitutional court in BVerfGE 54, 277 (292).

[48] Canaris, op cit, 577.

substantive elements of law which can even be influenced by the individual delivering a judgment.[49]

Given this concept of legitimacy the role of the state and its relation to private law rules can be described as follows: if private individuals seek the assistance of a formal procedure to sort out their conflicts and pursue their rights, rather than relying on the 'right of the stronger party', they also rely on the authority of an instance to govern the substantive law rules as well as the procedure. The compulsive element, which is essential to the enforcement of legal claims, is exclusively reserved for state institutions. Therefore, legislative and executive bodies within a state are equally essential to the conception and existence of law, both in a formal and substantive sense, and are closely linked to its legitimacy.

In the area of contract law, however, more than in other areas of law, the compulsive element is confined to the enforcement aspect rather than being found in the substance of the law. It is not the law that is compulsive but the enforcement.[50] The parties are entitled to rely on state organs to enforce the judgment based on the law. This law, contract law, derives its legitimacy to a great extent from its recognition among the individuals subject to it. Contract law has traditionally been formed out of established practice and tradition rather than by way of instantaneous short term political decisions. Historically, contract codes often incorporated and restated customary law. Certain substantive aspects of justice are thus decisive for the acceptance of law, specifically contract law. Legitimacy of law eventually depends on the existence of procedure and methods of enforcement, as well as on substantive qualities.

Legitimacy and justice are often understood to mean the same thing in the commercial world when referring to aspects of 'fair dealing'. This practice is not only a simplification and a colloquial use of the term, but is also a reference to the above mentioned substantive aspect of legitimacy. Two classical meanings of justice can be distinguished: *iustitia commutativa* and *iustitia distributiva*. A just order provides for the good distribution and balance of goods and charges, duties and rights. For merchants the principle of exchange is of central interest; the aim of fair exchange is regulated by rules of mutual legal relationships — contract rules. The substantive quality of contract rules will decide whether a legal system provides justice. Reciprocity is an essential feature for the merchant community and for commercial law; the theory of reciprocity is an equally basic condition for ethnologic thinking, 'as is the theory of gravitation in astrology'.[51]

'Balancing justice ... is to be found on the level of equality, among individuals of the same rank.'[52] This corresponds to the description of private law given

---

[49] Compare Chapter 5. See O Lando: '*Homo judicans*' Uniform Law Review 2/3 (1998), 535.

[50] Compare 5.3.

[51] Claude Levi-Strauss, *Strukturale Anthropologie* (1967), quoted in R Dreier '*Was ist Gerechtigkeit?*' *Juristische Schulung* (1996) 7, 581.

[52] Dreier, ibid, 580.

above,[53] and confirms the essential quality of contract law as distinct from regulating and subordinating law rules.

#### *1.1.3.3 Legitimacy of a-national commercial law*

The role of the state in private law comes to the fore if, and when, private individuals and their transactions cross national boundaries. Global markets invite transnational enterprises to operate all over the world simultaneously by way of corporate and financial networks powered by high technology.

> International production appears as a real challenge to the official allocation, among states, of the power of regulating the economy ... One of the primary causes of this situation is the emergence of the global enterprise. [54]

Contracts have been rejected as sources of law since Savigny.[55] They have been regarded as mere factual phenomena of legal reality. However, within the jurisprudential discourse about the existence and nature of *lex mercatoria*, the existence of an a-national private law is claimed.[56] Some even recognise self-governing bodies within the international merchant community, such as trade associations,[57] certain agencies or arbitration courts.

Teubner encourages a solution to the paradox of self-validating contracts:

> Any self-validating of contract leads directly into the paradox of self reference, into the contractual version of the Cretian liar paradox .... This underlying paradox is the principal reason why lawyers, as well as sociologists, declare self-validating contracts unthinkable and talk *lex mercatoria* out of existence .... Only on the condition that this paradox of contractual self-reference be successfully 'de-paradoxified' can a global legal system in economic affairs get off the ground. [58]

Teubner has the answer. It is embodied in:

> ... those commercial contracts that construct a so-called 'closed circuit arbitration' ... Apart from substantive rules it contains clauses that refer conflicts to an arbitration 'court'

---

[53] See 1.1.2.

[54] J-P Robé, 'Multinational Enterprises: The Constitution of a Pluralistic Legal Order' 45, 68. 'The existence of a global society' is a presupposition for the existence of transnational legal discourses. The global society has an economy 'that cannot be controlled by national policies' (H-J Mertens, '*Lex Mercatoria*: A Self-Applying System beyond National Law' in G Teubner (ed) *Global Law without a state* (Brookfield: Dartmouth, 1996) 4, 41, n 10).

[55] C F v Savigny, *System des heutigen römischen Rechts* (1840) Vol 1, 12.

[56] See Mertens, op cit, 31; G Teubner, '*"Global Bukowina"*: Legal Pluralism in the World Society' in G Teubner (ed) *Global Law without a state* (Brookfield: Dartmouth, 1996) 4, 3, 8: 'A war of faith'.

[57] Issuing widely used standard contract forms that are sometimes attached the quality of legal norms.

[58] G Teubner, op cit (n 56), 15.

which is identical with the private institution that was responsible for 'legislating' the model contract. This is the 'closed circuit'.[59]

Teubner recognises the existence of a *lex mercatoria* as a genuine, positive a-national law. He disapproves, however, of the theoretical foundations legal theory has been trying to build it on so far.[60] He claims that the theoretical justification of the *lex mercatoria* has been attempted by means of outdated conceptions (sic), and that where new approaches are undertaken, traditional arguments as to the requirements and nature of legal sources (based on the idea of national law and the identity of law and state) still prevail, and block the way to a reasonable, acceptable concept of a-national law.

Theories of legal pluralism will have to reformulate their core concepts, shifting their focus from groups and communities to discourses and communicative networks.[61]

These networks are *de facto* globalised today and are not confined to nation states. Global law is therefore the answer to this situation.

An equivalent to domestic institutions such as legislator and judiciary can be found on a global level in the existence of contracts, arbitration and quasi-legislative institutions such as The International Chamber of Commerce, The International Law Association, The International Maritime Commission, and others who often draft and issue the respective (standard) contracts or standard terms. UNIDROIT is such an institution too, when regarding the UPICC. One could say that there is a differentiation in the official and non-official sector of *lex mercatoria* which reflects the state functions of formal and judge-made law on the one hand, and contractual agreements created through party autonomy, on the other.

Private arbitration and private legislation become the core of a decision system which begins to build up a hierarchy of norms and of organizational bodies. [62]

It is the 'dynamics of interaction between an 'official' legal order and a 'non-official' one, which is constitutive for a modern legal system'.[63] In this sense Teubner conceives his pluralism in the world society: there are at present (at least) two systems of law co-existing. One is the traditional law of nation states and the other is the global law in the commercial world which is, of course, only fragmentary (*'fragmentierte Rechtsdiskurse'* – fragmented legal discourses) and is always related to specific areas which provide for a considerable differentiation:

The boundaries of global law are formed not by maintaining a core 'territory' and expanding on a federal basis as Kant perceived in terms of nation-states, but rather, by 'invisible colleges', 'invisible markets and branches', 'invisible professional communities', 'invisible

[59] Ibid, 16.
[60] Ibid, 8-11.
[61] Ibid, 7.
[62] Ibid, 17.
[63] Ibid.

social networks' that transcend territorial boundaries but nevertheless press for the emergence of genuinely legal forms. A new law of conflicts is emerging on the basis of intersystemic, rather than international, conflicts. [64]

The conflict solving answers in international dispute resolution are successfully taken from the international contract by arbitrators.[65] They reach decisions without expressly referring to national law and their awards are generally accepted by national courts if they are to enforce them. National law is vital to arbitration and at the same time to the scope of *lex mercatoria* or a-national contract law.[66] It does not, however, contravene its existence or effectiveness. The nation state thus seems more tolerant of a law of no origin than a law of another sovereign state. Apparently there are few instances of the invocation of public policy or mandatory rules of the forum which are to enforce arbitration awards.[67]

In this way a-national law exists outside international (interstate) relations and cannot be compared with legal provisions based on public international law and on the authority of international organisations. Teubner thus supports his 'pluralistic theory of norm-production'. He claims that concrete norms, positive law, are produced 'in national politics and in international political relations, ... in judicial processes within the nation-states and in international courts', as well as in 'global economic and other social processes'.[68]

From the point of view of other authors, common-lawyers as well as continental theorists, the unity of law and state cannot be evaded; a-national law is unthinkable. A contract has to be based on a national legal order and thus international disputes have to be solved by conflict rules and, on a global level, under the auspices of international conventions based in turn on international public law.

Given this approach of legal theory, states insist on their law being different from that of other states. The distinction is equivalent to the distinction between political spheres of influence and territories. Thus, with this view, the law of the forum is generally identical to the law of the nation-state.[69]

To question this proposition by suggesting legal pluralism in norm production means to suggest that on an empirical level there is law which applies in numerous countries, by way of uniformity of source, and thus dissolves the boundaries between the national legal orders in certain fields, namely within the fields established by the global networks.

---

64 Ibid, 7-8.

65 For further discussion see Chapter 7.

66 Compare Chapter 8 for discussion.

67 See Mertens, op cit, 37: 'On the contrary, most states tend not to object to the use of principles not linked to any particular national law ... or even recognize such legal principles as part of their own law.'

68 G Teubner, op cit (n 56), 11.

69 See Chapter 6 for further discussion.

### 1.1.4 Conclusion

Section 1.1 explained the relationship between sovereignty of nation states as it is understood in current legal doctrine and contract law in general. It identified doctrinal elements which lead to the exclusion of transnational uniform contract law from the catalogue of possible law rules for operating in international trade law. However, these seem to be outdated.

The doctrine of unity of law and state as described above cannot claim universal acceptance or authority. Too many instances, both historic and contemporary, of non-compliance with its presumptions occur, particularly when questioning the idea of unity and diversity of national laws. The section has provided evidence that alternative plausible concepts already exist and that they deserve more attention for the sake of the modern globalised role of contract law.

This particularly concerns the substantive source of law function of transnational commercial law rules: they can claim legitimacy according to established legal theory which traditionally recognises law rules originating and deriving authority from sources other than state organs.[70]

Diversity of laws, correctly understood in the sense of legal pluralism, rather than simply denoting substantive and territorial differences between national laws, thereby allows for transnational contract law to apply to international contracts as law governing the contract.

## 1.2 Distinctiveness of substantive contract law of distinct sovereign states

Section 1.1 described the role of the state when acting directly within the sphere of contract law. Section 1.2 now investigates the aspect of substantive difference and distinctiveness of national contract laws understood as an element of the diversity of national laws. It asks whether laws of nation states are in fact strictly different from each other, and whether this can therefore be regarded as a formative aspect of sovereignty of nation states. National law under traditional doctrine would then be created by the state organs and be the same throughout the territory (providing unity) while at the same time being different from the law of other nation states (providing diversity). Consequently, this would by definition exclude transnational uniform contract law rules from being law. This section asks whether such a concept of diversity of national laws still exists in modern nation states and if it can be maintained by analysing the role of foreign law.

[70] See Part 3 for further discussion.

### 1.2.1 Application of foreign law

The distinction between laws in different countries would be a mere formal one if it was exclusively based on the fact that law rules are created and enacted by distinct sovereign bodies of legislation. Legal doctrine which is critical towards the use of transnational law also derives authority from the existence of differences between the contents of the legal rules of each country.[71] However, in some instances these differences cannot be established very clearly; claims of public policy are often put forward very vaguely and *de facto* is very rarely invoked to defend against a norm of foreign origin. Matters of the application of foreign laws and the significance of rivalry between national legal systems are analysed in this section.

#### *1.2.1.1 Forum and territory*

The direct application of foreign law by a court might be regarded as proof of the existence of a forum extending beyond the reach of a national territory and as an instance of disparity between law and state. A court's forum can actually coincide with several political territories and several legal systems or, with no political territory at all. The former two options were a standard situation during the Middle Ages in Europe. The latter may be exemplified by the International Criminal Court at The Hague.

Application of foreign law has a tradition in twentieth century German jurisdiction: the *Reichsgericht* had a special '*Senat*' (chamber) dealing with the application of French law.[72] Legal theory though, points to incompatibilities of this practice with the rules of the court's constitutional framework, as well as, to the requirement of special knowledge on the part of the judges, which is difficult to guarantee.[73] English Courts do apply foreign law directly since they function as appeal courts in certain cases; the House of Lords apply the laws of Scotland and Northern Ireland which are regarded as foreign law.[74] Thus the application of foreign law seems not to be exclusively determined by political distinctions between states and nations, but rather, by territorial aspects of jurisdiction which is not necessarily identical with the territory where a certain legal system is applicable.

How is a rule recognised as foreign? One state may well comprise of different legal systems, such as the common law and Scottish law in the United Kingdom, still not every court within those states applies legal rules of different origin to every case. The Privy Council being an appeal court for Commonwealth countries also used to apply laws of different countries which were foreign to the state in

[71] As opposed to the same content of a rule applied in different countries (uniformity of source) see below, Chapter 2.

[72] French law, brought to Germany by Napoleon lived on as 'Rhenish Law', much valued by its subjects and sought-after even by other German states, namely Bavaria and Hessen-Darmstadt and Würzburg: see U Eisenhardt, *Deutsche Rechtsgeschichte* (2004) §55.

[73] See D Koch, *Sitzungsbericht*, 152.

[74] J G Collier, *Conflict of laws* (Cambridge, Cambridge University Press, 2001), 6-7.

which the court was located. The law might thus be allocated to a forum rather than to a state and its territory. The extent of a forum might differ from that of the respective state.[75] This model allows a wider view of the doctrine of legal sources including the court as another provider of law, rather than the legislator as a sole political entity providing law and legitimacy.

Foreign law, however, is applied by virtue of conflict of laws rules. English courts will only apply a foreign law rule which is brought before it as a fact, the party 'who relies on the rules of a foreign system of law must plead and prove them'.[76] The conflict of laws thus determines whether the *lex fori* or the *lex causae* is to be applied – the territorial aspect being seen from the viewpoint of the court concerned. Law is thus to be conceived as being connected with the matter to be decided as well as with the court, in that the court has a forum which can comprise of foreign law, as is the case in certain procedures before the House of Lords.

### *1.2.1.2 Legal theory*

The application of foreign law has always faced the need to be explained and justified by legal theory. According to the vested rights theory a right or claim could be enforced on the grounds that it had been acquired under foreign law and thus could not be disregarded in the domestic context. The legal result created by foreign law was to be respected and dealt with according to domestic law.

> A right having been created by the appropriate law, the recognition of its existence should follow everywhere. Thus an act valid where done cannot be called in question anywhere.[77]

> ... although the act complained of was subject to no law having force in this forum, it gave rise to an obligation, an *obligatio* which, like other obligations, follows the person, and may be enforced wherever the person may be found.[78]

These statements acknowledge the legal effects of foreign law rules. Nevertheless, the significance of the recognition of foreign law for the sovereignty of states has caused intense scholarly discussion. The idea of sovereignty seems to contradict the possibility of the application of foreign law. The application of foreign law is, however, motivated by *comitas*:

> There are two reasons why we do not automatically take jurisdiction or apply English law in all cases. First there is a historical concern with excessive assertions of sovereignty and possible foreign reactions to this. Secondly, there is a concern with fairness to the parties.[79]

---

75 A historic reality in Europe.

76 Collier, op cit, 33. See R Fentiman, *Foreign Law in English Courts* (1998), for an in-depth treatment of the subject matter.

77 J Beale, *Treatise on the Conflict of Laws* (1935) Vol 3, 1969.

78 Oliver Wendell Holmes in *Slater* v *Mexican National RR* 194 US (1904) 120, 126.

79 J Fawcett, 'The interrelationships of jurisdiction and choice of law in private international law' Current Legal Problems 44 (1991) 39, 49-50.

Fawcett refers to the fact that the choice of law rules increasingly serve to establish whether English courts have jurisdiction over a matter according to Order 11 of the Rules of the Supreme Court (RSC). These jurisdiction rules require the ascertainment of the applicable jurisdiction, while findings for example, as to the proper law of the contract, are reached at the trial stage. The reported cases mostly concern the discretionary decision as to whether service of the writ out of the jurisdiction is admissible under Order 11 r1 RSC Fawcett therefore, raises the question as to whether the influence of the choice of law rules on jurisdiction should be extended:

> There would only nominally be rules on both jurisdiction and choice of law. In reality only one set of rules would actually be of any real importance in any given case, the choice of law rules, and the decision on the applicable law. This is a very radical idea which has been justified on the basis that the underlying concern is the same in both the area of jurisdiction and choice of law, a concern with excessive assertions of sovereignty.[80]

Fawcett refers here to ideas put forward by American authors, suggesting that jurisdiction and the applicable law should coincide in such a way that a state exclusively applies its own law or refuses jurisdiction. This approach promotes the congruence of the political and territorial sphere of influence of a state and the jurisdiction of its courts by applying the *lex fori* to every case. Its application is based on a value judgment upon the content of a law rule or legal system with a view to achieving a just solution. One criterion is the underlying interest and legislative policy of the state whose law is considered to be applied, the 'governmental interest analysis'. In a search for the 'better law' the choice is most likely to be one's own law. Thus in the USA, the main field of application of this doctrine, the *lex loci*, is in tort cases due to the respective considerations. The US however, being mainly concerned with inter-state conflict of laws, cannot be simply compared to any other country whose conflict rules are predominantly made to deal with conflict cases involving fundamentally different legal systems of independent sovereign countries. Thus, English writers such as Fawcett and Collier reject the extreme approach to the role of choice of law as part of jurisdiction considerations. It was also rejected by the House of Lords in *Chaplin* v *Boys.* [81]

The view taken by Collier is the following:

> Two other considerations are either overlooked or minimised by these theorists. First, the object of the conflict of laws, as of any other branch of private law, is to advance the interests of private persons, not the state or government. Secondly, one of the interests that private persons (and corporations) have is in some measure of certainty about the law; whether their contract will be enforceable or not and what are their rights and duties under it ... to give some examples only of what they wish to know.[82]

---

[80] Fawcett, op cit, 49.
[81] [1971] AC 356 (HL).
[82] J G Collier, *Conflict of laws* (2001) 385.

Courts do give effect to private interests of this kind rather than expressly or de facto enforcing state or government interests or policies; despite being state organs in that they are established and paid for by public authorities. Courts enjoy independence in order to find the law and therefore they do not simply enact the will of the government. Their sphere of influence can thus differ from that of the state and its territory. The role of a court is not to exercise political power but to decide conflicts in this case between private individuals. The applicable law can thus be subject to discussion as far as this is relevant to the problem solving process.

In the area of contract law, the interest and policies of states or governments are supposed to be reflected in mandatory rules. The parties to a contract cannot deviate from those rules and this limits the parties' autonomy. If the parties seek the assistance of state courts[83] and legal services to enforce contractual rights, these provide an instance where citizenship and political objectives reach the closest possible connection in contract law. Otherwise the legal concept of a party to a contract does not necessarily presuppose, or coincide with, that of the political subject of a state such as formal citizenship. This idea has allowed the evolution of the connecting factor of domicile rather than that of nationality.[84]

The so-called theory of the *droit acquis* was taught among others by Pillet at the start of the last century;[85] he claimed that the rights acquired under a foreign legal system were to be respected and enforced if, and when, the domestic conflict of laws rules pointed to that foreign law. This was owed to respect for the foreign country's sovereignty (comity). A slightly different view is taken by the local law theory as put forward by Walter Wheeler Cook:[86]

> The forum … always applies its own law to the case, but in doing so adopts and enforces as its own law a rule of decision identical, or at least highly similar … in scope with a rule of decision found in the system of law in force in another state or country … The forum thus enforces not a foreign right but a right created by its own law.

This view is adopted and further pursued in Italy by Santi Romano.[87] The legal order is supposed to be exclusive. Foreign law cannot be recognised as such. It is to be introduced through the medium of conflict of laws rules which give effect to the foreign legal result. These theories are themselves discussed and adopted internationally without regard for the borders of nation states. They are a common matter of interest. Thus the (American) local law theory, is criticised by the (English) writer Collier, as being 'really pointless':[88] he regards both this approach and

---

83 As opposed to seeking arbitration proceedings.

84 See the Dutch author Ulrich Huber in his Treatise from 1715 (possibly first published in 1661) in G Kegel, *Internationales Privatrecht* (6th ed, 1987) 112; compare G Kegel and K Schurig, *Internationales Privatrecht* (2004) 176; Lorenzen, 'Huber's *De Conflictu Legum*' in *Selected Articles on the Conflict of Laws* (1947) 136-180.

85 Pillet: *Traité pratique de droit international privé* (1923) Vol 1, 11-18, 119-129; Pillet: *Principes de droit international privé* (1903) 495-571.

86 W W Cook, *The Logical and Legal Bases of the Conflict of Laws* (1949) 20.

87 S Romano, *L'ordinamento giuridico*, 1st/2nd edns 1918/1946.

88 J G Collier, *Conflict of laws* (2001) 382.

the vested rights theory as wrongly based on the concern that applying foreign law automatically means 'subordination to a foreign sovereign and legislator'.

> But this concern is baseless; ... [rules of law] are not all imperative. An English court does not, therefore, apply a foreign rule because it is bound by the foreign sovereign to do so, but because it is constrained to do so by English law to achieve justice and a satisfactory solution to the problem before it.[89]

Although Collier's understanding of these conceptions of the application of foreign law might take the constructivist views expressed thereby too literally, they are clearly based on the idea that there is something wrong with directly applying foreign law. The arguments supporting this seem not only to be very casuistic and thus overlook certain conflicts of law constellations, but also seem to be taken from areas of legal theory which do not correspond to the special situation of private international law. As Collier says they are 'perhaps connected with Austinian theories of sovereignty and with views such as Kelsen's that rules of law are built on sanctions.'[90] The position described here necessarily involves the private individual as being subject to its state's law in the sense of being subordinate. Private law and the conflict of laws in the area of contracts, however, deal with relationships between individuals on an equal level, a level of equal rights and powers.[91] Once private law is recognised and guaranteed in a political context it is certainly to serve the interests of these private individuals, as Collier phrases it.[92] Therefore theories about the application of foreign law and about the nature of conflict of laws rules as such, have to be judged by the degree to which they want to give effect to the interests of private parties. In this sense I agree with the criticism put forward by Collier towards the theories in contention.

### 1.2.2 Reception of foreign law

The sharp distinction between legal systems is blurred further through the reception of foreign legal rules. Legal theory has recently referred quite intensely to the reception of US law in European countries.[93] In the context of the development of a European contract law it is suggested, that the European states should mutually recognise their contract laws so as to give parties to a contract a free choice. [94]

Reception can take place in various ways. The traditional reception of a legal system by another or within a foreign territory has often been linked to political influence, direct imposition and force, as occurred when Roman law and French

89 Ibid.
90 Ibid.
91 See above.
92 See above.
93 But still not comprehensively enough, as Ugo Mattei sees it: U Mattei. 'Why the Wind changed' Am J Comp L 42 (1994) 195, 218.
94 C Kirchner: '*Europäisches Vertragsrecht*', 133.

law (*Code Civil*) received in Germany[95], when English law came into India during the time of the Empire ('English law circulated *ratione imperii*'[96]), and when American law came into Japan after World War II. There is, however another form of reception, the creation of 'legal transplants'.[97] This is the phenomenon of borrowing from other legal systems. The distinction between 'legal families' as is made by comparatists is not confined to nation states. It can extend beyond their borders, or not as far as, e.g. Canada. Distinct legal spheres such as the common law and the civil law have recently been examined as to their distinctiveness. By the use or creation of such transplants something called 'intellectual leadership' is established by a certain representative of a legal system: a state. But 'leadership' in this sense, is not acquired by political or military power, but rather, in the intellectual way, by choice not by imposition.

Mattei describes the historic move of intellectual leadership from French law to German law and to American law at present.[98] Examples of legal transplant from American law to German law are; the leasing contract, the new product liability law, as well as, the procedural rules on bankruptcy which aim to incorporate a similar solution to the 'Chapter 11' way of clearing personal debts. The use of American vocabulary in the German legal language as such is a symptom of the reception of American law: leasing, franchising, joint venture, merger, all acquire meanings in their own right and often lack a German translation. Mattei describes the profound influence of German refugee scholars in America inducing the formation of 'American intellectual leadership': the acceptance of cross-cultural scholarly activities is another factor of the spreading of legal solutions (the law making role of scholarship provided) over more than one country or legal system.

Legal science and legal education are certainly to be considered 'legal formants' in the sense of Sacco's concept.[99] They serve as a vehicle to import and export law between countries and legal systems. Reception means that features of a legal system are 'considered, discussed, copied or adopted'.[100] Since the law of a country on the one hand never exclusively consists of the positive law rules enacted by parliament or formulated by judges, but also of scholarly opinion and legal discourse which are influenced by foreign elements, domestic law is not pure in its substantive quality.

---

[95] See U Eisenhardt, *Deutsche Rechtsgeschichte* (2004) §§14, 55.

[96] Mattei, op cit, 201.

[97] See A Watson, *Legal Transplants* (1974).

[98] Mattei, op cit, 195.

[99] R Sacco, 'Legal Formants: A dynamic approach to comparative law (Inst II)', Am J Comp L 29 (1991) 343, 346; P-C Müller-Graff, *Gemeinsames Privatrecht in der Europäischen Gemeinschaft*, 13 with further notes; W Wiegand, 'The reception of American Law in Europe' Am J Comp L (1991) 230-233. 'The education of lawyers is a key function in the process of reception' (Wiegand, op cit, 146).

[100] Mattei, op cit, 201; see also the remarks in M P Furmston, *Cheshire, Fifoot and Furmston's Law of Contract* (2001) 15-16 describing the influence of continental jurisprudence on the development of English contract law in the nineteenth century, namely the reception of the teachings of Pothier and Savigny through English lawyers.

Thus, distinguishing between laws of different countries in a substantive sense by referring to the territorial and political boundaries of the nation state seems quite superficial.

### 1.2.3 Conclusion

Section 1.2 shows that there are no sharp distinctions between substantive national contract laws, but that borderlines are blurred by both historical and current practices of receiving and actively applying foreign laws. Therefore, the idea of diversity of laws flowing from the state as the sole source of law and providing an aspect of sovereignty of states is unsuitable for describing the nature of contract law.

## 1.3 Party autonomy: How autonomous is the individual?

The previous sections have dealt with the role of the state (1.1) and the role of the substantive law itself (1.2) in the doctrine of diversity of national laws and looked at how this enables or impedes the use of transnational uniform contract law. Section 1.3 examines the role of the individual. It asks to what extent individuals can create their own legal relationships and use state contract law at their discretion to govern their contracts. This leads to questions of party autonomy, freedom of contract and choice of law in general.

### 1.3.1 Choice of law

Party autonomy, allowing the choice of law governing contracts, is granted by almost every jurisdiction. It is disputed, however, as to what extent transnational law rules can be stipulated to be governing law, to the exclusion of domestic law, the so-called *kollisionsrechtliche Verweisung* or vocation. This choice would require transnational law rules to be applied in the same way as any other formal rule of law or legal system. Questions of conflicts with domestic law would arise in overlapping areas or where contents might be regarded as incompatible with national law. While Part 2 and Part 3 below provide a detailed account of the application of transnational law rules according to current legal theory and court practice, using the UPICC as an example, this section sets out the general setting for transnational law within conflict of laws doctrines without a reference to any particular set of rules.

#### *1.3.1.1 Common law*

At common law, party autonomy leads to the doctrine of the proper law of the contract.

English conflict rules accord to the parties to a contract a wide liberty to choose the law by which their contract is to be governed.[101]

The parties can choose the law of a country expressly, or the court will investigate their intentions by necessary implication.[102] The fact that foreign law appears as fact before English courts cannot be interpreted as a comparative reluctance to apply foreign law in relation to the situation under German conflict of laws rules, where courts investigate foreign law *ex officio*. The difference rather originates from the predominantly adversarial and more court-oriented procedural system in England: the territory of the law is conceived as being assigned more to a court and its forum rather than to the legislator representing a (nation) state. The English conflicts of law rules reflect the strong tradition of the courts. In fact the example of the domicile of a person forming a connecting factor shows a looser link to political borders than the German solution of choosing nationality as a connecting factor in comparable cases.[103] English traditional conflicts of law rules seem to be less politically oriented than German ones.

#### 1.3.1.2 The Rome Convention

Germany has adopted the provisions of the Rome Convention 1980 by way of the 'IPR-Gesetz' (1986) which reformed the EGBGB (*Einführungsgesetz zum Bürgerlichen Gesetzbuch* – Introductory Code for the Civil Code). In the UK this Convention was implemented by the Contracts (Applicable Law) Act 1989.

In German conflict law this led to a more liberal approach to party autonomy. Parties could now choose foreign law to govern their contract or parts of it even though it had no connection to any other state. Before, the provision relating to general contract terms had required a 'special interest' for the effective choice of foreign law rules (§10 No 8 AGBG). This provision was overridden by Art 6 §2 IPRG. Today the code says expressly, in Art 27 EGBGB, incorporating the Rome Convention, that the parties are free to choose the law governing their contract (para [1]) even in domestic cases (para [3]) – even though they cannot deviate from mandatory rules of the country with which the contract is most closely connected – and that they can change these provisions at any time *ex nunc* and *ex tunc*, (para [2]). Thus, at present, the only limitation to party autonomy in this respect, under German law, remains the relevance of mandatory rules of the 'proper law' of a contract which cannot be ruled out by *dépeçage*. The option of incorporating foreign law rules into the contract (*materiellrechtliche Verweisung*) will subject these to the interpretation rules relating to contractual clauses.[104] The general rules as to ascertainment of the applicable law still apply.

---

[101] *Amin Rasheed Shipping Corporation* v *Kuwait Insurance Co* [1984] AC 50, 61.

[102] Ibid.

[103] Succession cases.

[104] See OLG Hamburg IPRspr 1930 Nr 57. This is called '*materiellrechtliche Verweisung*' – substantive *renvoi*. G Kegel and K Schurig, *Internationales Privatrecht* (2004) 654.

### 1.3.2 Limits of choice of law: Doctrines of evasion and the role of mandatory rules

The incentive to choose the applicable law will mainly be an international aspect of the contract. Either because the parties reside in different countries or they are making a contract about goods to be shipped between different countries. The decision as to which particular system of law they would want to govern their contract is largely unlimited reflecting a wide range of motivations and reasons for a specific choice.[105] Is this choice always respected by courts? The parties' choice might pursue the aim of subjecting the contract to a 'neutral' law, which does not give either party an 'undue' advantage in that one of them might be more familiar with it, or simply that it is not the domestic law of either of them, thereby symbolising equal positions.[106] This suggests the attractiveness of a-national law for governing a contract which will be discussed later.[107]

Another motivation could be to find a legal system with a 'cheap quality' which provides little obligations and large benefits, eg, according to the amount of damages or extensive possibilities for terminating an agreement which has become economically unattractive. This motivation is often criticised as forum shopping and is sought to be prevented. The European Convention on the Recognition and Enforcement of Foreign Judgments (hereinafter Judgments Convention) is designed to regulate and minimise possibilities for forum shopping within the range of member states.

Evasion of the law sometimes has a taste of *au goût* attached to it. Indeed, French international private law knows the institution of *fraude à la loi.* This is unknown to English law in a doctrinal form. Evasion can be described as having a particular purpose and motivation behind, for example, the choice of law in an international contract. The fact that the law of Utopia is made, the applicable law to a contract which is concluded in England, could be regarded as being evasive if the parties particularly meant to escape English law. English jurisdiction is not necessarily avoided at the same time. This occurred in cases of 'evasive marriages' in former days where couples went abroad to make foreign legal provisions apply to their degree of marriage, or to their capacity. The legal issues arising from that marriage were nevertheless tried in England later since the married couple moved back to live in England.[108] This, however, led to the failure of the parties' intention. Evasion was not made an independent criterion, but led to the moulding of connecting factors which classified those cases as dealing with essential validity subject to the law of the domicile of the parties. In contract cases there is a requirement of good faith which can limit the parties' freedom to choose the law applicable to their contract. Express evasion of English law would contravene the bona fides doctrine. There is, however, no reported case where a choice of law

---

[105] See Chapters 7 and 8.

[106] See, eg, OLG München IPrax 86, 178 LS. This reminds us of diplomatic delegations meeting in a 'neutral' place (such as Geneva or Vienna) to negotiate delicate matters.

[107] See Chapters 7 and 8.

[108] See *Brook* v *Brook* [1858] 3 Sm and G 481; *Cheni* v *Cheni* [1965] P 85.

was struck out by English courts on these grounds.[109] Mandatory rules are incorporated in section 27 of the Unfair Contract Terms Act 1977. A choice of law made by parties to a contract which appears 'to have been imposed wholly or mainly for the purpose of enabling the party imposing it to evade the operation of this Act',[110] will not be given effect under its rules and party autonomy is thereby restricted.

Consumer protection is the most prominent area in private law where most states have provided for mandatory rules. In the area of commercial contracts the Carriage of Goods by Sea Act 1971 can serve as an example. The purpose of this Act is to give Article X of the Hague-Visby rules relating to the liability of parties to bills of lading – the force of law and the quality of a mandatory rule. It cannot be evaded by a choice of law clause pointing to a law which does not apply the Hague-Visby rules.

Evasion cannot be condemned generally as an impure practice, although 'the term is a loaded one, with connotations of shifty, underhand behaviour'.[111] However, Fawcett gives two reasons for which a choice of law should be regarded as undue evasion, other than simply being made in bad faith; cases of unfairness and where the attempted choice of law is against the national interest. Here, the motives of the parties have a specific quality which is subject to certain political regulatory interests, policies which are intended to override party autonomy. An important example where such a policy is enshrined in a statute is the Unfair Contract Terms Act 1977. The protection of consumers from exemption clauses is regarded as being equivalent to rules of public policy.[112] Therefore, the intention of parties of a contract to apply a foreign law in order to avoid this act is not against the state's interest merely because its own law is not applied. Balancing the parties' freedom of choice against the national interest only justifies a restriction of party autonomy if there is a 'strong social or economic policy'.

> The parties should not be lightly denied this right to choose. The balance only tips in favour of the interest of the state when the law which is being thwarted expresses a strong social or economic policy.[113]

In the commercial sphere, the Carriage of Goods by Sea Act represents such a policy; to avoid unfairness to one, usually weaker party: 'even in contracts between two large commercial undertakings one party may have the whip hand'.[114]

Do states protect the national interests and policies expressed in foreign laws? They do this if and when 'the national interest dictates that a foreign law should not be thwarted ... The only basis for a national interest in this situation is that of

---

109 See as examples *Vita Food Products* v *Unus Shipping Company* [1939] AC 277 and *Greenshields* v *Johnston* [1981] 119 DLR (3d) 714.

110 Section 27(2)(a).

111 J J Fawcett, 'Evasion of law and mandatory rules in private international law' Cambridge Law Journal 49.1 (1990) 50.

112 Law Commission, No 69, para 211.

113 See Fawcett, op cit, 53.

114 Fawcett, op cit, 52; see *The Hollandia* [1982] QB 872, [1983] AC 565 (HL) and *The Torni* [1932] P 78, 84.

considerations of comity of nations.'[115] This, however, is an exception as shown by the cases *Foster* v *Briscol*,[116] and *Regazzoni* v *Sethia*.[117] There, the enforcement of the obligations in contention involved the breaking of the law of a foreign friendly country in an extreme way which would not be comparable to cases where foreign law on exemption clauses is concerned. 'Given that English rules on exemption clauses give adequate protection to consumers it is hard to believe that considerations of comity dictate that more stringent foreign rules must be upheld.'[118] Fawcett here refers to cases to which English and foreign mandatory rules could apply accumulatively and thus compete. What about cases in which foreign mandatory rules apply in an area where English law does not know mandatory regulations, so as to supplement the English rules? The Rome Convention makes it clear that the mandatory rules of the forum can be applied without qualification to contracts that may otherwise be subject to foreign law by choice or under conflict rules. It thereby gives special protection to the interest of a forum to apply its own law. The parties' choice of law is thus disregarded as to the intended legal effect conflicting with the rules in question. The question remains, however, which mandatory rules of foreign countries may otherwise be applicable. If these rules express such a strong socio-economic policy every country could have an interest in having these rules applied: whether its law is the proper law of the contract, has the closest connection with the case, or is only remotely concerned by it. The Rome Convention says that 'effect may be given to the mandatory law of another country with which the situation has a close connection'. [119] This seems to leave discretion as to the application of the rules as well as to the manner in which to do so (direct or indirect). Fawcett calls it uncertainty.[120] It has to be considered whether this means uncertainty to the prejudice of contracting parties trying to choose a law to govern their contract, or to that of the court possibly trying the case with an underlying intention to give as much effect as possible to the *lex fori*.

### 1.3.3 Conclusion

The extent to which national laws grant contracting parties the freedom to choose the governing law for their contract determines the extent to which sovereignty is exercised over private individuals and dealings. It is also a measurement for the tolerance towards foreign law and therefore for the extent of distinctiveness between national laws in terms of forming clear borderlines in a substantive sense. This section has given account of the current status of this notion in national law and has shown why the nature of contract law (as opposed to other regulatory na-

---

[115] J J Fawcett, 'Evasion of law and mandatory rules in private international law' Cambr L J 49.1 (1990) 44, 53-55.
[116] [1929] KB 470.
[117] [1958] AC 301.
[118] Fawcett, op cit, 57.
[119] Art (7) (1) Rome Convention 1980 / Contracts (Applicable Law) Act 1990.
[120] Fawcett, op cit, 61.

tional law) and the status of the individual are the key arguments in determining the desirable scope of mandatory rules and choice of law rules regulating private dealings in modern nation states.

## 1.4 Conclusion

Chapter 1 identified relevant elements of legal theory relating to contract law in nation states which deny rules of transnational uniform contract law legitimacy and a substantive source of law function (1.1, 1.2) while limiting the choice of law capacities of private individuals (1.3). These are obstacles to the successful application of specialised transnational contract law rules and could be addressed as a form of 'legal conservatism', forming a barrier against the use of uniform law in international trade.

Chapter 1 has however, shown evidence that it is possible to integrate uniform law using other, equally traditional elements of contract doctrine by identifying and highlighting them in their wider context following a thorough review of underlying concepts both on a political and philosophical level.

The doctrine of unity of law and state which is a central element of traditional contract law doctrine cannot claim universal acceptance or authority. Too many instances, both historic and contemporary, of disparity between practice and its presumptions occur because its assumptions are uncritically extended from other regulatory law to contract law.

The concept of inevitable unity of law and state is an aspect of traditional theory built on outdated foundations as far as ideas stemming from the feudalistic and positivist eras underlie them. The modern nation state, however, is defined by its civil society and the equal relationship between citizens (contracting parties). The nature of contract law as a key element of free trade has to be revisited by revisiting practices of pre-nationalistic eras, for instance, the Middle Ages where the law merchant first evolved, throughout the history of the Hanseatic League or the evolution of English commercial case law.

There is a tendency of state organs and courts to prefer the domestic law and the *lex fori* to those of other countries via conflict rules, mandatory rules and doctrines of public policy and party autonomy which reinforces the impression that unity of law and state is inevitable. This practice forms an obstacle to the application of uniform contract law.

The concept of diversity of laws (1.3) is a consequence of this understanding of sovereignty and legitimacy, as the states are distinct from each other forming seemingly separate but homogeneous entities of national laws (unity). This is a questionable concept, however, because the borders between laws are blurred by reception, jurisdiction rules, international legal science and many other factors (1.2). It is not a static concept and is therefore open to adjustment. The sovereignty of states is not affected by a liberal application of party autonomy, as it is assumed by critics, and therefore does not need to be defended against a modern contract law doctrine (1.1, 1.3). A substantive source of law function of transnational commercial law rules is therefore possible even according to established legal theory which does traditionally recognise law rules originating and deriving authority and legitimacy from sources other than state organs.[121] Diversity of laws is correctly to be understood as legal pluralism.

In order to overcome these existing impediments against the use of transnational contract law in different domestic legal systems, it is therefore not necessary to invent a novel concept of contract law, but rather review positions which claim universal validity on a surface level and thereby form obstacles to the application of uniform law. The key aspect to be highlighted is the nature of contract law being private law regulating the dealings of private individuals. Their position within modern nation states has to be recalled in order to derive an appropriate role of national contract and conflict law. Such a review was carried out in this chapter and proves that uniform law can be integrated into the existing doctrine of contract law.

The process of reviewing such positions and highlighting supportive aspects of traditional legal theory in the different legal systems, however, forms an element of a novel methodology of international contract law.

[121] See Part 3 for further discussion.

# 2 Unity through uniform private law

The previous chapter dealt with legitimacy and functional source of law quality of uniform international law. This chapter explores the outward appearance and form of such law; it investigates its manifestation as one text and asks to what extent functional unity of legal solutions is attainable through drafting and interpreting of law rules.

This chapter explores the question of the nature and definition of the generic quality of transnational uniform contract law, with regard to the notion of unity. It asks whether uniformity is needed in international trade law and to what extent it is needed (2.1). It identifies arguments contesting the usefulness and achievability of uniformity on an international level and thereby highlights barriers to the use of such law rules. The chapter then investigates ways to remove obstacles to the use of uniform contract law in this area of theoretical dispute, including arguments relating to the idea of codifying rules of law in general (2.2).

Unity of laws on an international level, which form the opposite concept to diversity, can be understood in a number of ways. Uniformisation or unification of national laws is one possible meaning. The latter could be regarded an extreme move since it might realise all fears and expectations regarding a loss of sovereignty, or rather a shift of sovereignty onto the creator, the origin, of the (supranational) uniform source of law, eg, the EU and its institutions. Uniformity in a functional sense is the eventual aim of harmonisation efforts in the European Community. Within the scope of the Treaty, ie, the common policies, the ideal standard is to achieve the same legal solutions for a given problem in all member states. EC law appears as a uniform source of law in the form of the Treaty, Directives and Regulations as well as legally binding decisions by the Commission etc. Thus, it is one example, a form and manifestation of uniform transnational law since its legal effects extend across several national legal systems and originate outside these legal boundaries.

Another different form of transnational law source is the CISG, a multilateral Convention. This has the force of law in the signatory states (eg, Germany, not the UK), and appears as law in its original form without the interference of implementing legislation, thereby avoiding any alteration of the original text. The application of this Convention within domestic law is not part of everyday legal practice however, nor is it in education and contract drafting, or in court practice.[1] Instead, the Convention is often excluded by contract clauses, so the development of methodology in this field is not considered an urgent issue in legal science.

---

[1] See Chapter 8, eg, at 8.2.2.6 and 8.2.3.3 for further discussion.

Given the critical views on the role and quality of EC Directives,[2] this is surprising, considering the accessibility of the uniform source of law as a common text. The CISG encounters problems on the functional and substantive side in Germany, though. Some of its features are considered to predominantly belong to Anglo-Saxon legal systems, and these are often said to clash with certain aspects of German law. This view lacks a thorough methodological basis which would allow proper integration of transnational law rules into German domestic law. This study provides an example of how to develop such a specific method. The UPICC represent another type of uniform transnational law originating from yet another source, ie, a group of legal scholars rather than a political body.

## 2.1 Why uniformity?

This section asks for the need for unity and uniformity in international trade law. It follows up on critical arguments questioning the usefulness and desirability of uniform law.

The concept of uniform source of law is the core concept of unity in the law. The law materialises as one text which is applied by diverse users. Uniformity as an objective in international contract law is not self-explanatory. Regarding the UPICC, they are motivated by the actual needs for uniformity which require legal services to create and sustain uniform contract law on a transnational level. This is to be distinguished from the politically motivated driving force behind the uniformisation efforts, for example, on the community level where there are political powers in charge of creating new uniform legal sources.[3] The creation of a new source of law function equalling a political power, such as a sovereign entity, is not the objective of the UPICC and their creators.

### 2.1.1 Globalisation

One of the needs for uniformity emerges from the modern process called globalisation. 'International production appears as a real challenge to the official allocation, among states, of the power of regulating the economy.'[4] This is due to fewer trade barriers, interlocked financial markets and multi-national enterprises acting as 'global players' who are able to transfer workers, ideas, materials and products all around the world, so that in some cases it is hard to even establish the place (state) of their seat.

---

[2] See for instance T C Hartley, 'The European Court, Judicial Objectivity and the Constitution of the European Union' Law Quarterly Review 112 (1996) 95 and T C Hartley, *The Transposition and Interpretation of EC Directives: The British Viewpoint* (1997).

[3] The same applies to uniformisation efforts in the US such as the UCC or the Restatements of Contract Law.

[4] J-P Robé, 'Multinational Enterprises: The Constitution of a Pluralistic Legal Order', 45-79, 68.

Purely domestic legal systems, traditionally aimed at domestic legal situations, do not respond adequately to many of those constellations, both in corporate and contract law. Examples include commodities contracts being passed through chains of buyers and sellers which often cannot be allocated to a specific country by applying the characteristic performance rule.[5]

The above described theory of unity of law and state,[6] rooted in the era of the emerging idea of nation state and positivism, does not genuinely consider cross-border transactions because of its national viewpoint. On the contrary, modern developments, eg, incorporating the Treaty of Schengen within the EU, as well as an EU citizenship, deliberately facilitate unlimited mobility of persons, services and goods across borders. The requirement of transnational law is that of a transnational community which is only beginning to evolve. This transnational community is shaping up geographically through technical developments such as communication, technology and travel. Professor Fox explains that, 'not all law needs to be harmonized; one searches for the problems that most demand attention and for solutions that are feasible because they draw upon shared goals ...'[7] These shared goals form the community on an international level which gives itself its own rules. In this way, there is a general need for 'global law' because of the existence of a global legal space created by international trade.

The room for discourse, which Teubner describes and which he considers the source and catalyst for de-localised law, develops thereby in both an intellectual and geographical sense.[8] Eleanor Fox states: 'Disharmonies of law and procedure are costly and bothersome'.[9] She sees interdependence between increasing international transactions and activities, and the costs of having differences. Here, she describes the urge for uniform law: 'People begin to wish for harmonization in order to tidy up a messy world; they wish everyone would adopt the ideal standard, which is the one they like best'. They can, however, only be as consistent and homogeneous as is the respective community.

### 2.1.2 The costs of difference

The above mentioned 'costly and bothersome' differences among national contract laws and the diversity of conflict law create a need for uniform contract law.

The costs of difference can be precisely described in a monetary sense: the costs arising from the necessary research of the law applying to any transaction or involving a party from one or more foreign countries are those for legal consul-

---

5 Contained in the RC and implementing national legislation and see Chapter 6.

6 Compare Chapter 1.

7 E Fox, 'Harmonization of Law and Procedures in a Globalized world' Antitrust LJ 60 (1992) 593.

8 G Teubner, '"Global Bukowina": Legal Pluralism in the World Society' 12.

9 Fox, op cit, 593.

tancy, litigation and its economic risks.[10] Uniform law can reduce these costs to the extent to which true uniformity is achieved.

Professor Kramer, in his talk on the section on validity of contracts in the UPICC at the UNIDROIT conference in Basel, November 1997,[11] called diversity in private law '*disfunktionale Handelsschranken*' (dysfunctional trade barriers). Professor Kramer stated that the uncertainty about the applicable law very often compensates the interest tradesmen have in the deal, and thus many contracts remain unconcluded, but would come into existence if there was more certainty.[12] Those who decide to blindly take the risk of agreeing to the law of the other party's country to govern the contract often do so in order to save negotiating or because the other party is economically stronger. Often, the parties choose a 'neutral law' of a third country both being rather unaware of the solutions this law will provide in case of a dispute. These provisions are often made in the belief that the contract will be performed without problems. Indeed, most international contracts do not encounter any trouble while only a small number are brought before arbitral tribunals or state courts, who then have to deal with those contracts which were made with quite considerable unawareness of any particular legal system.[13] The stipulation of 'natural justice' or lex mercatoria as governing law is one frequent choice of law clause in such cases.[14]

### 2.1.3 Inverse conclusion: Indicators of acceptance

Another indication for the need of uniform law is the extent to which the UPICC have actually been accepted within the legal practice. Professor Bonell regularly reports on the development of their dissemination and use. From two surveys which were undertaken by UNIDROIT between 1994 and 1997 and by CENTRAL[15] it was apparent that many lawyers and arbitrators took recourse to the Principles and found them helpful.[16] The UPICC have actually found consid-

---

10 Compare Chapter 8, and see P Mankowski, '*Rechtswahl für Verträge des internationalen Wirtschaftsverkehrs*' RIW 1 (2003) 3, who calls them '*Rechtsermittlungskosten*' and '*Rechtsinformationskosten*'.

11 Conference paper, E Kramer, '*Die Gültigkeit der Verträge nach den Unidroit - Principles*' (1997), published as E Kramer, 'Contractual Validity according to the UNIDROIT Principles' European Journal of Law Reform 1.3 (1998/1999) 269.

12 Which can be brought about by more knowledge about the foreign law.

13 F Vischer, *Die Relevanz der UNIDROIT Principles für die richterliche und schiedsrichterliche Beurteilung von Streitigkeiten aus internationalen Verträgen* (1997).

14 See Chapters 7 and 8.

15 Center for Transnational Law at the University of Münster (Prof K P Berger).

16 Compare M J Bonell, 'The UNIDROIT Principles in Practice: The Experience of the First Two Years' Uniform Law Review 1 (1997) 34; M J Bonell, 'UNIDROIT Principles 2004 – The New Edition of the Principles of International Commercial Contracts adopted by the Institute for the Unification of Private Law' Uniform Law Review 1 (2004) 5 at 9, note 23.

eration in the drafting process of civil codes of countries which reformed their legal system after a political change, such as Estonia, the Czech Republic, Lithuania and the Russian Federation.[17] The Principles even influenced the drafting process of the new Dutch Civil Code and that of Quebec, as well as the Scottish and German Law Commission in the course of their work eg, the new law of obligations in Germany.

Non-English-speaking parties may find them translated into their language, but otherwise, a mutual understanding of the governing law is supported by referring to the UPICC as an international English language legal instrument. This applies of course, regardless of the alternative option to choose English law for reasons of language and the general popularity of the forum London for international dispute settlement.[18] This choice implies not just an English language governing law but provides a whole legal cosmos which the parties might not be familiar with. This is often overlooked in international contract drafting.[19]

In addition to the potential choice of law, uniform contract law can play the role of a model for contract drafting. The higher its quality in terms of skilful drafting, the greater its use for international lawyers. The UPICC have found high acclaim unanimously throughout legal science and practice for their high quality in this respect.[20]

### 2.1.4 Conclusion

Section 2.1 has shown that uniformity of laws is needed on an international level in trade law. It is not merely a theoretical subject but a real phenomenon in international trade, manifesting in trade relationships and the fact that uniform model laws and other examples of transnational law rules are well received in law reform and international commercial arbitration.

---

[17] Ibid. See also M J Bonell, 'UNIDROIT Principles 2004 – The New Edition of the Principles of International Commercial Contracts adopted by the Institute for the Unification of Private Law' Uniform Law Review 1 (2004) 5 at 7-8.

[18] One of a number of often rather irrational motivations for choice of law: see E Brödermann, 'Die erweiterten UNIDROIT Principles 2004' RIW 50.10 (2004) 721 at 722 et seq; P Mankowski, 'Rechtswahl für Verträge des internationalen Wirtschaftsverkehrs' RIW 1 (2003) 2-15; and see Chapter 8 below.

[19] See Chapter 8, and see P Mankowski, '*Rechtswahl für Verträge des internationalen Wirtschaftsverkehrs*' RIW 1 (2003) 2.

[20] Compare Mankowski, ibid; Kramer, op cit (n 11), 227; C-W Canaris, '*Die Stellung der* "UNIDROIT Principles" *und* "Principles of European Contract Law" *im System der Rechts*quellen' 5-31; R Goode, 'Usage and its Reception in Transnational Commercial Law' International and Comparative Law Quarterly 46 (1997) 1; E Brödermann, '*Die erweiterten* UNIDROIT Principles 2004' RIW 50.10 (2004), 721. See 2.1.3 below.

## 2.2 What uniformity?

The previous section dealt with the aspect of the necessity to use and create transnational uniform contract law. This section asks what form such law can take, what makes this law uniform, and what unity of laws might mean with regard to applying and interpreting such law in different legal systems and jurisdictions.

There are two sides of uniformity of law: uniformity of results and uniformity of sources. Uniformity of results in the application of the law is a popular demand and is mostly discussed under the heading of certainty and predictability in legal discourse. This presupposes uniform law sources as they are usually present on the domestic level. On a transnational and global level this means uniform sources of contract law for the merchant community. Besides the above discussed aspect of inherent legitimacy of transnational law, uniformity of transnational law is another quality of the law, namely the actual shape it takes: one form of appearance is written law rules which are ascertainable and accessible in the same way for everybody – such as the UPICC.[21]

Uniformity means recognisable manifestation and thereby distinction of law from non-law. Once again, one can realise a simultaneous occurrence of uniformity and distinctiveness, of unity and diversity. It is the degree of manifestation which determines whether or not transnational law, especially all phenomena which are called lex mercatoria, qualify as law in the eyes of the critical voices who tend to deny the lex mercatoria its source of law function without distinguishing individual phenomena within this complex of legal instruments.

The main argument against them being law is that they are vague and unascertainable, ie, non-law, not distinguishable from non-law and therefore not uniform. Teubner describes the paradoxical aspect of this process in-depth.[22]

### 2.2.1 Uniformity of results: The desire for certainty and predictability

Uniformity of law thus serves to establish certainty and predictability of the law. It is to serve the aim to submit people to the rule of law rather than to 'the rule of men' – law would otherwise be perceived as the 'creation of wilful interpreters'.[23] Certainty and predictability, however, are the core issues of misunderstanding between lawyers and businessmen confronted with questions of international trade law. Businessmen, who are after all the addressees of the transnational law rules, seek the same kind of certainty which allows them to create a strict timetable for the venture. The standard contract forms used in the commodities trade are good examples for such an understanding of certainty and predictability. The legal background for these transactions needs to be clear cut, allowing the merchants to

[21] Other possible non-written forms are custom or a body of case law rendered by arbitral tribunals. See Chapters 7 and 8 for further discussion.

[22] G Teubner, 'Breaking Frames: Economic Globalisation and the Emergence of the *lex mercatoria*' European Journal of Social Theory 5.2 (2002) 199.

[23] S Levinson, 'Law as Literature' 155.

decide on pricing, risk allocation and insurance requirements. This understanding of certainty is, in turn, the very reason why they sometimes fail to achieve this objective and, instead of smooth sailing, a dispute arises and litigation ensues.[24] It might be due to the businessman's orientation towards economical efficiency rather than towards mediation and conflict settlement that businessmen often feel they do not get what they want out of a legal dispute: justice.[25]

Predictability and certainty in the law is often understood to mean: one problem – one answer. The nature of contract law and legal reasoning never really reveals itself to many users of legal services. They tend to suspect too much discretion in the activities of the law-applying body, the court. They have a natural dislike for the dynamic character of the law which needs concrete application to a single case in order to manifest. This process has effervescent qualities for a trader who measures the value of his activities in hard money not learned speeches. However, '... it is sometimes said that certainty in the law is an illusion; and there is more than a grain of truth in this, once a dispute has gone to litigation'.[26] Not even a most elaborately formulated rule will open the paradise of complete certainty because it is 'not possible to devise any formula ... which will be adequate and appropriate for every possible contingency'.[27] This understanding of certainty means automatism. As much as this might be sought by the above mentioned business attitude this is wishful thinking and not attainable in legal reality.[28]

Predictability and certainty of law are one objective of codification and drafting techniques: effort is usually made to achieve the utmost precision and clarity in legal texts. The proper understanding of certainty has to be more complex: it is achieved through the method. Plausible solutions are reached by way of accepted methods. There is a range of solutions which is predictable, and certainty is limited to this range. Uncertainty remains an element of litigation as long as there are human beings involved.[29] Applying the law is nothing mechanical, but rather a creative act. To maintain standards of legitimacy and ultimately justice, the notion of procedure is therefore essential. [30]

---

[24] Compare *Richco International Ltd* v *Alfred C Toepfer International GmbH (The Bonde)* [1991] 1 Lloyd's Rep 136; *Richco International* v *Bunge (The New Prosper)* [1991] 2 Lloyd's Rep 92; see M Bridge, 'Good Faith in Commercial Contracts' 139 at 161-162 for analysis.

[25] Compare Chapter 1.

[26] G H Treitel, *Doctrine and Discretion in the Law of Contract* (1981) 3.

[27] New South Wales Law Reform Commission, quoted in Treitel, ibid, 19.

[28] 'The dream of a mechanical justice is recognized for what it is – only a dream and not even a rosy or desirable one.' A L Corbin, *Corbin on Contracts* (1964/2002) Vol 12, § 1136.

[29] Compare also Chapter 5 and see O Lando, '*Homo judicans*' Uniform Law Review 2/3 (1998) 535.

[30] See above, 1.1.3.2.

### 2.2.2 Uniformity of sources

Written law rules, codes, are the most prominent, visible, accessible form of uniform legal source. So, they are to be assessed here, with the UPICC as an example on the transnational level. This is not to question the existence of uniform case law on an international level, as well as general unwritten principles of law.

The concept of uniformity is a standard by which private law on an international level is measured. Transnational law is exposed to higher expectations as to the aspects of certainty and predictability. The latter qualities are not considered *conditio sine qua non* on the level of domestic law, but are readily used as an argument against the workability of transnational legal rules.[31] This might, however, reflect the generally increased level of uncertainty involved in transnational dealings. Higher expectations regarding international law, as opposed to domestic law, might be justified given that there is no state judiciary and legal administration on the international level – another argument against the existence and acceptability of transnational contract law.

One text – one legal solution. Frequent targets of criticism on the international level are EC Directives and multilateral conventions like the CISG. Such criticism, concerning clarity and certainty of the law, often refers to the idea of codified law in general, as well as to written law on an international level from where it is to be applied in different jurisdictions, often indirectly through another transforming process of implementation. Again both the function and the form of the law are to be looked at: the codification as a manifestation of legal source and the quality of the text – the drafting technique.

#### *2.2.2.1 Uniformity through codification on the domestic level*

Codified and non-codified law mark the poles traditionally represented by the civil law and the common law systems, and hence one of the marked differences between English and German law. The UPICC – as a written source of transnational contract law – are therefore subject to discussion with regard to this aspect. Codifications and statutory law perpetuate the legal rule through one textual formulation. Sceptics consider this technique utterly inflexible. What if times change and with them the problems demanding legal solutions?[32] Flexibility to sceptics is an inherent opposite to codification. However, this does not appear to aim toward the idea that statutes cannot easily be adapted to different situations, but rather at the experience that the formulation of statutes can display a stifling quality.

This is a drafting style often serving the aim of certainty and clarity. However, experience shows that even the most carefully drafted contract can encounter un-

---

[31] See for instance K P Berger, *The Creeping Codification of the Lex Mercatoria* (1999) 5-6 who provides an in-depth analysis of the status quo of the discussion about the *lex mercatoria*.

[32] 'That rules of law can be stated with verbal exactitude and unvarying uniformity and that they can be applied to the changing facts of life with logical certainty is an illusion from which our leading jurists do not suffer' (Corbin, op cit, Vol 12, §1136).

foreseen problems and leave questions open. How can a statute be expected to exceed this degree of certainty while covering a wider scope? Regarding the quality of the formulation, the example of the BGB is useful. A few remarks are therefore to be found below.[33]

#### *2.2.2.1.1 The value of codifications in civil law and common law traditions*

In 1986 Hein Kötz commented on codification efforts of the Law Commission concerning the law of contract in England in his fifteenth Clore Lecture held at the LSE in London.[34] He takes a comparative look at the attitude towards codification in common law countries from the perspective of a civil lawyer.

> No one in England seems to object to the judges using vague and indeterminate concepts and particularising them as cases come up so long as these concepts are common law concepts created by the judges themselves, as when a judge in an action for damages for negligence decides whether the defendant's conduct has been that of a reasonable man who took reasonable care to avoid an unreasonable risk of causing injury to others. But when it comes to legislation, the parliamentary draftsman, if he can be persuaded to use a broad term like 'reasonable', seems to be under an irresistible urge to teach the judge a lesson on what 'reasonable' really means, and while the words commonly used for that purpose are no-doubt well meant they exude, at least to a Continental lawyer, a somewhat condescending and pedagogical flavour. [35]

It is Kötz's point that the language used in certain examples of English legislation is nothing less broad and general as a typical civilian counterpart. Such an example is provided by comparison of the formulations used in the Unfair Contract Terms Act 1977 as well as the German Standard Terms Act (AGBG), 1976. Hence, this argument is unsuitable for backing the distinction of written law in civil and common law spheres and the dismissal of codification as such.

The forms of manifestation of the law in written texts range between the maximum accepted degree of vagueness and the required degree of certainty. According to Kötz, these are reflected in English law by the extremes of case law on one end, consisting of nothing else but a sequence of cases, one being a precedent for another; a 'wilderness of single instances'[36] with the acceptance of general principles of law existing independently from the cases[37] as an intermediate form, and at the other end of the scale, the claim that a code is required to 'cover every foreseeable situation'.[38] Statutes do not always live up to the latter expectation. Criti-

[33] 2.2.2.1.2.

[34] H Kötz, 'Taking Civil Codes Less Seriously' Modern Law Review 50 (1987) 1.

[35] Ibid, 4-5.

[36] Ibid, 5-6.

[37] 'English law contains a number of doctrines of great breadth which are more powerful than any of the decisions on which they are based or in which they are applied.' (F H Lawson, 1977, quoted by Kötz, ibid, 5).

[38] Kötz, ibid, 5.

cal arguments either target the codes' 'vague generalities' or 'rigorous inflexibility'.[39]

The purpose behind codification is to mould the law into a more accessible form; 'to make the law manageable and findable, and to provide a language in which a meaningful discourse between lawyers can take place'.[40] The often cited conflict between the role of Parliament and that of the judiciary regarding the creation of law by drafting legislation, is said to be meaningless by Kötz in those cases where a generally accepted principle of common law is put into the shape of a codification (restatement) because of the use meant to be made of it, in either form of existence.[41] Kötz recalls the limited use of taking specific continental Civil Codes as a point of reference for value judgment about codification in general, since each of them was created within a different political, historical and social setting. These codes were drafted 'in other countries, at other times and for other reasons'.[42] Only the technique of codification ought to be taken into account, though. There are different stages of generality and particularity which can be realised by skilful draftsmen. After all, legislative drafting is an art. The subject to be regulated determines how much flexibility is needed or how much precision is required.

This applies to domestic matters as well as to transnational contract law.

> He (the draftsman) must steer the best course available by finding language that strikes an apt balance between certainty and flexibility and facilitates the orderly development of the law without unduly fettering judicial creativity. [43]

Kötz, in the end, makes the same observation as Hartley,[44] when he states:

> Indeed all codes, partly from age, partly from the intention of their draftsmen, partly from mere oversight, leave wide gaps which cannot be filled by the available statutory rules. [45]

The process of reaching decisions within the framework of such a typical imperfect code is the same on both a domestic and an international level. The general problem of uncertainty and open-textured terms in a code can be approached by way of established techniques applied in case law as well as by recurring to pre-code legislation or judge-made law and customary law.

---

39 Ibid, 14-15.

40 Ibid, 6. Another aim is, of course, to make the law accessible for 'everyman' which was the republican postulation at times of parliamentary discussions of the BGB in the nineteenth century: see 5.3 below.

41 Ibid, 6.

42 Ibid, 8.

43 Ibid, 9.

44 Looking at EC Directives, T Hartley, 'The European Court, Judicial Objectivity and the Constitution of the European Union' Law Quarterly Review 112 (1996) 95; see also 2.2.2.2 below.

45 Kötz, op cit, 11.

To illustrate this further, the controversy around the notion of good faith in English law can serve as a reference: it is often accused of inducing the use of 'visceral justice'.[46] However, open-textured terms occur regularly in English law, they must be filled with legal meaning by objectively formulated principles. Such principles exist in English law in connection with the use of judicial discretion conferred to courts under doctrines such as the doctrine of frustration and many other instances in contract law.[47] Apart from the various instances where contract law is applied by reference to reasonableness, a few examples from statutory law might illustrate the point; the Sale of Goods Act 1997 not only provides, in s 17(1), that for the passing of property 'at such time as the parties so intend', but also that for the ascertainment of this intention 'regard shall be had to the terms of the contract, the conduct of the parties and the circumstances of the case'. This is a clause of remarkable vagueness.[48] Nevertheless, the vagueness of s 17(1) 'has not in practice caused unacceptable uncertainty because it is supplemented by statutory guidelines and by principles derived from an extensive body of case law'.[49] Note also Treitel's example: 'an Act of 1854 (now repealed), which required certain terms in contracts for the carriage of goods by rail to be such as the court found reasonable'.[50] Interestingly enough, the court practice resulting from the application of this Act, which became known as 'the doctrine of the "fair alternative"',[51] found its way into modern law: 'a modified version … appears as a statutory guideline (applicable to contracts for the supply of goods), in the Unfair Contracts Terms Act 1977'.[52]

Treitel gives many more examples from case law and statutory law, and they are worth studying to demonstrate the extent to which English law is suffused with open-textured rules and terms. The vagueness of which has been subject to criticism but nevertheless they are standard tools in English legal practice. Section One of the Law Reform (Frustrated Contracts) Act 1943, confers discretion to the courts regarding the expenses and benefits incurred by the parties which might be subject to reimbursement. Section 1(2) confers a free discretion while s 1(3) provides a 'guideline', as Treitel puts it,[53] to the courts.

The important thing to note is that the use of these rules illustrates 'that they provide different legislative techniques for producing a balance between certainty and discretion'. [54]

---

46 M Bridge, 'Good Faith in Commercial Contracts', 140.

47 For an in-depth analysis see G H Treitel, *Doctrine and Discretion in the Law of Contract* (1981).

48 Compare *Varley* v *Whipp* [1900] 1 QB 513, 517.

49 Treitel, op cit, 14. By statutory guidelines further legislation is meant, here, SGA 1979 s 18 (see *Benjamin's Sale of Goods* (1974) ss 291-391; 1400-28; 1556-61; 1689-1703).

50 Treitel, ibid, 15.

51 Ibid.

52 Ibid. The doctrine said that it was 'reasonable' according to the Act, 'if the carrier gave the consignor the option of sending the goods either at the carrier's or at the consignor's risk, of course at differential rates'.

53 See for more details Treitel, ibid, 18.

54 Ibid.

### 2.2.2.1.2 Example: The BGB

One example of domestic unification of private law[55] is the enactment of the German BGB in 1900. When the BGB first came into force it replaced a large number of *Partikularrechte*, about 39 of them, which were feudal laws of different regions applying to different areas of life, partly stemming from the Middle Ages; the *Gemeines Recht* (common law); the Saxon Civil Code (1863); the *Preußisches Allgemeines Landrecht* (Prussian Civil Code, 1794); Rhenish Law (including the Code Civil, 1804); Danish Law (1863); and Austrian Law (ABGB 1811).

Application of contract law was subject to one instance only (*Reichsgericht* – Imperial Court) which could be perceived as *conditio sine qua non* for uniformity by guaranteeing a uniform application and interpretation.

The uniform application of this law did not naturally follow the introduction of the code immediately. Judges resorted to pre-code law in order to interpret certain passages which might have left gaps open. A common interpretation grew out of the activity of the *Reichsgericht* and later the *Bundesgerichtshof.* The methods of interpretation, however, had been the result of scientific research of almost a century. The evolution of interpretation methods occurred independently of the introduction of new legislation. Legal science had been a strong factor in building the law before the BGB came into force. Thus, gaps and general clauses provided little difficulty since judges and lawyers were accustomed to resorting to science and general principles to develop the law further. The technique in a code like the BGB is the formulation of abstract sentences that are to be interpreted and can cover as many instances of real life as possible.[56]

Skilful drafting of codes is what is needed for such a project. This approach avoids trying to pre-formulate every possible twist of life and thus becoming too literal. General clauses are therefore sometimes the last resort for the objective to provide for as much substantive value as possible. Vague formulations, gaps, *Generalklauseln*, open terms, require an agreed method of application and interpretation. After all, applying law is not an automatic mechanism but a process taking place in a human brain, sometimes a process of negotiation and interaction between several individuals.[57] The outcome can never be certain or foreseeable. The way in which German domestic law deals with gaps and open terms can serve here as another example of how wrong common prejudices about the static character of the legal families and their attitude towards fundamental and constituting principles of their system actually are, and how the civil and the common law can use the same techniques. Also, a first reference is made to a substantive rule of the UPICC, which will be the subject of Part 2.

---

[55] Including many examples of successful drafting meeting Kötz's description quoted above, 2.2.2.1.1.

[56] The BGB claims to be formed of a comprehensive, scientific legal system the original claim of which was to provide for the possibility of deducting a logically founded and thus guaranteed solution for every case; see *Münchener Kommentar, 'Einleitung'*, No 19.

[57] Compare Lando, op cit (n 28), 535-544 and see Chapter 8.

In German law, general clauses (*Generalklauseln*) provide for judge-made law to be developed. This practice is well established and has produced the doctrines of *culpa in contrahendo* (pre-contractual liability), positive *Vertragsverletzung* (damages for negligence in the course of contractual performance),[58] and *Drittschadensliquidation* (damages for third parties). These doctrines are all unconnected to the wording of the statute at first sight and seem to grant claims which were not provided for by the legislator. The most dramatic case is that of the doctrine of frustration of contracts (*Wegfall der Geschäftsgrundlage*)[59] which is to fill a gap discovered in the wake of the First World War concerning the validity of long-term contracts.

Under German law supervening events are generally addressed under the heading of impossibility.[60] It is a different approach from the common law one in that it focuses on the nature of the event rather than on the commercial purpose of the contract. The only instance where a German judiciary was forced to pay tribute to the commercial purpose of the contract is the doctrine of *Fehlen oder Wegfall der Geschäftsgrundlage*, the lack or the subsequent disappearance of the commercial basis (of a contract). This doctrine was in fact first accepted and developed by the judiciary (*Reichsgericht*) after World War I in the wake of political and economical upheaval.[61] Many contracts and intended businesses could not be implemented as planned due to tremendous changes in the underlying circumstances. A substantial amount of business transactions were desperately affected by hyper-inflation and destruction of goods and production facilities by the war. The same applied, of course, after World War II when the *Oberster Gerichtshof für die Britische Zone* (OGH) and the *Bundesgerichtshof* (BGH) continued to apply the doctrine, thereby moving further away from the pure exceptional and emergency-induced character of the first instances of its recognition.[62]

---

[58] Now §280 BGB (2002).

[59] Now §313 BGB (2002).

[60] See 2.2.2.2.2.

[61] The creators of the BGB had not followed Windscheid's 'doctrine of the assumption' (Bernhard Windscheid, '*Die Lehre von der Voraussetzung*' in AcP 78 (1892) 1); see Mot I, 249. During the times of gross inflation after World War I Oertmann (*Die Geschäftsgrundlage*, 1921) developed his doctrine of the *Geschäftsgrundlage*, the commercial basis. Taking these writings together with certain provisions in the BGB (§§321, 610) into account the *Reichsgericht* recognised the so-called *clausula rebus sic stantibus* and granted relief in cases mostly concerned with price adjustment to parties affected by the inflation. Examples are RGZ 50, 255, 257; 60, 65, 68; 100, 129, 130; 103, 3; 107, 151, 153. See also K Zweigert, and H Kötz, *An Introduction to Comparative Law* (1998), 518-524.

[62] See BGHZ 25, 390 where the parties, after the currency reform (RM to DM), had based their price (for some disowned property) on the then accepted exchange rate of 10:1 for the new currency (DM) which was subsequently changed for this particular claim to a relation of 1:1. This was a typical example of a situation where the change of the basis of the contract was beyond the parties' control and could not have been foreseen. A later case, BGHZ 47, 48, 51, concerned the price of land sold for building purposes, but development was not allowed later. BGH NJW 67, 721 and JZ 77, 177 were similar cases. See also BGH LM No 83 at §242 (Bb).

This, and most other doctrines mentioned above, are based on the principle of good faith as is expressed by §§157, 242 BGB, the provisions relating to the construction of contract clauses and *Treu und Glauben.*[63] The principle of good faith provides another traditional conflict between the common law and the civil law worlds.[64] The reason for granting special relief in the above mentioned cases was the disturbance of the overall equilibrium of the contract, just as Art 6.2.2 UPICC describes it. *Wegfall der Geschäftsgrundlage* does not automatically discharge the parties of their original obligations. The legal effect is the adaptation of the contract terms by the court.[65] The UPICC provide for renegotiation by the parties, which is a solution more suited to commercial men rather than the general public and consumer contracts.

#### 2.2.2.2 Uniformity on the international level: Examples of uniform law sources

In order to examine the quality of international contract law as to the degree of its uniformity, three different types of international law may serve as examples for written uniform international sources of law: the CISG, EC Directives and the UPICC.

CISG, which emerged originally as a convention, has now been turned into domestic codifications in many countries. In most cases it has not been altered through implementing legislation. Its rules are thus subject to judicial review and thus to interpretation by judges, but also by users such as lawyers and merchants

---

Following the German reunification similar problems were met by the enactment of numerous pieces of legislation such as the *DM-Bilanzgesetz* (DM balance law) which grants a possibility of adaptation of the price in its §32 II. Other laws relate to pre-unification debts (*Altschuldengesetz*, excluding the application of the doctrine), adaptation of interest rates (*Zinsanpassungsgesetz*). Regarding sales contracts there is only one special constellation where sales effected under the urge of emigration to the West which is regulated in the *Vermögensgesetz* (wealth law). All other sales contracts concluded before 9 October 1990 remain valid and are not affected by the political changes, KG OLG-NL 96, 76. Overall, this modern situation of fundamental change has been handled with much more preparation and sophisticated foresight than the previous ones which were of course set in a situation of chaos and subsequent lack of judicial organisation and preparation, eg, regarding technical facilities and personnel. For further reference see Görk, *Deutsche Einheit und Wegfall der Geschäftsgrundlage* (German unity and the doctrine of lack of the basis of the transaction), 1995.

63 For the old doctrine and jurisdiction, see D Medicus, *Bürgerliches Recht* (1991) No 165a; K Larenz, *Allgemeiner Teil des Deutschen Bürgerlichen Rechts* (1983) 382; K Larenz, *Lehrbuch des Schuldrechts. Erster Band: Allgemeiner Teil* (1982) 297; H Hübner, *Allgemeiner Teil des Bürgerlichen Gesetzbuches* (1996) §42 D I; MüKo and Roth §242 Nos 535 et seq (compare §313 BGB (2002)); and see K Larenz and M Wolf, *Allgemeiner Teil des Deutschen Bürgerlichen Rechts* (2004) §38.

64 With regard to the UPICC I suggest dealing with this doctrine under the principles developed in the context of applying any open textured terms in English law.

65 §313 BGB (2002); for case law and doctrine see H Hübner, *Allgemeiner Teil des Bürgerlichen Gesetzbuches* 1996, §42 D V, 468; BGHZ 47, 48, 51; 70, 47, 51.

who become parties to contracts under CISG. These rules can now be understood and interpreted differently in different jurisdictions according to different languages and legal techniques.[66] CISG contains certain internal rules concerning interpretation (Arts 8-13) as well as the rule in Art 7 which provides for external interpretation methods, in order to give effect to the international character and the purpose of the convention.

Uniform application is ensured in most international Conventions and Model Laws through the insertion of a clause into international codifications. An example is provided by Art 7 CISG. Section (2) of this Article provides a standard of interpretation by pointing to the 'general principles underlying this convention'. Thereby, it intends to suggest that there exists a common understanding of the regulated matters extending beyond the literal meaning of the convention. This is the potential enabling lawyers and contracting parties to apply the convention in a uniform way. The final outcome of any application still depends on the technicalities of interpretation which differs between legal systems. Once the interpretation has to leave the framework of the literal text and the 'underlying principles', and resort to the conflict of laws according to Art 7(2) CISG, there is, of course, a strong possibility that the uniformity can get lost and turn into diversity or entropy and thus possibly the state in which the law of international sales was before CISG came into existence.

These ambiguities and sources of uncertainty are typical of any written law and by no means specific to international law as opposed to domestic law. Specific problems of international uniform law are, however, said to arise from different textual versions such as differing translations and unsuitable drafting techniques.

##### *2.2.2.2.1 Textual understanding*

Applying law in the form of a written text can take the form of interpreting literature. It is the perception of words. Language has a great significance here. A common understanding of certain words is important to successful communication. But at the same time one would not expect a greater certainty of the law than the meaning of words can ever have. Certainly, interpreting legal texts requires insight into special characteristics of each language, such as the subtle change of expressions over time, once a legal text is of any age:

> Consider, for example, the vicissitudes of the description of a person as 'sentimental'. The Oxford Dictionary tells us: 'Of persons, their dispositions and actions; characterised by sentiment. Originally in favourable sense: ... refined and elevated feeling. In later use: Addicted to indulgence in superficial emotion; apt to be swayed by sentiment.' What has been a term of praise became one of mild reproach. What would be the task of a lawyer, then, if asked to construe a trust instrument written in 1720 establishing scholarship for 'sentimental' youths?[67]

---

[66] Compare in this chapter at 2.2.3.

[67] S Levinson, 'Law as Literature', 157.

And what that of the merchant reading a code dating from fifty years earlier in our fast moving times? One only has to think of the grand expression 'good faith'.[68] Is this not a rather outdated use of language? Is this expression suitable for certain and predictable results?

> … the plain-meaning approach inevitably breaks down in the face of the reality of disagreement among equally competent speakers of the native language.[69]

So, is a certain uncertainty, disagreement and implied unpredictability not immanent to uniform domestic contract law? To the extent that this is tolerated on the domestic level, it should be on the international level, too. Certainly, complete uncertainty cannot be the nature of law and its application, either. Applying law generally implies the need to create the missing bit between the abstract formulation and the real case to be decided. This process is innate to any written law. This is not an argument specifically affecting international codifications.

EC directives, to provide an example, often display deliberate textual openness since they are usually not directly binding but are to be implemented into domestic legislation. They are meant to be models leaving space for the creative spirit of legislators, ie, to the sovereignty of the member states. This is the theory of harmonisation. The creation of ambiguities in directives and other EC instruments is said to stem from deliberately ambiguous formulations, either because a final decision as to the meaning was diplomatically avoided and could not be reached, or because it was subject to a 'deal', as in an example given by Hartley.

Uniform application of EC law, and especially EC directives, was discussed at a comparative law conference in Graz, 1997. Trevor Hartley commented on the lack of clarity in EC directives from the point of view of English law,[70] especially referring to Regulation 1612/68; Directive 68/360; *R* v *The Immigration Appeal Tribunal, ex parte Antonissen*.[71] Hartley reported on the specifically English approach to interpretation of statutory law, while referring to the opinion given by the House of Lords in the *Webb* case[72] on the interpretation of domestic law according to EC directives. Linguistic uncertainty for him is one of the first and most obvious reasons for distortions of meaning of EC directives which are meant to be applied equally in all member states. These directives serve as one single source of law just like CISG does for its member states and the UPICC can do for parties who choose them. However, Hartley demonstrates different legal meanings of the term 'goods' in the Unfair Contract Terms Directive.[73] He points to the fact that the Directive was originally drafted in French, in which 'goods' is to corre-

---

[68] Contained in Art 1.7(1) UPICC. '*Treu und Glauben*' in German is also an outdated use of language.

[69] Levinson, op cit, 158.

[70] Compare T C Hartley, 'The European Court, Judicial Objectivity and the Constitution of the European Union' Law Quarterly Review 112 (1996) 95 and T C Hartley, *The Transposition and Interpretation of EC Directives: The British Viewpoint* (1997).

[71] Case C-292/89 (1991) ECR I-745 ( paragraph 18 of the judgment).

[72] *Webb* v *Emo Air Cargo* [1995] 1 WLR 1454.

[73] Directive 93/ 13, OJ 1993 L 95/29.

spond to '*biens*' which covers land, as opposed to the English meaning of 'goods', referring only to movables. Is now the scope of this Directive different in French and English speaking countries? Do the translation and formulation have to be adjusted according to the true meaning of the Directive? Which is the true meaning?

#### *2.2.2.2.2 Drafting technique*

A high standard and quality of drafting technique and legislative concept is specific to any written law and equally important on both the municipal and international level. It is unjustified to allow a lesser standard to any of these types of law. The UPICC provide a successful example regarding the drafting of individual rules and consistency of the whole set.[74] Therefore they are well suited to serve as a model for new domestic legislation in the field of international commercial contracts. Unfortunately, recent German law reform projects have not implemented the high standard of clear drafting and conceptual consistency provided by the UPICC,[75] neither in the area of the law of obligations, nor in that of international commercial arbitration. While the new law on arbitration is discussed in Chapter Eight, the following section will give a brief example of failed integration of international law into novel German legislation.

The UPICC introduce the concept of non-performance giving rise to autonomous contractual rights. In German contract law, non-performance (*Nichterfüllung*) appears in damages provisions merely as a measure for damages,[76] §325 BGB,[77] and is mentioned in §326 BGB[78] as a ground for liability in damages of the defaulting party. Nevertheless non-performance is not specifically defined in the BGB, and it does not entitle ensuing contractual rights as an independent contractual remedy or defence. Therefore, the notion of non-performance as used in the UPICC might at first sight be considered an instance of incompatibility and thus, lead to more entropy in international contract law. In fact, the BGB used to employ the highly sophisticated concept of 'impossibility'. Cases that would fall under non-performance rules in the UPICC would be solved under impossibility or defective performance rules in the BGB. One objective of the recent reform of the BGB was the simplification of this over complicated section of the code, as well as its adaptation to international standards and models. Traditionally, the concept of breach of contract as it is contained in the CISG, or the concept of non-performance of contractual obligations as contained in the UPICC, are recognised as originating from common law jurisdictions in Germany. In order to come up

74 This will be discussed further in Part 2; compare also the acknowledgements by B Fauvarque-Cosson, 'Comparative Law and Conflict of Laws: Allies or Enemies? New Perspectives on an Old Couple' AmJCompL 49 (2001) 416; Canaris, op cit (n 19), 5; U Drobnig: 'The UNIDROIT Principles in the Conflict of Laws', Uniform Law Review 2/3 (1998) 385; Goode, op cit (n 19), 1; P Mankowski, '*Rechtswahl für Verträge des internationalen Wirtschaftsverkehrs*' RIW 1 (2003) 2.

75 As well as by the PECL.

76 Eg, in §§325, 326, 338, 340, 463, 538, 545, 635 BGB.

77 On impossibility on the debtor's part.

78 On delayed performance.

with a similar concept the new concept of 'breach of duty', or breach of obligation (*Pflichtverletzung*) was introduced into the new law of obligations. This does not seem to be a convincing solution, however, given that it introduces another term, meaning yet something other than the above mentioned two international sets of rules, also something other than the English concept of breach of contract, so this *aliud* results in even more variety of concepts on the scene of contract laws, and hence, more entropy instead of harmony of standards on an international level.

The new term suggests a confusing proximity to the concept of breach of contract which stems from a fundamentally different understanding of contract. A fundamental change of understanding of contract, however, cannot have been the aim of the German legislator.

Obviously therefore, the legislator did not take existing and suitable examples of modern international contract law into account, probably due to the lack of formal authority of the rules as discussed above.[79] The persuasive force of the UPICC,[80] however, was of no interest to the legislator which shows that other interests, certainly purely domestic ones rather than those of international trade, were observed in the drafting process.

It confirms the above mentioned theory, that traditional doctrine focuses on, and confines itself to, the nation state and ignores the international dimension of modern developments of the law in the course of the evolution of global trade and the EU.

Besides this effect, the law reform has brought about various difficulties in the application of newly introduced concepts because it disturbs the consistency of the traditional system of German contract law, which is an important constituting element for legal reasoning in German legal practice.[81] The lack of thorough doctrinal foundation of the new concepts and notions[82] highlight the importance of the UPICC as a prototype for international contract law in the field of commercial contracts. The UPICC provide a comprehensive solution for a whole area of contract law using the notion of non-performance which includes defective and late

---

[79] An absence of coordination in the sense described by P J-J Hering and A J Kanning, 'Unifying Commercial Laws of Nation-States, Coordination of Legal Systems and Economic Growth' (accessed online 2004: http://ideas.repec.org/p/dgr/ummet/2002027.html).

[80] Compare Part 3.

[81] For an in-depth analysis of this problem, compare J Kohler, '*Rechtsetzung im demokratischen Rechtsstaat und Rechtswissenschaft – Anmerkungen zu Stil und Bedeutung neuerer Gesetzgebung*' *Kritische Vierteljahresschrift für Gesetzgebung und Rechtswissenschaft* 4 (2002) 369. There are numerous instances of flawed drafting in the new civill code, both in terms of breaches of established concepts and textual weaknesses, compare eg, the provisions regulating the new rules on time limits.

[82] Another example is the notion of consumer which is alien to German law otherwise. German law deals with a very unique distinction of merchants and non-merchants and important legal consequences are attached to this definition. The Commercial Code (*Handelsgesetzbuch*) is based on this distinction.

performance.[83] Questions of defective performance are dealt with by Art 7.1.4 and 7.1.5. Under German law questions of hardship and *force majeure* need to be distinguished from, and sometimes resolved under, the rules relating to defective and late performance, too.[84]

It would be a recommendable solution to provide for a law relating to specifically defined international commercial contracts, which then expressly introduced specific theoretical concepts distinct from traditional domestic law. This would clearly mark and justify the introduction of new paradigms for special subjects to be resolved under specialised law. It would avoid the dilution of traditional concepts by flawed drafting and conceptualisation. Such a technique would be in line with both the established German doctrines of *Sonderprivatrecht der Kaufleute*, the special law merchant, as well as the doctrine of *lex specialis*.[85]

### 2.2.3 Uniformity of application and interpretation methods

One of the main objections to the idea that uniform law can exist at an international level is the absence of a common instance functioning as an interpreter of the law. Application of uniform law, such as CISG, for example, is said to inevitably lead to a modification of that law, to the creation of new difference which is then often called 'harmonisation' (indicating that there is still some common feature left) as opposed to 'uniformity'. It has to be asked whether this kind of modification, arising from applying the law, is not innate to applying any law. [86]

Uniformity is a matter of definition and depends strongly on the purpose it is trying to achieve. Uniform international law is predominantly defined by its purposes and sources, rather than by the technically uniform nature of the results when applied to concrete cases. The determination of the purpose of unified international contract law is the decisive argument needed in order to assess the degree of uncertainty and lack of clarity which is tolerable, or, to what extent precision and uniform interpretation methods are required and indispensable.

Interpretation and application beyond the literal terms of the codification, convention or model law is inevitable. As to the BGB it has already been said that probably the largest component of legal questions, arise from gaps in legislation.[87]

[83] Art 7.1.1 UPICC, 'non-performance defined': 'Non-performance is failure by a party to perform any of its obligations under the contract, including defective performance or late performance'.

[84] Eg, temporary impediment. In the area of discrepancies between the parties' expectations and reality the law relating to defective performance is applicable: If goods or services suffer from a defect, if they do not comply with the employer's or buyer's expectations, there are remedies granting damages, a right to rectification, a right of termination and a right to reduce the price: §§633-636 BGB for service contracts, §§459 et seq BGB for sales contracts.

[85] See Chapter 8.

[86] Compare 2.2.2.2 and 2.2.2.2.1.

[87] See Heck, *Gesetzesauslegung und Interessenjurisprudenz* (1914) s 174, quoted in *Münchener Kommentar, Einleitung*, No 64.

If we were to find the larger amount of legal problems to be solved under diverse domestic laws and interpretation methods rather than under international law, this would not frustrate the purpose of unified codification as long as there were suitable methods of integration and application, within domestic legal systems, available.

A model for internationally 'unified' interpretation of legal rules is sometimes seen in the jurisdiction of the ECJ. Open textured formulations in regulations or conventions have often given rise to the development of more concise formulations by the judges justifying decisions which then form a network of guidelines or even judge-made law.

True uniformity is therefore often said to be available only in this and similar areas of international law where a common judicial body is available. We subject our legal conflict or quest to the judges. We accept their judgments due to their institutional power but also, and only if, their judgments are 'reasonable'.[88] If they are not, we take them to the next instance or constitutional court or otherwise, if there was none of those, we would gradually lose faith in the law and evade it.

Indeed, methods of interpretation used by the ECJ as well as the formulation of its rulings are considered a source of 'uncertainty' by some.[89] Methods of interpretation are themselves to be agreed; as far as they concern the international level and a transnational forum, this process requires its own specific method and understanding. Common methods of interpretation are essential tools for achieving uniformity.

## 2.2.4 Conclusion

This section has demonstrated that unity of laws manifests through uniformity of sources, not uniformity of results. This means using codified systems of transnational law on an international level to provide this form of uniformity for international commercial contracts. Uniformity of results cannot be expected from uniform contract law on application in national legal systems. This is not the aim of uniform law neither on a domestic nor on an international level. This also means that skilled drafting of such rules[90] and a practice of applying written law, especially open-textured terms,[91] are a condition of the successful use of such law within national legal systems. If this is recognised, a successful use of transnational contract law even in common law systems is possible. Such a way of using

---

88 See G Graff, 'Keep off the grass, Drop Dead, and other Indeterminacies: A Response to Sanford Levinson', 179. There the polarity between the two perceptions is illustrated: interpretation as 'unchallenged authority of divine commands' against no authority whatsoever except the 'coercive authority of institutional force' and certainly an attempt to mediate.

89 Hartley's example: *Torfaen Borough Council* v *B&Q plc* Case C-145/88 ECR 3851 (1989). See T Hartley, 'The European Court, Judicial Objectivity and the Constitution of the European Union' Law Quarterly Review 112 (1996) 95.

90 See 8.1 below.

91 Compare Chapter 4 below.

uniform law is guided by the uniform law itself under its interpretation provisions as incorporated, eg, in Art 7 CISG. It requires an agreed method of operating such law within the area of international trade law. This can become a methodology of international contract law as suggested in this study. The understanding of the nature of applying written law and textual understanding of its rules implies the acceptance of the simultaneous existence of unity and diversity in the law as a general phenomenon which is not only typical for transnational law. Creating a method of working with this paradox is the task of a specific methodology of international contract law.

## 2.3 Conclusion

This chapter has explained an important aspect of uniform transnational contract law; it has shown what uniformity of law means, how it is to be defined. Namely two aspects have been distinguished: uniformity of sources on the one hand and uniformity of application and its results on the other. The former is achievable through transnationally used uniform sources and texts, the latter is commonly understood to provide 'certainty and predictability' in the law and is not normally achieved, not even on a domestic level.[92] Based on this understanding it follows that uniformity of laws cannot be universal (unifying all the law of all the nations), but is fragmentary and confined to branches of trade or a geographical network of trade relations. Uniform contract law arises where there is need for it. The need (incentive) exists in the area of international commercial contracts in an international community of merchants which is not defined by political or geographical borders. The degree and quality of uniformity is determined by the needs for uniformity.

Unification of laws and uniformity of international contract law are not a goal, in itself it provides no self-fulfilling purpose. The uniform character of transnational law is kept up by discourse and common practice. It would be wrong to expect uniformity of results through the application of uniform law and therefore deny the prospects of transnational law by pointing to the absence of supranational state court control (2.2.3).[93]

[92] Certainty and predictability in transnational law can be advanced by a competent discourse producing accepted standards. This discourse does not need to be embodied in a state court structure. The emergence of courts on a transnational level is not excluded, anyway. There are already bodies like the ICC and their arbitration institutions; compare below, Part 3.

[93] Compare also Chapter 8.

# Conclusion (Part 1)

Part 1 of this study has identified the origin of obstacles to the successful use of transnational uniform contract law arising from legal theory in modern nation states; an unreflective use of traditional concepts of contract law doctrine (Chapter 1) as well as, erroneous expectations towards the function of uniform law (Chapter 2).

Part 1 of this study also described and identified aspects of the legal nature of uniform contract law; its position within traditional legal doctrine of contract law and its generic quality and definition as uniform law in general. Part 1 has also shown ways in which problems posed by traditional concepts and the current superficial understanding of uniform contract law can be overcome:

Through revisiting and reviewing the use and understanding of traditional concepts, through deeper analysis of the application of equally traditional concepts and addressing the law in an appropriate context, which allows the integration of uniform contract law into domestic legal systems. This process and practice forms an element of a novel methodology of international contract law.

# Part 2 Methods of applying uniform private law within domestic legal systems

## Introduction

The previous section (Part 1) looked at general aspects of legal theory with regard to applying transnational rules of law. This second part explores the ways in which the UPICC, as a specific set of uniform law rules, can be integrated into domestic law on the level of substantive law and by concrete practical application of individual rules. It identifies the second major obstacle to the use of transnational uniform contract law; the application process of such law by national lawyers. It inquires whether this process reveals or presupposes a specific methodology of international contract law and how difficulties applying uniform law within national legal systems can be overcome accordingly.

The two domestic legal systems under which the principles are analysed are English and German law. These two legal systems represent two of the major 'legal families' in the Western world. English law has laid the foundations for the whole of the common law world, especially the Anglo-American jurisdictions which are given special consideration in this section. German law represents the so-called civil law jurisdictions. This may sound somewhat of a simplification since the civil law jurisdictions themselves are very different from each other.[1] German law, however, differs most significantly from English law in many aspects of contract law and the law of civil procedure.

Part 2 therefore asks how the UPICC as novel international contract law blends with the standards of substantive law of these two European jurisdictions. It investigates whether the UPICC are compatible with English (Chapter 4) and with German law (Chapter 5), investigates what their quality as rules of law are, and whether they offer advanced solutions to selected problems in domestic contract

[1] See for instance the following quotation by John P Dawson: 'The contrast between the French and the German treatment of specific performance is among many demonstrations of the great differences between the "civil law" systems. Despite their long exposure to ideas derived from Roman law, each of the "civil law" systems is the product of independent values and objectives from the society it purports to regulate.' (J P Dawson, 'Specific Performance in France and Germany' Michigan Law Review 57 (1959) 495, 525).

law on the level of international contract law. It examines the question of how obstacles to the use of transnational uniform contract law created by a flawed application technique can be overcome both from a substantive law aspect as well as from a methodological viewpoint. Another general concept examined in Part 2 is the idea of applying a codified contract law within the context of English law as a common law system. Both Chapters 4 and 5[2] analyse aspects of the codification of contract law throughout European history, in order to suggest possible answers to questions of the integration of uniform contract law into a common law system.

[2] Compare 4.1.3. and 5.3. below.

# 3 Performance of payment obligations in the UPICC

Chapter 3 analyses the meaning and scope of Art 7.2.1 UPICC in the context of international building and construction contracts. This rule provides for a right to require performance of payment obligations.

The chapter asks how Art 7.2.1 UPICC is to be applied according to an autonomous interpretation technique and researches answers to the questions brought up by scholars in connection with this rule of the UPICC. This involves a discussion of aspects of specific performance, the enforcement of payment obligations, and cancellation rights in building contracts under the UPICC as well as under English (Chapter 4) and German, domestic contract law (Chapter 5).

The extensive scope of the principles invites a discussion of contracts other than those for the sale of goods in order to establish the compatibility of the UPICC with domestic legal systems. The commentary of the UPICC very often refers to construction contracts to explain the scope and meaning of single provisions. I have therefore selected the example of international building and construction contracts to conduct an exemplary discussion of selected provisions of the UPICC and the potential of their application within domestic legal systems.

## 3.1 Starting point: Article 7.2.1 UPICC and scholarly critique

This section introduces one specific article of the UPICC, a written rule of uniform contract law. It sets out the wording and literal meaning and asks how this rule can be applied to individual cases within a domestic law setting. It pinpoints one specific problem raised by a scholar in the course of her research on the scope of payment obligations in the UPICC.

### 3.1.1 Articles 7.2.1 and 7.2.2 UPICC [1]

Art 7.2.1 UPICC is located in Chapter 7 of the UPICC on non-performance, in its second section entitled *Right to Performance*. It provides for the enforceability of payment obligations:

Where a party who is obliged to pay money does not do so, the other party may require payment.

Here, the UPICC establish their concept regarding performance of contractual obligations. They generally recognise a direct self-executing right to performance and at the same time determine the way monetary obligations are to be dealt with under their regime. The right to performance is further described by the subsequent Art 7.2.2 UPICC, *Performance of Non-Monetary Obligation*, which reads:

Where a party who owes an obligation other than one to pay money does not perform, the other party may require performance, unless;

(a) performance is impossible in law or fact;
(b) performance or, where relevant, enforcement is unreasonably burdensome or expensive;
(c) the party entitled to performance may reasonably obtain performance from another source;
(d) performance is of an exclusively personal character; or
(e) the party entitled to performance does not require performance within a reasonable time after it has, or ought to have, become aware of the non-performance.

### 3.1.2 Scholarly critique

The wording of Art 7.2.1 UPICC has provoked some objections because it does not contain express limitations. It is said that this provision grants an unqualified right to performance of the monetary obligation.[2] Professor Schwenzer accepts that no other European jurisdiction supports specific performance to such an extent, and she mentions the duty to mitigate loss as a possible limitation to the scope of Art 7.2.1 UPICC.[3] Above all she misses a right of cancellation in the Principles. This criticism is based on the understanding that the monetary obligation is not to be qualified by any limitation under the Principles. It is considered an overly rigid expression of the principle of *pacta sunt servanda* especially since a cancellation right is not included which could even force an unwilling party to consummate a transaction which is of no interest to them. It would follow that the

---

[1] Articles of the UPICC will also be quoted without express reference in the following, eg, Art 7.2.1.

[2] I Schwenzer, *Erfüllung und Schadensersatz nach den Unidroit – Prinzipien* (1997) 4-5, (conference paper); published as I Schwenzer, 'Specific Performance and Damages According to the 1994 UNIDROIT Principles of International Commercial Contracts' ELR 1 (1998/1999) 289.

[3] Ibid, 295.

Principles do not provide the potential to create uniformity in international contract law[4] because they are incompatible with national law, at least in this area.[5]

Professor Schwenzer's article provides an excellent starting point for a thorough analysis and interpretation of the UPICC not only because it is the first and probably the only one dealing with the subject of specific enforcement and damages in the Principles, but also because it provides an example of applying the Principles in a way which is very typical for a national lawyer.[6] It is because of this phenomenon that uniform private law falls short of its true potential.

Another noteworthy aspect of Professor Schwenzer's article is that it is a civil lawyer who shows great concern about the scope of the right to performance in a uniform law model. Traditionally, the common law systems are sceptical about the use of performance provisions in international sets of rules[7] which are obviously created according to the civil law model. Civil law systems are said to support specific performance often equalled with specific enforcement, much more generously than common law jurisdictions. It is therefore all the more surprising that with regard to Art 7.2.1 UPICC the concern about rights to require performance can be said to have been raised from both sides; the above mentioned criticism is expressed by a civil lawyer pointing out that the UPICC create an exaggerated and unacceptable emphasis of specific performance by the way Art 7.2.1 UPICC is formulated. The common law position can be presumed to be equally critical given the legal situation under Art 28 CISG.[8]

## 3.2 Towards a methodology of transnational contract law: Doctrinal foundations

The following section explores the compatibility of the UPICC with English and German contract law and asks how they can be integrated and how conflicts arising out of differences between the transnational and the national regimes can be solved.

An autonomous interpretation method as suggested here presupposes the conception of the UPICC as a comprehensive and self-sufficient body of rules and their application as the law governing the contract to the exclusion of national law (*Kollisionsrecht*), in the first place. National contract law would then serve to supplement the UPICC where they do not provide answers to certain questions of law or fact, either because they are outside their scope or because there is a gap. This technique corresponds to standard methods of applying CISG and other interna-

4 Ibid, 295.
5 Ibid.
6 See below 3.2.
7 Compare Art 28 of the 1980 Vienna Convention on the International Sale of Goods, CISG.
8 See 4.1.1 below.

tional conventions within a domestic context.[9] It requires the UPICC to be compatible with national contract laws which means it must be possible to overcome existing differences by applying established techniques.[10]

### 3.2.1 Autonomous method of applying Art 7.2.1 UPICC

An autonomous method of applying Art 7.2.1 UPICC starts by looking at the wording more closely. The wording of Art 7.2.1 UPICC reveals that it actually presupposes the payment obligation rather than creating it.[11] Hence, considerations must focus on the question of whether or not there is a payment obligation to be performed in the first place. This question has to be determined relying on the rules of the UPICC. It is different from the method applied by Professor Schwenzer in her study,[12] where she does not mention the existence of a valid obligation as a prerequisite for Art 7.2.1 UPICC to take effect. She would, however, do so applying domestic law. Instead of doing so here, she jumps to the question of whether a duty to mitigate can provide a limitation to Art 7.2.1 UPICC.[13] This deficiency of methodological coherence regarding the application of law on a domestic level on the one hand, and on an international level on the other, is a source of misunderstanding in the area of application of international uniform law rules. It also characterises the often alleged deficiency of such law; it is truly the deficiency on the part of its users.

The following sections highlight some issues of legal theory which were brought up in the context of the above described critique of Art 7.2.1 UPICC. Viewing these together is a formative process for the development of a potential novel doctrine of transnational contract law. It is also part of an appropriate method of application of transnational law; keeping the background in perspective and in the user's awareness. Even using domestic legal concepts as an argument in the context of such an application process[14] requires revisiting these concepts in order to justify the argument.

---

9 Compare, eg, F Ferrari, '*Das Verhältnis zwischen den Unidroit-Grundsätzen und den allgemeinen Grundsätzen internationaler Einheitsprivatrechtskonventionen*' *Juristenzeitung* 1 (1998) 9 and F Ferrari, 'Defining the sphere of application of the 1994 "UNIDROIT principles of international commercial contracts"' Tulane Law Review 69 (1995) 1225.

10 The legal prerequisite for applying the UPICC as the law governing the contract (*Kollisionsrecht*) are supportive conflict of law rules in domestic legal systems. These are discussed below in Part 3.

11 See below 3.3 for further discussion.

12 I Schwenzer, 'Specific Performance and Damages According to the 1994 UNIDROIT Principles of International Commercial Contracts' European Journal of Law Reform 1 (1998/1999) 289.

13 Ibid, 295: 'A first possible interpretation would seek to apply the duty to mitigate as stated in Art 7.4.8…'.

14 Such as reservations against specific performance or good faith in English law.

Some of the objections raised against rules of transnational law such as the UPICC are based on unfounded preconceptions brought about by domestic law. This chapter will therefore revisit conceptions of English and German law in order to demonstrate that a correct understanding of one's own legal background is essential for the successful application of transnational law.

The following sections, Chapters 4 and 5, therefore analyse the right to require payment, specific performance and cancellation rights in English and German law responding to the above mentioned critique. They show how Art 7.2.1 UPICC is successfully to be applied within the context of both these legal systems, namely by analysing the scope of the primary right to require payment under the UPICC, as well as under current English and German law,[15] and by explaining the respective areas of both legal systems where clashes are to be found and defining what requirements have to be met in order to overcome these difficulties.

The Principles fulfil a prime category of compatibility with domestic law and practical workability as the law governing international commercial contracts (*Kollisionsrecht*) due to their high level of drafting technique and consistency. This is a paramount quality compared to highly specialised and fragmented solutions of standard terms and general trade usages[16] tailored to match the needs of diverse branches of international trade.[17]

### 3.2.2 Conclusion and structure of autonomous methodological approach

The previous two sections of Chapter 3 have shown how one particular rule of uniform law can be misunderstood and have also explained a concept for a more successful method of application. This is called an autonomous interpretation, which will be extended in the following chapters by a historical perspective element. In the following, Art 7.2.1 UPICC will be analysed according to an autonomous interpretation, primarily, by taking other rules of the UPICC into account and more specifically, by analysing the scope of the primary right to require payment.[18]

Chapters 4 and 5 below, then analyse the right to require payment, specific performance, and cancellation rights in English and German law responding to the

[15] Considerations of mistake, frustration, *force majeure* and hardship as well as good faith aspects which are possible defences against payment claims are disregarded here.

[16] Such as INCOTERMS.

[17] Compare P Schlechtriem, 'Termination and Adjustment of Contracts' European Journal of Law Reform 1.3 (1998/1999) 323: '... a legal counsellor will check the Principles point by point so as to determine whether and to what extent they conform with the client's interests and expectations'. This biased quality of trade standard and standard contract forms may have supported the traditionally critical attitude of English Courts to the use of a-national law in international commercial arbitration: compare 5.1.1 and 8.2.2.2; see also *Charnikow* v *Roth Schmidt & Co* [1922] 2 KB 478.

[18] Considerations of mistake, frustration, *force majeure* and hardship as well as good faith aspects which are possible defences against payment claims are disregarded here.

above mentioned critique. They ask how Art 7.2.1 UPICC can be successfully applied within the context of both these legal systems, and by explaining the respective areas of both legal systems where clashes are to be found – what requirements have to be met in order to overcome these difficulties.

## 3.3 Scope of the payment rule in Art 7.2.1 UPICC

This section explores the inherent limitations that are contained within the UPICC but not in the form of express limitations. The logically preceding question of the existence of a valid payment obligation is the true limitation of Art 7.2.1 UPICC.

### 3.3.1 The legal nature of the right to performance in Art 7.2.1 UPICC

The wording of Art 7.2.1 UPICC suggests that the existence and the maturity of the obligation are conditions for payment:

Where a party who is obliged to pay money does not do so …

Thus, this rule does not establish the payment obligation itself but rather presupposes its existence. It describes the breach of an obligation as well as a remedy for this breach.

There is no provision in the UPICC which constitutes this underlying payment obligation. Regarding the specific purpose of the UPICC, it seems difficult to expressly state each of the parties' duties since those will depend on the contract type they have concluded. The UPICC relate to all kinds of commercial contracts. So, the only reference made by the Principles concerning the establishment of the respective obligations is in Art 5.1 *Express and Implied Obligations*: 'The contractual obligations of the parties may be express or implied'. Although the Principles then refer to the details of performance such as modalities of payment, place of performance, quality of performance, etc, the actual content of the obligations to be performed has to be formulated in the contract.

Some insight as to the intended meaning of Art 7.2.1 UPICC can be gained by looking at the reception of comparable rules in other international conventions such as ULIS and CISG which are well introduced and established. The question of whether a payment obligation exists is therefore one which concerns the type of the actual contract under consideration and is thus a question to be answered according to the special circumstances of each case.

Payment, despite being one out of countless possible obligations in a contract, can be said to be the common denominator in most of them. Therefore, this specific obligation can be isolated and treated separately from other, non-monetary obligations. This justifies the decision of the authors of the UPICC to create Art 7.2.1, separate from Art 7.2.2 UPICC. But does it also justify the special treatment as to the lack of express limitations, eg, in the form of a legitimate interest or a mitigation provision?

Under CISG the obligations of seller and buyer are constituted through separate rules. The seller's general obligations under a sales contract are established in Art 30 CISG while the following Articles refer to the more detailed aspects of the sale, such as time and place of delivery of goods and documents (Arts 31-34 CISG), as well as conformity of the goods (Arts 35-44 CISG). The buyer's obligations (to pay the price and take delivery of the goods) are written down in Art 53 CISG again, and are followed by detailed provisions as to the modalities of payment (Arts 54-59 CISG), and taking delivery (Art 60 CISG). Remedies for breach of contract by both seller and buyer are then stated separately relating to each party to the contract in the sections following the description of the parties' obligations. The 1964 Hague Convention follows the same pattern; the wording of Art 56 ULIS expressing the obligation of the buyer to pay the price, differs from that of Art 53 CISG in that it uses the word 'shall' rather than 'must'. Apart from that they are identical. The same applies to Art 18 ULIS compared to Art 30 CISG, where the slight differences seem to be merely editorial.

By way of an inherent interpretation of the UPICC, however, these limitations can be found within the whole system of the Principles. Art 7.2.1 UPICC does not answer the question as to when payment actually becomes due. A contractor can only have a right to claim any sum of money if the payment obligation is mature. In most cases the contractor, by common usage, will have to perform first. Especially according to Art 6.1.4(2) the non-payment performance in building contracts will be the one to be rendered first. Therefore, the employer will not be 'obliged to pay money' unless any work has been carried out. This is, in itself, a basic limitation to payment claims which is contained in Art 7.2.1 UPICC. The wording at least provides expressly for an existing and valid monetary obligation, it does not create such an obligation. Whether or not the right to performance granted by Art 7.2.1 is an overly rigid one, requires further investigation.

The Principles contain a right to cure, provided for in Art 7.1.4 and 7.1.5 UPICC. The contractor could 'retract his repudiation' (ie, cure his anticipatory non-performance in the terminology of the Principles) under Art 7.1.4. One objection to this solution could be that the Principles deal with anticipatory non-performance in Art 7.3.3 and 7.3.4 in the section on termination (see 7.3 below). These provisions could therefore be meant to regulate remedies relating to this special case of non-performance exclusively, not allowing for an application of the provisions on cure. Art 7.1.4(2), however, provides expressly that 'the right to cure is not precluded by notice of termination'. Because of this link any doubts should be removed.

Art 7.3.3 reflects the innocent party's option to terminate the contract in case of anticipatory breach. Art 7.3.4 (second phrase) provides for the option of the 'injured party to terminate the power of retraction by indicating to the repudiating party that the injured party considers the repudiation final'.[19] It also confirms that no explicit notice of repudiation, ie, non-performance has to be issued in order to entitle the aggrieved party to the said remedies. On the part of the party in breach, the employer, it is vital to decide whether Art 7.1.4 and 7.1.5 can be applied beside the previously mentioned ones. This could be answered in the affirmative if the anticipatory non-performance is at the same time regarded as a breach of an already existing obligation of holding oneself willing and able to perform. [20]

There is also a right to withhold performance in the Principles, Art 7.1.5(2) UPICC which adds to the options the contractor has in this case.[21] The provision also leaves all other remedies available which affirms the freedom the aggrieved party has under English law in case of anticipatory breach, Art 7.1.5(4).

Can the performance of the contract be forced upon the unwilling party in order to obtain the right to claim the price under the UPICC?[22] In most building contract cases, co-operation of the employer (eg, as site owner where the contractor needs access to the site) is required.[23] Do the Principles give the contractor the opportunity to force performance upon the employer by way of Art 7.2.1?

The problem has been discussed in the context of CISG. In sales contracts a similar problem can occur where a buyer has not received the goods but the seller requires payment under Art 62 CISG. Bearing in mind, that other than in Art 7.2.1 UPICC, Art 62 CISG also explicitly provides for the buyer's obligation to take delivery, coerced performance may create an unwanted result for both parties. This is illustrated by Honnold[24] in his example:

Example 28A: Seller, a Stockholm furniture manufacturer, and Buyer, a furniture distributor in Buenos Aires, made a contract for Seller to ship 500 of its standard coffee-tables to Buyer. Before Seller shipped, Buyer learned that customers in Buyer's area did not care for these items. Buyer telexed these facts to Seller, requested cancellation of the shipment, and offered to compensate Seller for any loss on the transaction. Seller replied: 'Shipping as ordered. Require you to pay the agreed price'.

The first question arising here is that of the systematic difference between the payment of the price and payment of a sum to 'compensate any loss on the trans-

---

[19] R Goode, *Commercial Law* (2004) 128; E A Farnsworth, *Contracts* (1990) 668; *United States* v *Seacoast Gas Co* 204 F2d 709 (5th Cir); UCC 2-611(1); Restatement Second §256.

[20] Relying on an interpretation taken from English contract law.

[21] Compare UCC 2-609 (1) and (4); restatement Second §251 for contracts other than contracts for the sale of goods.

[22] Obviously, the defendant did not try to contravene the performance through the plaintiff, and thus issues of consent as an argument supporting the price claim could have been discussed in the case.

[23] In *White and Carter (Councils)* v *McGregor* [1962] AC 413 the recognition of the performance of the contractual obligation by the plaintiff was only possible because no co-operation of the defendant was necessary. See below, Chapter 4, for further discussion.

[24] J O Honnold, *Uniform Law for International Sales under the 1980 United Nations Convention* (1999) No 193, 1.

action'. Would these two sums be equal? Why is it significant whether the seller's claim is labelled 'performance' or 'damages'?

### 3.3.2 The wording of Art 7.2.1: Unqualified right to performance? Debt or damages?

Art 7.2.1 UPICC reads: '... the other party may require payment' and not 'may require performance'. Is payment thus not regarded as performance in this case? Does it allow for an award of damages instead of one for payment of the price?

Under CISG and ULIS, compensation of the loss would cover any difference in market prices that arise on resale of the goods. This is not necessarily identical with the original contract price. The situation would be different, of course, in cases where the buyer has received the goods: 'When the buyer has accepted the goods the seller's legal remedy to recover the price normally resembles an action to collect a debt implemented by execution on the debtor's property'.[25] However, English law has always had a preference for the remedy of damages, even where a party is entitled to 'the monetary equivalent of performance', compelling performance by the breaching party is not normally available.[26]

The second question concerns the behaviour of the seller: should it be protected by the law? Honnold points out that in this case the seller is clearly the party who can resell the goods more efficiently than the buyer, since not only is the seller 'regularly engaged' in selling these goods, but also the goods are not wanted in the buyer's place which puts him in an unfavourable position. In this, and similar situations, the substantial transportation costs common in international sales can augment the waste involved in forcing the completion of an unwanted transaction.[27] This argument must be all the more true in international building contract cases where the unwanted completion of a project would involve the construction of plants that cannot be resold or removed easily at all. The UPICC must therefore provide a satisfactory solution to the problem of coerced performance.

To answer this question Art 7.2.1 UPICC cannot be applied on its own. The complete system of the UPICC has to be taken into account. With regard to CISG, inherent limitations are recognised and discussed by Honnold,[28] who especially mentions the principle of good faith as an interpretation maxim. CISG contains provisions other than Art 28 restricting the right to performance. Just like CISG, the UPICC contain an interpretation rule in Art 1.6 which provides for the observance of the international character of the Principles (Art 1.6(1)). Therefore, with regard to various factual circumstances, an analysis of the conflict solving quali-

---

25 Honnold, op cit, 345.

26 A H Kastely, 'The Right to Require Performance in International Sales: Towards an International Interpretation of the Vienna Convention' Washington Law Review 63 (1988) 611. See Chapter 4 for further discussion.

27 Honnold, op cit, No 193, 1.

28 Ibid, No 285.

ties of the Principles themselves has to be undertaken first in order to answer questions arising in the course of their application. [29]

Again, the main concern of possible critics of the UPICC is that due to the conception of contractual performance in the Principles, unwanted and inappropriate results are achieved by a lack of express limitations, or exceptions, to the right to require performance of payment obligations in Art 7.2.1 UPICC. This concern is well illustrated by considering a situation of construction contracts, where, according to Art 6.1.4(2) UPICC, the contractor's non-monetary obligation will be the one to be rendered first and might be used to unduly compel performance.

The express requirement of a legitimate interest – one potential inherent limitation – is missing in the Principles. It could, however, be derived from the underlying principles of the UPICC by interpretation.[30] Of course, one could argue that the duty to perform the monetary obligation ought to be supplemented by an express exception or qualification providing for a requirement of a legitimate interest. The requirement of a legitimate interest of the creditor and a duty to mitigate loss may be expressly inserted into Art 7.2.1 UPICC perhaps in the course of an updated second edition.

### 3.3.3 Termination and non-performance under Arts 7.3.1, 7.3.3 UPICC

The contractor might regard an express rejection of performance at any stage of the performance of the contract as an anticipatory non-performance as provided for in Art 7.3.3 UPICC. The apparent similarity of this expression and its counterpart in English law (anticipatory repudiation) raises one main problem of the application of transnational uniform law; the problem of the misleading similarity of language and wording often disguising a difference in meaning upon superficial understanding, the problem of *faux amis* (false friends).[31] The concept of anticipatory breach set up in the UPICC should not be construed as being identical with the English anticipatory repudiation. Nevertheless, this notion has to be introduced here for purposes of comparison as the corresponding concept under domestic English law. It needs to be established here whether the solution in the UPICC is

[29] See also Kastely, op cit, 645 who emphasises that this method 'suggested a basic tenet of statutory construction'.

[30] A similar position is taken under German law where the difference between the formal nature of a contract debt and that of a damages claim in the civil code causes conflicts in the reception of the UPICC: see below.

[31] 'No introduction to the French language would be complete without the traditional list of *faux amis*': E A Farnsworth, 'The American Provenance of the UNIDROIT Principles' Uniform Law Review 2/3 (1998), 402. Farnsworth gives a few examples in his note No 36. Another noteworthy example might be one reported on the Bristol Congress 1998 by the Canadian Reporter on the UNIDROIT Principles: the English protocol of a court session reported that 'the witness had a change of heart' which was translated officially into the French version as 'the witness had a heart transplantation'.

compatible with English law, or whether it is irreconcilable and remains a foreign element. [32]

In order to provide a defence against, or limitation to, the right to require payment, the intention not to pay for the contractor's services would have to amount to a fundamental non-performance as stated in Art 7.3.1(1) UPICC:

A party may terminate the contract where the failure of the other party to perform an obligation under the contract amounts to a fundamental non-performance...

According to the guidelines given in section (2) of Art 7.3.1, the intention not to pay the contract price would easily have to be regarded as being fundamental. Especially lit (e) can be assumed to be applicable in case the contractor has already contributed to the realisation of the project, eg, not only by buying material but also by commencing the building work. He might also have entered into further obligations himself, such as leasing machinery, and liabilities might arise out of such arrangement for the supply of equipment. The announcement of the non-performance by the employer might be regarded as 'intentional or reckless' (Art 7.3.1(e) lit (c)).

The contractor would then have a right to terminate the contract. He would notify the employer according to Art 7.3.2(1). The contract would thereby be terminated and both parties released from their obligations, Art 7.3.5(1). The contractor could also not claim performance anymore. The obligation to pay money arising from the contract would thus be discharged by remedies contained in the UPICC, other than express limitations as in Art 7.2.2. Anticipatory breach in combination with termination would provide for the right defence against a claim under Art 7.2.1.[33]

Of course, in this situation the other party, the contractor, is required to take action and exercise a right, the remedy of termination. The employer depends on the contractor's decision in this respect. This is not satisfactory from the employer's point of view. But what can a party expect if they were in breach of contract?

This section has explained and highlighted the conditions and defences contained in the UPICC that apply and are available to parties obliged to pay money under Art 7.2.1 UPICC. These make up for the limitations of this right to performance when viewed together.

## 3.4 Conclusion

Chapter 3 has identified and analysed a specific mindset of national lawyers dealing with international uniform law which impedes the easy and successful application of such law.

---

[32] In Chapter 4 below.

[33] Claims arising out of secondary monetary obligations such as damages or restitution claims are disregarded here.

Compatibility of uniform contract law with national (domestic) contract law is often denied due to a superficial attitude towards the application of international private law rules:

Some scholars allege that the UPICC contains an overly rigid right to performance of payment obligations rendering this rule incompatible with domestic contract law. This view, however, results from an insufficient application technique in practice, namely, the fact that the UPICC are not seen as a comprehensive set of rules. Solutions are therefore not taken primarily from the Principles (according to an autonomous interpretation technique) but instead, Art 7.2.1 is viewed as an isolated rule. The appropriate autonomous interpretation of the UPICC carried out in this chapter, has revealed, however, that there are sufficient inherent limitations within the Principles to safeguard against excessive effects of their payment obligation,[34] namely the logical precondition of validity and maturity of the obligation and the defences and remedies against the claim itself, as well as against breach of contract contained in the UPICC. Some scholars allege an overly rigid right to performance of payment obligations in the UPICC by merely looking at Art 7.2.1 on its own, disregarding all other rules of the UPICC and thus declaring this rule incompatible with domestic contract law.

The interpretation method, applied by the national lawyer in the example introduced in this chapter, forms an obstacle to the smooth application of the UPICC. This is because a lesser standard of diligence is applied to the international rule than would have been standard practice dealing with the same rule in national contract law. The appropriate autonomous interpretation of the UPICC carried out in this chapter, however, has revealed the full potential of an individual rule of uniform contract law.

The fact that two different standards are applied means a shift from domestic to uniform international law of which national lawyers are unaware. Consequently, there is no explanation for this shift from one level to another and application of double standards in traditional contract law practice and hence, a flaw in methodology.

An appropriate attitude of the national lawyer towards uniform contract law and practice of its application, however, is not the development of a hybrid attitude and mindset of national lawyers, but rather the consequential application of existing domestic standards to international uniform law rules. The solution is to maintain the same high quality in methodology as is standard practice in domestic law. This seems to be commonplace, but, as shown in this chapter, is not a common standard in the treatment of uniform law at present.

The autonomous interpretation method is to be further explained and demonstrated by thorough comparative analysis in the following chapters of Part 2, where the legal concepts addressed in this section are examined in national legal systems, namely the English (Chapter 4) and the German (Chapter 5), in the light of the UPICC and their critics' opinion.

[34] Compare also 6.3.2 below.

# 4 Exemplary application of the UPICC in the context of English law

The previous chapter established the scope of Art 7.2.1 UPICC according to an autonomous interpretation technique, and highlighted specific questions brought up in the course of applying UPICC in practice and research. These questions are now further analysed with regard to English law.

Chapter 4 investigates how difficulties in the area of substantive contract law can be met when applying the UPICC within the English legal system. It asks whether clashes between concepts used in the UPICC and English contract law, which seem to be irreconcilable, can be overcome. The main concept analysed under this aspect is that of specific performance. The chapter explains the status quo of the legal position of contractors and employers under current English law regarding payment obligations in building and construction contracts and compares this position with that under the UPICC. This serves to answer the question whether the UPICC's solution is compatible with English law, and, where it seems to differ from English law, how a solution can be achieved using established application techniques according to an autonomous interpretation method as suggested in Chapter 3.

## 4.1 Compatibility of the UPICC with English law

Section 4.1 considers the difficulties arising in the course of applying the UPICC in the context of English contract law and asks how these could be overcome by revisiting traditional concepts and historic developments of European legal history.

At first sight, the UPICC appear to meet with considerable difficulties when applied by common lawyers. The provision on monetary obligations in Art 7.2.1 UPICC could be regarded as incompatible with English law because of fundamental differences in underlying concepts. Monetary obligations are described by Art 7.2.1 UPICC in a general way and are subjected to the right to performance as in civil law jurisdictions, thus making Art 7.2.1 UPICC a type of claim derived from the law of obligations. It clashes with the concepts of specific performance, breach of contract and the procedures for recovering debts and awarding damages under English law. This is because requiring performance is not generally available for monetary obligations in common law jurisdictions.[1] Monetary obligations themselves do not give rise to a homogeneous type of claim.[2]

Art 7.2.1 UPICC poses complex questions of legal methodology in the context of English law since it involves specific performance of contractual payment obligations. The formulation 'may require payment' is obviously tailored to reflect the discretionary nature of the remedy but is employed here in connection with the claims stage of the contractual relationship, or, respectively, the duty stage rather than the enforcement stage.[3] Clarification is therefore required with regard to the use of the term. As much as the formulation may have been intended to provide scope for the corresponding discretionary remedy of specific performance under English law, it still might not be easily integrated into legal procedure due to the rule's structural resemblance with the law of obligations.

The term specific performance is commonly only used to denote a remedy to enforce non-monetary contractual obligations other than payment obligations. The discretionary and subsidiary nature of the equitable remedy distinguishes this legal instrument from the continental idea of a claim based on the primary obligation to pay the contract price. The applicability of specific performance under English law is not self-evident from the principle pacta sunt servanda. Specific enforcement of the primary payment obligation is addressed expressly only in the Sale of Goods Act 1979 s 49(1) and (2), providing for the action for the price. This is mainly due to the history of the court system and procedural law in England. Even though payment obligations can generally be subject to specific performance under English law, it might be technically difficult to base such a claim on Art 7.2.1 UPICC and thus integrate the provision into English contract law.

The expression specific performance, in English law, can in fact be generally applied to the enforcement of primary contractual obligations. It does not exclusively denote the remedy for non-monetary obligations in a procedural sense, drawing on the tradition of the ancient formulas and real actions.[4] It therefore covers instances of debt claims, including the action for the price.[5] This does not affect the position regarding actions for damages for breach of contract, which as paramount remedies, traditionally enjoy a privileged role in common law jurisdictions compared to civil law systems.

This use of terminology notably involves a shared value with civil law jurisdictions in that it acknowledges the general availability of specific enforcement of contractual claims, without discrimination as to their monetary or non-monetary nature. This might be regarded as bridging the gap between the two systems and hence, between the UPICC and English law.

To follow therefore, is an analysis of the scope of the remedy of specific performance in English law, in other international conventions, and in other European

---

1 See below for further discussion.

2 See below for further discussion.

3 Because the UPICC do not deal with procedural but with substantive law.

4 Compare M Bridge, *Sale of Goods* (1988) 718-719 and n 306; G Jones and W Goodhart, *Specific Performance* (1996) 6 et seq.

5 Compare G H Treitel, *The Law of Contract* (1999) 944.

and common law jurisdictions, in order to provide arguments promoting the integration of Art 7.2.1 UPICC into English law, using the term specific performance in the above described sense.

A brief recollection of the historic development of the role of specific performance under continental European jurisdictions reveals the core of the conflict underlying the discussion of Art 7.2.1 UPICC.[6] An example is given by a description of the concept of *astreinte*,[7] and its development and current role in French law.

### 4.1.1 Requiring performance and payment obligations in international contract law

International contract law models utilise a special technique of working with payment obligations in close context with requiring performance. This is irritating from a common law viewpoint, where the action for the price, damages for breach of contract, and performance of non-monetary obligations, are traditionally subject to different treatments from each other.[8] International contract law models have been striving to blend common law and civil law notions forming new concepts. The terminology in international contract law rules is designed to include ideas derived from the law of obligations which recognises a right to require performance of monetary obligations.

A right to 'require performance' is expressed in Art 46(1) CISG:

> The buyer may require performance by the seller of his obligations unless the buyer has resorted to a remedy which is inconsistent with this requirement.

The seller's right to performance is contained in Art 62 CISG:

> The seller may require the buyer to pay the price, take delivery or perform his other obligations, unless the seller has resorted to a remedy which is inconsistent with this requirement.

The provisions use the particular terminology ('requiring performance') of the uniform law conventions that had been adopted internationally before; the 1964 Convention relating to a Uniform Law on International Sales, ULIS, granted rights to require performance in various provisions: eg, Art 24(1)(a), Art 42 and Art 55(2), etc. The expression corresponds to 'specific performance', the 'common law parlance'.[9] Art 61(1) ULIS reads:

> Where the buyer fails to pay the price … the seller may require the buyer to perform his obligation.

---

[6] See 4.1, below.

[7] 4.1.3.2, below.

[8] See below for further discussion.

[9] J O Honnold, *Uniform Law for International Sales under the 1980 United Nations Convention* (1999) No 279.

Both CISG and ULIS, however, contain provisions which restrict the right to performance under their regime in cases where the law of the forum does not recognise specific performance to the same extent as the Conventions; Art VII of the Hague Convention and Art 28 CISG, both state that the courts cannot be forced to grant judgments for specific performance unless they would do so under their domestic law.

Apart from this more procedural limitation to the right to performance under these conventions, there are express limitations to the right itself. Under Art 46(1) CISG there is the limit of the 'inconsistent remedy' resorted to by the buyer, and equally under Art 62 CISG, by the seller. Also, in ULIS as well as under CISG there are provisions protecting the commercial interests of the parties by allowing, even requiring, replacement transactions. CISG does not allow the buyer to compel delivery of substitute goods in cases of minor defects (Art 46(2) CISG), while ULIS even provides explicitly for the replacement purchase of goods by the buyer 'if it is in conformity with usage and reasonably possible', Art 25 ULIS. In this case the buyer cannot 'require performance'. The rule even provides for the contract to be ipso facto avoided if these requirements are satisfied.[10] The corresponding provision concerning the seller's right to performance (the payment of the price) is Art 61(2) ULIS.

Despite these efforts to compromise, neither of the main international sales law conventions have come into force in the United Kingdom because of these disparities which have been regarded as incompatible with English law so far. The UPICC follow a tradition established by international codifications and conventions of uniform private law,[11] by including the principle of requiring performance. However, the UPICC do not contain the possibility of a reservation like the one of Art 28 CISG. Therefore, the chances of their success in the sphere of English law appear to be only minute at first sight.

### 4.1.2 The law relating to specific performance of payment obligations in common law jurisdictions

In order to prepare the ground for the analysis of the UPICC from the point of view of English law, this section provides an overview of the position regarding the enforcement of contractual payment obligations under English law. American law is taken into account where it helps to emphasise the English, and thereby, the

---

[10] Since it is not easy to establish in a given situation whether these requirements are satisfied or not, in my view a great uncertainty as to the validity of the contract and the parties' mutual obligations is created by Art 25 ULIS. The existence of usages and reasonableness has to be established prior to the decision whether the contract 'shall be avoided'. Due to the openness of the terms it does not seem practical for merchants to deal with this provision.

[11] Such as the 1980 United Nations Convention on Contracts for the International Sale of Goods (CISG), or the 1955 Uniform Law on International Sales (ULIS) enacted by the 1964 Hague Convention relating to a Uniform Law on the International Sale of Goods (the Hague Convention).

common law position in a wider sense. This is done by contrasting solutions in both jurisdictions which are related through the bond of traditional common law.

Despite modern developments there still remains a difference in Anglo-American law, especially in English law, regarding the origins and the effect of the action for the contract price (specific performance) on the one hand, and a damages claim for breach of contract on the other. These two concepts need to be treated separately and require different procedural steps for their enforcement.

Regarding the extent of enforceability of payment obligations, it can be said that under English and American law, the contractor cannot generally insist on performing the contract (subject to certain exceptions) by simply relying on his right to performance, even though the original contractual payment obligation might entitle him to specific performance. There are limitations to the right to performance, particularly regarding price claims, based on the equitable principle of a legitimate interest in the enforcement of the contract against a party in breach. These can even amount to a duty to mitigate loss in the form of a duty to terminate the contract. It shows that the overall situation regarding the outcome of cases and the eventual position of the debtor under Anglo-American law resembles very much that under German law, where there is by law a general right of cancellation for an employer in building and construction contracts (before the completion of the work) coupled with a modified payment obligation in case of a cancellation.[12] The existence of doctrinal difficulties and peculiarities [13] provide for another similarity of this particular area of contract law.

The Sale of Goods Act 1979 (hereinafter SGA) deals with the enforcement of the seller's right in s 49(1). It provides for an action for the price, but only where the property has already passed onto the buyer at the time of the breach of the contract. The buyer's remedy for breach of contract is described in SGA 1979 s 52. Specific performance can only be sought for contracts for specified or ascertained goods. The court retains its discretion even then.[14] The Uniform Commercial Code (hereinafter UCC) of the United States, provides for specific performance for the buyer in Section 2-716. It does not require the passing of property prior to a right to specific performance, but limits this remedy to cases where 'the goods are unique or in other proper circumstances'.[15] Apart from this restriction the remedy is quite far reaching, concerning the content of the decree to be granted by the courts,[16] as well as the possibility of *replevin*,[17] involving seizure of the goods and their delivery to the plaintiff.

---

[12] See 5.1.2 and 5.1.3, below.

[13] Such as the question of a gradual disappearance of the distinction between debt and damages claims in common law jurisdictions, 4.2.5, and the problem of classifying the modified payment obligation in §649 BGB as a 'disguised damages provision' under German law, 5.1.3, below.

[14] 'If it thinks fit': SGA 1979 s 52(1).

[15] UCC 2-716(1).

[16] 'The decree for specific performance may include such terms and conditions as to payment of the price, damages, or other relief as the court may deem just': UCC 2-716(2).

[17] UCC 2-716(3).

The seller's right to recover the price is regulated by UCC §2-709. Full recovery of the price is only provided for where the buyer has 'accepted' the goods. Otherwise, §2-709(1)(b) UCC, only grants specific performance in case of 'identified goods', and 'if the seller is unable after reasonable effort to resell them at a reasonable price, or the circumstances reasonably indicate that such effort will be unavailing'.[18] The foremost concern against specific performance is that of coerced performance.

The legal effect of specific performance in English law is that a court order instructs a party to perform the contractual obligation in question. The remedy is an equitable one and is only available where damages are not considered by a court as being adequate. Even in a 'contract to pay money' 'specific performance ... could be granted in a proper case'.[19] Specific performance is thus not generally excluded for monetary obligations under English law. In contracts for the sale of goods, however, it is rarely granted since 'other goods of a similar kind can be purchased and the difference assessed in damages'.[20] This position is well reflected in CISG as well as in ULIS.[21] It is also present in the limitations to the right to performance in Art 7.2.2(b) and (c) UPICC.

The remedy first appeared in the form of a decree issued by the Equity courts. These were enforced by the courts fining non-complying defendants for 'contempt of court' which could lead to imprisonment.[22] 'Equity does not act in vain.'[23] Due to this, history specific performance is sometimes considered an overly-rigid remedy in a contractual context.

> In the common law system, the sanction was both severe and effective, since specific performance was enforced by penalties such as fines (or, in some jurisdictions, even by imprisonment for contempt of court) ... it was in view of the undue harshness of that remedy (particularly in the context of international sales) that the drafters of the 1964 ULIS had rightly limited the role of specific performance ... [24]

---

[18] This provision is much clearer than the provision in ULIS which requires the seller to find a replacement deal since it relates to facts rather than speculative elements such as usages and general chances to resell.

[19] *Beswick* v *Beswick* (1967) 2 All ER 1197. A husband had concluded a contract with his nephew to pay a weekly sum of £5 to his widow in return for the sale of his business. She was granted specific performance by the House of Lords.

[20] D Keenan, *Smith and Keenan's English Law* (2004) 394.

[21] Arts 25 and 61(2).

[22] See also the remedy of replevin in §2-716 UCC, discussed above.

[23] *Tito* v *Waddell* (No 2) [1977] Ch 106, 326.

[24] Prof Farnsworth in Summary Records of the First Committee (18th meeting); UN Doc A/CONF97/C1/SR18 (1980), 328, 330 on the United States proposal to limit the performance remedy in Art 46 CISG.

## 4.1.3 Common origins of specific performance in European jurisdictions

Payment obligations arising from promises to pay a price for the supply of goods or services have a common origin in European jurisdictions. Money judgments were the most common relief given in Roman legal practice, and this remained a predominant fact under early English law. German law as an example of civil law, together with most European legal systems, also has a Roman heritage. Therefore, the development of the law relating to payment obligations needs to be explained in this wider context.

### *4.1.3.1 Roman law and the reception through the Bolognese glossators*

The development of the two apparently adverse poles of specific performance and damages has very much been influenced by procedural facts and circumstances concerning the actual execution of judgments, which were relevant in the respective eras of their use. In the classical Roman period the praetorian procedure involved *iudices* to render judgments against litigating parties.[25] These lacked a sort of power and authority of a central power to enforce decrees, in the form of for example, physical force. This was more up to various occurrences of private self-help; it was the judgment creditor who exercised measures like killing or enslaving of the defendant in cases of disobedience to the award obtained. In England, during the twelfth century, this important power to command which was held by kings, was 'made available to private litigants' by way of the royal courts.[26] It may have been this difference in procedure and distribution of power which contributed to the development of the two ends in performance claims, represented by the common and the civil law. In fact, despite certain procedural means, either written law or practice,[27] granting a certain use of force to aid enforcement of money judgments even in the classical Roman period, [28] the money judgment remained the most common, and effectively the only, form of award a party could obtain:

> As has been said, the general principle of praetorian procedure at the time he (Celsus) wrote was that all obligations were translated into money judgments, whether they involved doing, not doing, surrendering specific property or anything else. [29]

---

[25] D Liebs, *Römisches Recht* (Roman Law) Vol 465, 1999, 37 et seq; for general reference see also F Wieacker: *Der Prätor*, 83-127.

[26] Dawson: 'Specific Performance in France and Germany' Michigan Law Review 57 (1959) 495, 497.

[27] See the comment by Dawson, that a certain clause extending the traditional money judgments was recorded and inserted into the *Corpus Iuris* by later compilers; Dawson, ibid, 500.

[28] If the defendant had the property sued for, a clause would be inserted into the judgment ordering it to be taken away from him *manu militari officio iudicis* (by military force on the authority of the *iudex*).

[29] Dawson, op cit (n 26), 501.

This practice was recorded by the Bolognese glossators during the mediaeval Holy Roman Empire and preserved by the Roman law tradition spread over Europe throughout its reign. Aspects of specific performance started to evolve in the form of concerns such as: 'If you have sold bread, have not delivered it, and I have died of hunger, will a money judgment suffice?'[30] In addition, there was the notion that a 'promisor', who paid damages instead of performing, was merely doing so relying on a privilege given by law.[31] One innovation of that period was that the distinction between obligations 'to do', and obligations 'to give', resulted into different legal consequences. The commentator Baldus stated that no one could be compelled to perform, specifically a promise to build a house since 'this would be a kind of servitude', especially if this performance extended over a period of time.[32] So, the opinion was that only promises 'to give' could be enforced to be specifically performed, whereas any breach of promises 'to do' were sanctioned by damages: *nemo potest praecise cogi ad factum*. It is noteworthy that the mediaeval Italian glossators did take notice of an ancient opinion that, 'in obligations "to do" the promisee might often have no interest of his own that performance might serve',[33] but in general, their practice of dealing with the material they studied was purely academic and without any consideration for the great time spans that lay between the time of the creation and practice of the ancient Roman texts and their then contemporary revival. Thus they tended to take the *Corpus Iuris* at face value and delivered a law to their contemporaries, and even generations after them (by learned interpretation), which was full of restrictions in substance and content, taken mainly from sources which were derived by way of technical and merely terminological reproduction. There was little regard to the factual necessities from where the legal solutions recorded by the Roman authors had come into existence. Contemporary legal practice and legislative activity should not copy this technique.

#### *4.1.3.2 Specific performance in the form of* astreinte *in French law*

The *astreinte* seemingly found its way into the UPICC in Art 7.2.4 – 'Judicial Penalty'. This penalty is payable to the aggrieved party on non-compliance with a court order to perform. Although it does not 'exclude any claim for damages' (Art 7.2.4(2) UPICC), the Principles do not refer to the French practice of keeping the astreinte – a preliminary means of enforcing the court order. Therefore this provision has been criticised as not complying with domestic rules.[34] In fact, German

[30] Martinus of Bologna, quoted by Haenel, *Dissensiones Dominorum* (1834), 46-48, 93-94 and 597.

[31] Ioannis Bassianus quoted by Accursius in the gloss to D.19.1.1.

[32] Baldus, commentary on C.4.49, quoted by Dawson, op cit (n 26), 504.

[33] Dawson, op cit (n 26), 505

[34] I Schwenzer, '*Erfüllung und Schadensersatz nach den Unidroit – Prinzipien, 1997*' / I Schwenzer, 'Specific Performance and Damages According to UNIDROIT Principles of International Commercial Contracts' European Journal of Law Reform 1 (1998/1999) 289-303; cf also the official commentary to the Principles, Art 7.2.5 Nos 1-7.

law does not recognise any punitive damages (in accordance with French law) and would not recognise a regulation formulated in this way, especially since the penalty is payable to the other party. Penalties like this can, however, be agreed by the parties: §§339-345 Bürgerliches Gesetzbuch (Civil Code; hereinafter BGB).[35]

The influence of theoretical authority of the Roman authors and the glossators reached far into the eighteenth century when the Code Civil was drafted under the prominent contribution of the French lawyer, Pothier.[36] His interpretation and compilation of past and present legal writings and practice resulted in an upholding of the statement, *nemo potest praecise cogi ad factum*. This led to its penetration of the new legislation regarding specific performance and infiltration into much of the law of obligations. Again, procedural circumstances of that era might have supported the rather uncritical acceptance of the old restrictions in substance as the royal courts were established by the crown under the Ancien Regime, having a vast amount of power through saleable and inheritable offices, as well as largely uncontrolled legislative powers. The legal views, which impose a substantive restriction of the means of enforcing obligations by rigid measures, meant at the same time a restriction of judicial powers. This was welcomed by the libertarian movement, formed during the times of the Revolution, who were fighting against arbitrary power exercised not only by the courts. Also, the Code was drafted within a short period of time – commanded urgently by Napoleon.[37] This, among other things, obviously hindered a thorough scrutiny of the underlying dogmas and doctrines.[38]

Without going into too much detail of the various expressions of specific performance within the Code Civil, two developments are to be mentioned: the remedy of *astreinte*, and the treatment of obligations 'to give'. This latter type of obligation is strongly determined by the mechanism cast in Articles 1136, 1138, 1583, 938 and 1703, which establish the passing of title by mere agreement. Thus, obligations to transfer assets as in contracts for sales, gifts and exchanges are subject to direct execution ie, seizure of the assets. 'The doctrinal writers, at least, all claim that direct execution is available to buyers of both land and goods, and the fact that so little litigation on the subject has spilled into the law reports seems to

---

[35] *Bürgerliches Gesetzbuch*, 18 August 1896, first published in *Reichsgesetzblatt* (1896) 195; C H Beck'sche Textausgaben, '*Bürgerliches Gesetzbuch mit zugehörigen Gesetzen und EG-Richtlinien*', 105 ed, 10 April 1999.

[36] Pothier provided with his *Traités* some of the most important sources of the '*ancien droit*' on which the Code Civil is based: see M Stolleis (ed), *Juristen – Ein biographisches Lexikon von der Antike bis zum 20.Jh* (1995) 174.

[37] See Dawson, op cit (n 26), 510.

[38] Ibid, 508: 'There was no inherent reason … why French law could not have developed a rational system of contract remedies and freed itself from hampering restrictions that the glossators had derived from Roman law … This kind of distinction (ie, between promises "to do" and those "to give") could have been brushed aside by an original mind, well informed on French practice and capable of undertaking a fresh analysis of the problem.' This Pothier was not, according to Dawson at this point.

lend some support for the claim.'[39] The general rules for protection of ownership are the vehicle for facilitating this result. Regarding the obligations 'to do or not to do', another way had to be found. Under Art 1142 Code Civil:[40] 'Every obligation to do or not to do is resolved in damages in case of non-performance by the obligor'. The *astreinte* as a 'mode of coercion' as Dawson puts it, began to develop from 1804. This was a provisional, and 'comminatory', order by the court to pay a fixed sum of money unless the required performance was rendered. These judgments were revoked and transformed into definite damages awards once the required act was done; very often the money payable under the *astreinte* amounted to fantastic sums. Besides raising a procedural problem (offending the rules of *res iudicata*) the fact that the money was in fact never paid, but the *astreinte* only used as a threat, resulted into practical difficulties after World War II when, in times of housing shortage following large population movements, it extended to numerous cases of unsuccessful eviction of illegal occupants of residential property. Courts resorted to an attempt to extend their powers by changing their provisional judgments (derived from Art 1036 of the Code of Civil Procedure as well as from *coutume jurisprudentielle*)[41] into final damages awards; *astreintes non-comminatoires*.[42] This attempt was contravened by legislation in the form of the statute of 21 July 1949, which declared 'that every *astreinte* attached to an order for eviction from housing was necessarily merely 'comminatory' and must be reduced to simple damages after the tenant had finally left'.[43] Punitive damages were consequently counteracted as they violated the principle that damages, 'no matter to whom they are paid, are arbitrary and cannot be subjected to any kind of definite rule'.[44] Nevertheless, to French courts they appeared to remain the only solution to the problem which the lack of persuasive qualities of the *astreinte* posed to the plaintiff parties.

These considerations ought to have shown the critical attitude to coerced performance in the civil law systems, in order to have counteracted a general concern in the common law world about the notion based on the argument of mere origin from the law of obligations.

---

[39] Dawson, op cit (n 26), 511. See also Planiol and Ripert, *Traité Pratique de Droit Civil Français* (2nd ed, 1954) §779; Garsonnet and Cézar-Bru, *Traité de Procédure Civile et Commerciale* (1913) §6; Baudry-Lacantinerie and Barde, *Traité Théorétique et Pratique en Droit Civil* (2nd ed, 1900) §364.

[40] *Code Civil: Textes, jurisprudence, annotations* (Paris: Dalloz, 2005).

[41] See Dawson, op cit (n 26), 520.

[42] *Semaine Juridique* (1946) II 3079 (5 March 1946); D 1948 135 (7 November 1947).

[43] Dawson, op cit (n 26), 521; Planiol et Ripert, op cit, §795 quatre.

[44] Kayser, *Revue Trimestrielle* (1953) 209, 243-244; Dawson, op cit (n 26), 523.

## 4.2 Scope of employer's rights under construction contracts under English law

The previous section, 4.1, described general doctrinal difficulties in contract law which might impede the application of UPICC under English law as a specialised law governing international commercial contracts. These difficulties arising out of the notion of specific performance can be overcome by a thorough analysis of underlying principles also referring to historic developments.

This section asks how the UPICC can contribute to reaching solutions in the specialised area of construction contract law. It analyses the existing law, and the scope of payment claims under English construction contract law, in order to compare the solution suggested by the UPICC.

The Commentary of the UPICC very often refers to international construction contracts to explain the scope and meaning of single provisions. These are typically contracts involving large engineering projects where the parties (persons or corporations) reside in, or operate from, different countries and where the project is possibly to be completed in a third country. Contracts of this kind often involve third parties playing a key role in the legal process of the performance of the contract, eg, architects, consultants and sub-contractors. Special payment mechanisms, as well as financing procedures protect the interests of the parties. Projects of this kind are mostly long term commitments and involve special risks which would not occur in 'one-off' transactions such as contracts for the sale of goods. This contract type can serve here to explain the relationship between English law and the UPICC in terms of compatibility and methods of integration. The above mentioned, Art 7.2.1 UPICC, concerns the legal position of the employer in a construction contract and his payment obligation in case of subsequent events affecting contractual performance. The employer's rights and defences are the subject of the following discussion.

### 4.2.1 Standard terms and practice of contract drafting of international construction and building contracts under English law

International construction contracts are commonly concluded under the standard forms of the various Professional Institutions such as the JCT (Joint Contracts Tribunal Ltd, formed in 1931) 'Standard Form of Building Contract' or the specialised forms for large construction projects.[45] These forms are intended to help standardise, and thereby simplify and professionalise, the procedure of concluding contracts involving the planning of large, or international, projects. They do, however, not rule out contract law. Domestic contract law is applicable to international

---

45 See A Pike, *Engineering tenders, sales, and contracts: standard forms and procedures* (1982); for details and the latest versions of the forms (2005) go to www.jctltd.co.uk, where the forms can be purchased for use.

construction or building contracts[46] under the conflict of laws.[47] Non-English parties will often not agree to a standard contract issued by an English professional agency.

On the level of contractual performance, international projects depend to a great extent on political events in the countries involved. Although security bonds and insurances are involved in the process in large projects to back payment mechanisms – embargoes, export regulations, currency fluctuations and building regulations can interfere with such projects in a major way. The employer might be deprived of the whole purpose of his intended project by an embargo or other change of legislation which, for example, renders the production of certain substances illegal. Currency fluctuations can also greatly affect the economic balance between the parties.

The specific character of construction contracts, both domestic and international, originates in special circumstances such as the great time span involved and the tendency of problems to create 'domino-effects'.[48]

The parties will provide for most of these typical risks in their contracts. Contract law solves problems reaching beyond the scope of the contract. Therefore, the law should provide for the corresponding categories. Although, this is often not the case with domestic law in general, English law has a tradition of giving consideration to commercial matters and the practices of international trade developed through centuries of seafaring.[49] It is likely, therefore that the UPICC cannot offer novel solutions in the area of substantive law, but will have to stand the compatibility test if they are to be an instrument of neutral transnational contract law.

### 4.2.2 Speculative aspects of international contract practice and contractual performance

What would be the position of an employer in an international building contract who suddenly changes his mind, withholds all payments and announces his intention not to pursue the contract any further? What is the position regarding his obligation to pay the price and to have to consummate the transaction even though it might be of no interest to him?

Under English contract law, no right of cancellation as such exists. The parties are free to include it in their contracts, though. Standard contracts will usually not

---

46 A May, *Keating on Building Contracts* (1995).

47 Discussed in Chapter 6, below.

48 The threat of the anticipated domino-effect in the 1999 crisis of the large German building concern Phillip Holzmann was so intense that the German government even resorted to anti-liberal measurements in order to avoid insolvency among hundreds of companies involved in Holzmann-projects and the loss of thousands of jobs. The government consented to guarantee loans given by the banks in order to facilitate restructuring of the concern. The business nevertheless eventually declared bankruptcy. See, eg, *Frankfurter Allegemeine Zeitung* 26 November 1999, articles on pp 1, 13 and 17.

49 Compare Chapter 8, below.

provide for any right of cancellation as such. Contract forms, such as the JCT 2005 Form, or the BEAMA Conditions of Contract (E), are drafted by the respective professional institutions representing the contractors.[50] Therefore, in this respect, regard is not made to the interests of the employer.[51] An unqualified right of cancellation is not contained in any standard form. A right of cancellation on special grounds is sometimes included in building contracts.[52] There are instances of termination provided for, given that certain factual circumstances occur. These are called forfeiture clauses.[53] In addition, general rules of law apply.

Relying on the principle in *White and Carter (Councils)* v *McGregor*,[54] the contractor may decide to compel the employer to proceed with the transaction. In order to perform a building contract, access to the site is essential to the contractor. Standard forms provide for the contractor's right of access. The employer's interest in this case is not only to defend against the payment obligation arising out of the contract but also to stop the actual performance of the building work. Therefore a legal possibility needs to operate in his favour allowing him to terminate the contract.

The extent to which a legal system supports the enforceability of contractual obligations, by for example specific performance, reflects the degree of intensity with which the keeping of legal promises is emphasised in the domestic legal order. One aspect concerning the significance of strictness of a binding promise is the change of circumstances after the promise is given. A subsequent change of mind of a party to a contract can have various reasons and some of them, certain motivations, are recognised as valid points by the law. These instances are reflected in the rules relating to mistake and frustration, rescission, cancellation, repudiation, termination, etc.[55]

In trade relationships the speculative aspect of contractual agreements is an important factor to be considered.

> At the time the agreement is made, each party has reason to suppose that it will be profitable for that party. A party may, however, err in calculating the net benefit to be anticipated from performance of the agreement, or circumstances may change so as to disappoint that party's initial hopes. A contract that the party once thought would be profitable may turn out to be unprofitable. If it is profitable for the other party, should the reluctant party be compelled to perform? [56]

---

[50] JCT: Joint Contract Tribunal; BEAMA: British Electrical and Allied Manufacturer's Association Ltd.

[51] This has already given rise to criticism and ultimately to reform of the standard forms( eg, A May, *Keating on Building Contracts* (1995) 527) and compare the situation in Germany at 5.1.1. below.

[52] See, eg, *Hounslow London Borough Council* v *Twickenham Garden Developments Ltd* [1971] Ch 234.

[53] See, for an example, clause 27 of the 1980 JCT Form, published in A Pike, *Engineering tenders, sales, and contracts: standard forms and procedures* (1982).

[54] [1962] AC 413; see further discussion below, 1.5.4.

[55] These are excluded from this study.

[56] E A Farnsworth, *Contracts* (1990) 846-847.

Farnsworth mentions the 'economic theory' as an underlying justification and modern doctrine enforcing and strengthening traditional common law decisions. Modern (American) common law finds support in this theory for the existing manner of solving contract cases of 'efficient breach' where there is a 'redistribution of wealth' as a consequence:

> The party in breach may gain enough from the breach to have a net benefit, even though that party compensates the injured party for resulting loss, calculated according to the subjective preferences of the injured party .... and economic theory not only sanctions but encourages breach. [57]

It is obvious that in a legal environment where merchants are specifically addressed by a set of rules like the UPICC these considerations are particularly attractive.

German 'common law', the *gemeines Recht*, which was in use until modern codifications like the Commercial Code (*Handelsgesetzbuch* or HGB) and the Civil Code (*Bürgerliches Gesetzbuch* or BGB) were enacted, strongly emphasised the 'keeping of the promise', and was hostile towards withdrawal and other means of discharging a contract other than by performance.[58] The merchant community, however, had always postulated, even since the Middle Ages, a legal solution which allowed for a quick discharge or termination of contracts as in cases of non-payment or defective performance.[59] It is said that the BGB contains more flexible solutions in this respect, so that the modern rules give effect to the traditional preference of the trading world.[60] This question deserves further discussion in the light of the UPICC. [61]

On commodities markets, contracts are of a considerably different kind from consumer contracts. Not only is a number of up to a hundred contracts all relating to one and the same consignment of cargo perfectly common, but hedging transactions and trading in futures are essential in modern agricultural commerce. All these contracting parties deliberately benefit from speculative aspects of their agreements. It is their vital interest to engage in paper trading, encouraging the activities of speculators: 'Paper trading creates liquidity, and liquidity tends to even out prices so as to remove the more extreme cyclical swings.' [62] In addition to this the ready use of technical rejection rights are an important means for gaining

---

[57] Farnsworth, op cit, 847; see also R Goode, *Commercial Law* (1995) 26.

[58] See Hager, '*Der Gedanke der Solidarität in der Lehre vom Synallagma im Deutschen und Internationalen Schuldrecht*' in *Kolloquium aus Anlaß des 75. Geburtstags von Ernst von Caemmerer* (1983) 29.

[59] For mediaeval merchants in the Netherlands, see Miteis, *Rechtsfolgen der Leistungsverweigerung beim Kaufvertrag nach niederländischen Quellen des Mittelalters* (1913) 17, 72 et seq.

[60] F Nicklisch, '*Empfiehlt sich eine Neukonzeption des Werkvertragsrechts? – unter besonderer Berücksichtigung komplexer Langzeitverträge*' JZ 39 (1984) 757, 760.

[61] See 5.8.

[62] M Bridge, 'International Private Commodity Sales' Can Bus LJ 19 (1991) 485, 486.

flexibility and taking advantage of specific market conditions. In this respect, among commodities traders, emphasis of loyalty towards the contract or the other contracting party – in order to maintain any future goodwill – does not seem to be the most prominent feature of the rules.[63] This means that not only are special forms of agreement and practices used to bargain, but also the contract law itself, namely the provisions on breach of contract.

Substitutional relief, such as awarding damages rather than specific performance, serves the attitude of aiming for relief on breach of promises, rather than for preventing such breach; 'Our system of contract remedies is not directed at compulsion of promisors to prevent breach; ... Its concern is with a different question: how can people be encouraged to deal with those who make promises?' [64]

It is this speculative element which makes a right of cancellation a paramount demand made by German authors towards the UPICC.[65] German,[66] Swiss,[67] and French[68] law also contain a right of cancellation.[69]

### 4.2.3 Cancellation rights, breach of contract and anticipatory repudiation in English law

Since most building contracts do not contain a stipulation providing for a general right of cancellation, the employer's announcement to step back from the contract and not pay any money due under the agreement is regularly dealt with according to the rules relating to breach of contract.

However, an illustration of the law relating to cancellation of building contracts is provided by the Hounslow case.[70] A cancellation clause was contained in condition 25(1)(b) in the contract incorporating a RIBA standard form between the Hounslow London Borough Council, as employers, and Twickenham Garden Developments Ltd, as contractors. The employers were entitled to give notice to terminate the employment if the contractors failed to proceed 'regularly and diligently' with the work. The employers gave notice but were refused a mandatory injunction on motion expelling the contractor from the site which they sought. This was decided because there were some doubts as to the valid determination of the contractor's licence to occupy the land and the subsequent arising situation of trespass to be recognised.

The Hounslow case shows that the right of cancellation was only provided for in a restrictive way, in that notice was not to be given 'unreasonably and vexa-

---

63 See Bridge, op cit, 488.
64 Farnsworth, op cit, 840.
65 Schwenzer, op cit.
66 §649 BGB.
67 Art 377 OR.
68 Art 1794 CC.
69 For further details see 5.8.
70 *Hounslow London Borough Council* v *Twickenham Garden Developments Ltd* [1971] Ch 234.

tiously'.[71] The speculative element occurring under a general right of cancellation as, eg, under German law [72] is thereby counteracted. If the contract was thus not validly determined by the Hounslow Borough, the employers were to be regarded as being in breach of contract. The contractors then had a right of election whether to continue or to terminate the contract.

If the employer announces to the contractor prior to taking up any work that he has no intention of paying the contract price and that he will refuse to accept the intended work this would be an anticipatory repudiation and thus a breach of contract.[73] Under English law the maturity of the payment obligation is thus not a condition for a breach of contract.[74] Formally the common law solution resembles that of the UPICC. It has to be established however, to what extent the views taken on anticipatory breach can be applied to payment obligations such as those addressed in Art 7.2.1 UPICC; it has been contested that anticipatory breach can occur in unilateral contracts, or those bilateral contracts where one obligation is fully performed and just the obligation to pay money remains.[75] The latter case might occur where the contractor has completed the work entirely and only the contract price remains outstanding. This seems unlikely to occur under most building contracts since they usually provide for payment in instalments, on presentation of certificates after completion of building sections, as the work progresses.

### 4.2.4 The aggrieved party's options on anticipatory breach under English law

The contractor has several options regarding reacting to the breach. Even if he treats the contract as discharged[76] this does not necessarily free the employer from paying a sum of money since he might be liable in damages.[77] The contractor, as the aggrieved party, is discharged of his remaining duties. There is, however, generally one possibility that might match the employer's interests in this case. The employer can retract his repudiation before the contractor has reacted to it in a way which would lead to a discharge of the contract. This would suit him when the reason for him to withdraw from the contractual agreement is, for example, adjusting to a change in market prices; he could repudiate on finding a better offer which even compensates potential damages, and retract if this chance falls flat.[78] It

[71] [1971] Ch 234.

[72] See below.

[73] *Hochster* v *De la Tour* 1 Ellis & Bl 678, 118 Eng Rep 922 (Queen's Bench 1853).

[74] Especially taking Goode's view into account, who states that in fact the employer is in breach of an already existing obligation at the time of the repudiation: the obligation to hold himself willing and able to pay; R Goode, *Commercial Law* (2004) 126.

[75] *Brown Paper Mill Co* v *Irvin*, 146 F 2d 232 (8th Cir 1944); *Phelps* v *Hero* 215 Md 223, 137 A 2d 159 (1957); see E A Farnsworth, *Contracts* (1990) 659.

[76] See D Keenan, *Smith and Keenan's English Law* (2004) 386.

[77] Ibid, 386.

[78] Compare Farnsworth, op cit, 669; *Taylor* v *Johnston*, 15 Cal 3d 130, 539 P 2d 425 (1975); Goode, op cit, 127.

is doubtful however, as to whether this is a suitable option in building contracts, since it is unlikely that the costs of breach could leave alternative employment lucrative. In the Hounslow case the employers probably sought to complete the work with another contractor facing excessive delays under their existing contract. The court acknowledged this interest, but preferred the view that 'a contract remains a contract even if, or perhaps especially if, it turns out badly'.[79] The contractor, on the other hand, is not forced to wait until the employer chooses to retract. His rights are balanced by the possibility of treating the contract as terminated after taking notice of the repudiation.[80] In the Hounslow case, the duty not to exercise the right to give notice 'unreasonably and vexatiously' was a safeguard against any speculative action on the employer's part.

### 4.2.5 Compelling performance and enforceability of the contract by action for the price

As mentioned above, under Anglo-American law the contractor is generally not obliged to accept the employer's repudiation. He can keep the contract open:

> Repudiation is not something that calls for acceptance when there is no question of rescission, but merely excuses the innocent party from performance and leaves him free to sue for damages.[81]

Does it therefore follow that the aggrieved party is entitled to enforce the contract, relying on the payment obligation against the will of the party in breach?

In *White and Carter (Councils) Ltd* v *McGregor*,[82] a contract was concluded providing for the advertisement of the defendant's business through the plaintiff's advertising contractors. Although McGregor (the employer) expressed his unwillingness to perform the contract before any work was carried out, the plaintiffs did in fact perform the contract, by placing metal plates on rubbish bins delivered to local authorities, for the agreed period of three years. They then claimed the whole sum due under the contract. The House of Lords awarded the contract price as a recoverable contract debt, not as damages.[83] The court held that the contractor had the right not to act on the anticipatory repudiation and not to terminate the contract. There is, however, a limit to this option of the contractor:

> ... where performance is so obviously commercially wasteful and of no benefit to the guilty party that the innocent party cannot be said to have a legitimate interest in continuing the contract.[84]

---

79 Megarry, J [1971] Ch 234, 269.

80 Farnsworth, op cit, 668; see UCC 2-611 (1); Restatement Second §256.

81 Laskin, JA in *Finelli et al* v *Dee et al*, 67 DLR (2d)(31 January 1968), 395.

82 [1962] AC 413.

83 Ibid, 435.

84 R Goode, *Commercial Law* (2004) 127, quoting *Attica Sea Carriers Corporation* v *Ferrostal Poseidon Bulk Reederei* [1976] 1 Lloyd's Rep 250 and *The Alaskan Trader*

This view was also indirectly taken by Lord Reid in *White and Carter* where he contemplated that the plaintiff's action would have failed had the defendant shown that the contractor had no legitimate interest in performing the contract in that case.[85] It was pointed out that this legitimate interest could have been denied if the contractor had a duty to mitigate his loss under the circumstances; eg, if he had an opportunity to obtain another customer. The contractor could thus not be obliged to terminate the contract under a duty to mitigate.

The restraint of the legitimate interest is derived from general equitable principles which apply to a case depending on the facts. An unfettered right of election by the innocent party on breach of contract is not recognised. In *Clea Shipping Corporation* v *Bulk Oil International, The Alaskan Trader,*[86] the chartered vessel broke down requiring expensive repairs, whereupon the defendant charterer gave notice of their intention to end the contract. This was regarded as repudiation. The plaintiffs claimed that they had a right of election as the innocent party and decided to keep the contract open. They sought to keep the (prepaid) hire as contract price instead of having to sue for damages after termination. Lloyd J held that the plaintiffs had no legitimate interest in this case to uphold the contract and could thus be forced to accept damages and not the sum due under the contract after the actionable event had occurred.

The contract price was awarded in *White and Carter* because of the fact that *White and Carter* were able to carry out their contractual performance without the cooperation of the employer. It was because of these special circumstances that *Finelli et al* v *Dee et al* was distinguished from the previous case later; the plaintiff (the contractor) paved the driveway of the defendant employer in the absence of the owner against the owner's will. The owner (employer) had expressed the intention to end the contract by oral notification on the telephone prior to any performance, which had not then been scheduled. This was received and possibly agreed to by one of the contractor's employees. Leaving the question of a rescission of the contract open, Laskin J held that in either case (rescission or repudiation), the contractor was not entitled to recover the contract price:

> ... and without wishing to embark on any issue as to trespass, the plaintiffs, in my view, were obliged to give previous intimation to the defendant that they were prepared to do the work called for by the contract and proposed to do it on a certain day. This, of course, was not done.

Damages cannot normally be awarded instead of the contract price, since under an action for the contract debt damages are not the normal remedy to an actionable event.

This is true notwithstanding the fact that, where the two sums happen to be equal the two claims appear to be the same and are sometimes not clearly distin-

[1984] 1 AllER 129; see also *White and Carter (Councils) Ltd* v *McGregor* [1962] AC 413.

85 Lord Reid in *White and Carter (Councils) Ltd* v *McGregor* [1962] AC 413, 431 (HL),

86 [1984] 1 All ER 129.

guished under English law,[87] but more commonly so under American law where the law has developed a more blurred distinction between actions for debt and those for damages.

Thus, it is understood that in *White and Carter* the defendant employer was not successful in claiming a failure to observe a duty to mitigate on the contractor's side, because this was irrelevant in the context of an action for the contract price as a debt.[88] This general position has equally been valid under US law where it was expressed in 25 CJS, Damages, §34, 708 (1966); that the duty to mitigate leaves the action for the price untouched.[89] The decision in *White and Carter*, however, has not received a positive reaction in the US[90] where an earlier case, *Rockingham County* v *Luten Bridge Co*,[91] provided the basis for the modern legal situation;[92] the County had employed the plaintiff contractor to build a bridge over a street and subsequently notified them that they regarded the contract to be void. By then, the costs of the work already carried out had amounted to $1,900. The contractor carried on performing the contract and claimed $18,000 nine months later as part payment. The appeal court held that the contractor had been under a duty to avoid unnecessary losses subsequent to the notification by the defendants (a repudiation of the contract) and that he should therefore have stopped the building work on the bridge which had become worthless to the employer after the County's underlying street building project had been cancelled. The contractors were awarded the costs up to the time of the repudiation, but were refused the subsequent incurred costs as contract price. The reason why the duty to mitigate loss (originally developed in the context of damages) was introduced into that case of a price claim, was that the plaintiff was deemed to have attempted to evade his otherwise arising duty to mitigate by performing the contract.[93] In this way action for the contract price (specific performance) will usually fail if a damages claim

87 G H Treitel, *The Law of Contract* (1991) 896, n 33; see also Goodhart, LQR 78 (1962): 263, 270.

88 Chitty and Harris, *Chitty on Contracts: General Principles* (1994) Vol I, 26-060; P S Atiyah, *An Introduction to the Law of Contract* (1995) 432. Neufang thinks that the different opinion of Treitel (Treitel, op cit, 900 et seq) is just a way of justifying the result of a decision using an alternative dogmatic argumentation: P Neufang, '*Erfüllungszwang als* "remedy" *bei Nichterfüllung*' (1998) 77.

89 Ibid.

90 See, eg, W Bishop, 'The Choice of Remedy for Breach of Contract' J Legal Stud 14 (1985) 299; E Yorio, *Contract Enforcement, Specific Performance and Injunctions* (1989); S Williston, *Williston on Contracts: A Treatise on the Law of Contracts* (1968) Vol II.

91 35 F 2d 301 (4th Cir 1929).

92 The first case of this kind is said to be *Clark* v *Marsiglia*, 1 Denio 317, 43 Am Dec 670 (NY 1845) where the owner of some paintings repudiated a contract for the restoration of his paintings, which were subsequently finished without his consent. The court denied that the restorer could claim the price, but did not mention any duty to mitigate expressly – possibly in order to observe dogmatic clarity; see Neufang, op cit (n 88), 78, n 294.

93 Williston, op cit, Vol 2, §1301 p 80 et seq; A L Corbin, *Corbin on Contracts* (1951) Vol 4, §981 p 936; *Wilson* v *Western Alliance Corp* 715 P 2d 1344, 1346 (Or Ct App 1986): 'We do not agree, however, that non-acceptance makes the repudiation a nullity.'

would lead to a different result, and therefore become the subordinate form of remedy. In the US the action for specific performance is therefore practically regarded as a special form and a measurement for damages, even a sub-division of a damages claim.[94] Accordingly, the action for the price is not directly regulated anymore in the Restatement (Second) which even points to the rules about damages.[95]

Some early evidence for the connection between the concepts of debt and damages under English law may be *Slade's* case,[96] where 'damages ... for the whole debt' were the subject.[97] In the context of an action of *assumpsit*, there are instances of overlap in the use of both terms.

In relation to an action for the contract price, the abstention from any subsequent performance after repudiation or other breach of contract is regarded as the required contribution to mitigate the loss. There are, however, instances where just that could actually amount to a bigger loss for the innocent party; where a contractor has a special interest in performing a contract, other than that to claim the contract price, the courts might grant specific performance, ie, award the contract price on completion of the agreed work as the appropriate remedy on the facts of the case. This was so decided in *Bomberger* v *McKelvey*,[98] where the contractor had completed the work despite the employer's repudiation. The contractors in this case were in need of the material which there was shortage of at that time, and they were to obtain the material from the demolition of the house – the agreed work. The argument behind this decision can be seen in the consideration that, unless the employer lacks a legitimate interest in the performance of the contract, the contractor's duty to mitigate his loss can only be satisfied by performing the contract.[99] The contractor's loss would otherwise be part of the calculation of damages.[100] Another specific interest of a contractor in performing the contract could be a special advertising effect[101] or, in international contracts, the company's introduction to new markets.

There is, overall, clearly a temptation to regard the claim for the contract price on full performance despite prior repudiation as nothing else but a mathematical transformation[102] of the damages to be awarded in case of an accepted breach of contract. This view corresponds to a recognised method of calculation of damages, as in §2-708(2) UCC, for cases in which a covering transaction cannot be seen as a mitigation of loss because the party was in fact in a position to deliver to both the original, as well as to the replacement buyer, and his loss is really caused by a decrease in turnover.

---

94 See Neufang, op cit, 79.

95 Restatement (Second) Contracts, Ch 16, Topic 2, Introductory Note.

96 (1602) 76 Eng Rep 1074 (KB).

97 Ibid, 1077.

98 220 P 2d 729 (Cal 1950).

99 See *Bomberger* v *McKelvey*, 220 P 2d 729 (Cal 1959) 733.

100 E A Farnsworth, 'Legal Remedies for Breach of Contract' Colum L Rev 70 (1970) 1145, 1162.

101 E Yorio, *Contract Enforcement, Specific Performance and Injunctions* (1989) 351.

102 See Restatement (Second) Contracts, §349, Comment a.

## 4.3 Conclusion

The notion of specific performance as it occurs in Art 7.2.1 UPICC is not a general obstacle to the integration of the UPICC into English contract law. This is because this notion to some extent only serves as a label for distinguishing aspects of civil law systems from English law and the common law in general on a merely surface level.

An appropriate application of the relevant provisions of the UPICC needs to be carried out against a comparative background in order to accommodate the international character of the transnational contract law into the national legal systems. Chapter Four has shown that recourse to, and recapitulation of, historic developments allow a comprehensive understanding of certain general concepts of contract law, such as that of specific performance in a national legal system. This understanding of a national lawyer's own national law will allow the integration of transnational uniform contract law.

The true meaning and use of the concept of specific performance (of payment obligations) in civil law systems does not justify the strict reservations made by common lawyers against the notion. Civil law traditions show exactly the same reservations against any potentially overly rigid effects of specific performance in its rudimentary sense.[103]

The analysis in this chapter has proven that, because English law takes an almost identical attitude towards coerced performance as the UPICC, it is not justified to regard Art 7.2.1 UPICC as a legal import from civil law systems and introduce a legal position strongly opposed to by the common law sphere

The process of revealing and reviewing the underlying aspects of national legal concepts forms part of the suggested method of applying uniform international contract law. It prevents conclusions drawn on a superficial basis which provide obstacles to the application of such uniform law.

Due to the nature of the common law and the role of modern statutory English contract law, the integration of the UPICC into English law depends strongly on the willingness of English courts to do so, rather than on positions adopted within legal doctrine. Therefore such developments cannot be anticipated in this study.[104] Given the traditional support of commercial aspects in English contract law,[105] it can be expected however, that the courts will be in favour of the integration of uniform law rules into English law to the degree that a need for uniform transnational law manifests.[106]

---

[103] Compare also 5.3, below.
[104] Compare Chapter 8.
[105] Compare also Chapter 8.
[106] Compare Chapter 2.

# 5 Exemplary application of the UPICC in the context of German law

The previous chapter analysed the position of the UPICC under English domestic contract law, this chapter now identifies potential clashes between individual rules of the UPICC with German substantive contract law and asks if, and how, these can be overcome.

Exemplary, as introduced in Chapter 3, is again demonstrated by analysing Art 7.2.1 UPICC; providing for a right to require payment in international commercial contracts and is set into the context of international building and construction contracts. This procedure allows the detailed examination of specific instances of successful application of uniform contract law in a national legal system.

The lead question is still taken from Professor Schwenzer's criticism as set out in Chapter 3, where she asks how Art 7.2.1 UPICC (regulating payment obligations) can be integrated into domestic legal systems, given that it is drafted without express limitations to the right to require performance, unlike the rule in Art 7.2.2 UPICC regarding non-monetary obligations.

The chapter carries out a review of underlying theoretical concepts and current legislation in order to suggest ways of application and integration of the UPICC into substantive German contract law. It also asks, what the meaning of the general concept of specific performance is, particularly in the context of the historic development of codified modern German contract law. This recourse further purports to the analysis of the understanding of civil law concepts in common law systems and English law in particular, following the findings of Chapter 4. Both chapters thereby highlight ways of reconciling and integrating the solution of the UPICC into common law as well as into civil law jurisdictions. They look at possible underlying common origins of both legal systems, which could help to develop a modern approach to international contract law doctrine and the methodology of its application.[1]

German private law is firmly grounded in the belief that law has to be scientifically developed. The BGB was created by the end of the nineteenth century as a result of intense scholarly work. It consists of interrelated provisions which form a network of obligations, remedies and defences aimed at providing a general instrument for finding an answer to every problem that could possibly arise. The rule of law is affected by this systematic, 'scientific' way in which results are

[1] Compare 5.3 below.

achieved.[2] Legal method and the carefully planned doctrinal system of the legislation are designed to provide orientation and to facilitate consistency of legal decisions all the way through the hierarchies of judicial reasoning.

One of the major principles of German contract law is the synallagmatic (reciprocal) structure of the contract. A contract consists of mutual and corresponding rights and obligations. These obligations each have an individual life of their own and there are specific means to discharge obligations and to enforce rights.

Under German law, any result derived from a legal rule thus has to be reconciled with the doctrinal basis of the contract law. This is one of the major sources of misunderstanding in the application of uniform private law rules. Awareness of this problem is one of the most important demands to be put forward to a German lawyer if they are to apply the Principles in an appropriate way, giving effect to Art 1.6 UPICC.[3]

This chapter explains how both employer and contractor under building contracts can discharge the payment obligation, to what extent German law supports compelling performance, and the weaknesses of current German contract law regarding the regulation of building contracts.

## 5.1 Payment obligations in building contracts under German law

This initial section of Chapter 5 considers the current status of payment obligations in building contracts under German domestic contract law. It sets out the current legislation applicable to the *Werkvertrag*, comprising building contracts, and compares the position with the UPICC rules, highlighting questions which could be addressed under the heading of this novel uniform law. These are, in particular, questions of cancellation rights and the ensuing right to require payment in the current German contract law which have given rise to reform proposals, but have not benefited from recent enacted law reform.[4]

---

[2] K Larenz, *Allgemeiner Teil des Deutschen Bürgerlichen Rechts* (1983) §4III (79); K Larenz and M Wolf, *Allgemeiner Teil des Deutschen Bürgerlichen Rechts* (2004) §4; see also J Kohler, *'Rechtsetzung im demokratischen Rechtsstaat und Rechtswissenschaft – Anmerkungen zu Stil und Bedeutung neuerer Gesetzgebung' Kritische Vierteljahresschrift für Gesetzgebung und Rechtswissenschaft* 4 (2002) 369.

[3] Compare 3.2.2.2, above.

[4] The reform of the law of obligations by legislation enacted on 26 November 2001 reforming parts of the BGB (*Gesetz zur Modernisierung des Schuldrechts*, BGBl I, p 3138), effective from 1 January 2002 and applicable to contracts made after 31 January 2001 (Art 229 §5 EGBGB), has not changed the payment rule in the *Werkvertrag* which is discussed here. New rules which differ in wording and position from the old legislation are marked BGB (2002) in this text, eg §313 BGB (2002), and rules of the previous edition of the BGB are marked (old), eg §324 (old) BGB. Those old rules still apply to contracts made before 31 January 2001 (Art 229 §5 EGBGB) which, in the area of construction contract law, will still quite often occupy the courts since they are often long-

Building contracts are generally governed by the rules relating to the *Werkvertrag*, contracts for works and services in the *Bürgerliches Gesetzbuch* (Civil Code; hereinafter BGB)[5] §§631-650. Also, the parties can choose to make the *Vergabe- und Vertragsordnung für Bauleistungen, Teil B* ('Standard Terms for Building Services, Part B', hereinafter VOB/B)[6] part of their contract. These rules are the most widely used standard terms in this area of contract law and regulate many of the issues contained in British standard contracts such as the contract price (§2), liability and risk (§7, §10) and co-operation of the employer (§6). They are not formal legislation, though in Part A they contain guidelines for procurement that are binding for the public sector to prevent discrimination and violation of competition rules.[7] Part C relates to technical standards of the building contract. The VOB were first drafted and published by a commission of the ministry of finance, the *Reichsverdingungsausschuß* in 1921-26. Its successor, the *Deutsche Verdingungsausschuß für Bauleistungen* (DVA) issued several updated versions. The current version of Part C is from 1996 and Parts A and B were last revised in 2002. The VOB are not currently qualified as being trade usage or common usage: they are standard terms.[8]

The rules on the *Werkvertrag* fit a small-scale business, but they are largely supplemented by standard terms[9] and are subject to extensive judge-made law in the field of large construction projects.[10]

---

term agreements and take a long time to be brought before the courts, often following arbitration or ADR. Therefore, the source materials relating to this part of the study are quoted from both eras, ie, pre- and post-reform legislation. The scholarly opinions analysed here mostly originate from and refer to the pre-reform era due to the nature of the subject matter. This fact allows a thorough demonstration of the doctrinal development and background of the new post-reform contract law. For further discussion of the reformed BGB, see below: 5.1.4, 6.3.2, 8.2.3.2.1.

5 *Bürgerliches Gesetzbuch*, 18 August 1896, first published in *Reichsgesetzblatt* (1896) 195; C H Beck'sche Textausgaben, 'Bürgerliches Gesetzbuch mit zugehörigen Gesetzen und EG-Richtlinien', 10 April 1999; BGB (2002), eg, in *BGB – Bürgerliches Gesetzbuch*, annual editions (eg, 53, 2003 or later) Beck – *Texte im dtv* (Munich, Deutscher Taschenbuchverlag) and a synopsis is published by Beck in *Neues Schuldrecht: Genegnüberstellung BGB neu-alt mit Nebemgesetzen* (Munich, Deutscher Taschenbuch Verlag, 2002).

6 Text published among others by H Kuß, *Verdingungsordnung für Bauleistungen (VOB), Teile A und B mit Erläuterungen* (1997).

7 EC Directives 71/305/EEC (26 July 1971 / 21 July 1989) and 90/531/EEC (17 September 1990 / 14 July 1993, 93/38/EEC) also concerning purely domestic procurements, ECJ in EuZW 1996, 506. Based on these directives, the 1993 version of the *Haushaltsgrundsätzegesetz* 1969 was issued as well as the *Vergabeverordnung* 1994, which regulate public procurement. For texts see H Kuß, *Verdingungsordnung für Bauleistungen (VOB), Teile A und B mit Erläuterungen* (1997).

8 Palandt and Heinrichs, *Bürgerliches Gesetzbuch* 2006 Einf v §631, No 4.

9 H-L Weyers, 'Welche Ergänzungen …' in *Gutachten und Vorschläge zur Überarbeitung des Schuldrechts*, ed Bundesminister der Justiz (Cologne, 1981) Vol II, 1115. Examples are the ECE (United Nations Commission for Economy) clauses of March 1957 in the German version, published by Maschinenbauverlag, Frankfurt, and the joint 1968

Large projects, such as the acquisition of industrial plants, the construction of underground transportation systems, power stations or railway bridges, can of course, be subject to various areas of private law since they do not, in their complexity, fit into the standard categories of specific contract types of the BGB. Contractual arrangements relating to such projects can range from leasing to building contracts including hire, purchase, contracts for works or services, all in one complex agreement. [11]

The requirement of maturity of an obligation contained in Art 7.2.1 UPICC, 'who is obliged to pay money', under German law regarding *Werkverträge*, is contained in §641 BGB.

Under a building contract the contractor can only demand performance on completion and acceptance (*Abnahme*) of the work by the employer, §641 I BGB. If, as in large construction projects, building work is completed in subsequent stages, payment is due on acceptance of each agreed partial stage. Payment is then dependent on issuance of the *Aufmaß*,[12] usually the architect's certificate testifying the stage of the progress. VOB/B terms[13] contain detailed regulations as to the necessary requirements (*Feststellungen*) preceding payment, including rules concerning the bill.[14] The architect's certificates are deemed to represent the culmination of a joint investigating activity and consent of both parties that the performance of the contractor has been completed, and they constitute the maturity of the payment obligation.

In fact, this area provides a good example for a demonstration which will indicate the extent to which German law as a civil law system depends fundamentally on judge-made law and how decisions of the Federal Court can have quite large scale economic effects. Following extensive discussion in the 1950s, the Federal Court (*Bundesgerichtshof*, BGH) established its opinion, in a decision of 26 November 1959,[15] that contracts employing architects were to be classified as *Werkverträge*, as regulated in §§631-652 (old) BGB, and thus subject to the thirty years' time limit under §195 (old) BGB. Then, unexpectedly in 1972,[16] the Court changed its opinion and maintained that architects were regularly employed under contracts for services, and the time limits for their right to claim the contract price was two years – according to §196 I No 7 (old) BGB. The profession faced mil-

---

clauses of the metal and iron producing and manufacturing industries. See also P Joussen, *Der Industrieanlagen-Vertrag* (1981).

[10] R Grimme, '*Die Erfüllung beim Werkvertrag*' Vol 105, 1987; F Nicklisch, '*Empfiehlt sich eine Neukonzeption des Werkvertragsrechts? – Unter besonderer Berücksichtigung komplexer Langzeitveträge*', JZ (1984) 757;

[11] See Joussen, op cit (n 8), 7; Nicklisch, op cit (n 9), 757, 758, 761.

[12] §14 No 2 VOB/B; H Kuß, *Verdingungsordnung für Bauleistungen (VOB) Teile A und B mit Erläuterungen* (1997) §14 VOB/B, Annotation No 18 et seq. Compare *Vergabe- und Vertragsordnung für Bauleistungen* (2006) §14 and see below.

[13] Kuß, ibid, §14 VOB/B, Annotation No 21; *Vergabe- und Vertragsordnung für Bauleistungen* (2006) §14; OLG Hamm, BauR 1996, 739.

[14] §14 VOB/B.

[15] BGHZ 31, 224.

[16] BGHZ 59, 163 (165) = NJW 1972, 1799 (1800).

lions of losses but despite vigorous opposition by legal writers[17] the court did not see a need for intermediate solutions.[18]

The law relating to building contracts is governed by a rather fragmentary set of rules which have not been fundamentally reviewed since the enactment of the BGB. In reality, many of its solutions do not quite live up to the requirements of modern industrial practice.[19]

Certain contract types, brought about by modern times, have now been subjected to new legislation. One such contract, the travel contract (§§651a-m BGB (2002)) was incorporated into the BGB. Complex long-term agreements dominate modern commercial activities,[20] and when compared with the time when the BGB was drafted, securing transactions against currency fluctuations are now among the most important challenges to the law.

Efforts for reform have been made since the early eighties. The Federal Minister of Justice (*Bundesminister der Justiz*) has commissioned numerous reports and proposals on different areas of the private law. A commission was formed (*Schuldrechtskommission*), a group of experts who worked on the subject over many years. In 1992, the commission published their final report.[21] The proposal received a positive reception by the practitioners on the Annual Meeting of German Lawyers (*Deutscher Juristentag*, DJT) who voted for the proposal to enter legislative procedure. However, the proposal was not taken any further than that and it was not directly made a basis for the recent reform of the BGB.[22]

The reluctance may have stemmed from the fact that the proposal favoured some fundamental changes and innovations within the system of the BGB. In order to rectify frequent problems concerning the interrelationship of rules governing defective performance and guarantee (*Mängelrecht, Gewährleistungsrecht*) on the one hand and *Leistungsstörungen* (eg, impossibility) on the other, the experts considered the notions of fault, 'breach of duty' or 'breach of obligation', better starting points for developing legal solutions.[23] This solution resembles the Anglo-American approach to contract law which regards the 'breach' as a pre-requisite for remedies and has actually now been incorporated into the new law of obliga-

---

17 Many architects had relied on the thirty-year time limit and not yet collected their outstanding balances. See Ganten, NJW 1973, 1165; Jagenburg, NJW 1973, 1721 (1728); Schneider MDR 1973, 305. Nowadays the situation has changed again: the contract employing an architect 'is to be treated according to the rules of the *Werkvertragsrecht*', BGH NJW-RR (1989) 1248-1250, 1249.

18 BGHZ 60, 98(101).

19 Not even after the recent reform of 2002: compare 5.1.4, 6.3.2, 8.2.3.2.1 below.

20 In 1983 DM10bn gross production value was reached by construction businesses employing 20 and more people (*Statistical Yearbook for the Federal Republic of Germany 1983*, 203). See also M Bridge, 'Does Anglo-American contract law need a doctrine of good faith?' Can Bus L J 9.4 (1984) 397.

21 *Abschlußbericht der Kommission zur Überarbeitung des Schuldrechts*, 1992.

22 See below, Chapter 8.

23 Palandt and Heinrichs, *Bürgerliches Gesetzbuch* (2001) Vorb z §275 Nos 4 and 5. Compare Palandt and Heinrichs, *Bürgerliches Gesetzbuch* (2006) Vorb z §275. In my opinion, Heinrich Stoll's terminology should have been followed: compare Chapter 8.

tions,[24] leaving the rules on *Werkvertrag* and cancellation unaltered. The Draft Principles of European Contract Law (PECL) pursue this approach as well.[25]

Therefore, in the absence of thorough modernisation and reform of domestic contract law, a set of rules like the UPICC may serve as a solution in the field of international construction contracts. More specifically, relating to construction contracts, discussions took place among participants and delegates of the private law section of the 55th German *Juristentag* in Hamburg, 1984. Details of payment practice were subject to suggestions for altering and extending the provisions regulating the matter in the BGB. Some lawyers however, are of the opinion that appropriate solutions can be reached on the basis of existing provisions if thoroughly assessed and applied.[26]

The provisions regulating building contracts form complex interactions between the rules on cancellation, those on late performance, and the right to withhold performance, as well as the doctrine of 'positive breach of contract' (positive *Vertragsverletzung*).[27] They pose difficult questions of classification regarding the contract type in practice, and the lack of clarity regarding the relationship of the different areas of law often leads to lengthy court procedures.

A good example is the judgment of the Federal Court, *Bundesgerichtshof* (BGH), of 16 June 1972.[28] On purchase of a piece of land and house under a contract of 28 June 1966, the parties agreed that the vendor should carry out certain repairs and finish building work in exchange for DM28,000 which formed part of the whole contract price of another DM55,000. Being dissatisfied with the vendor's efforts to realise the desired results, the buyer withheld DM25,000 and had the work carried out by a third party by means of the sum withheld. The plaintiff vendor claimed payment of DM25,000 as the contract price. The defendant claimed a right to set-off against the plaintiff on the vendor's delay and a right to damages thereupon. At first instance (*Landgericht*) the plaintiff was awarded DM23,333.90, including interest. The second instance, the *Oberlandesgericht* Karlsruhe,[29] rejected the defendant's appeal. The court obviously regarded the contract exclusively as a sales contract. Therefore, they could not find any justifications for the withholding of DM25,000, neither in the provisions on the synallgmatical contract (§321 BGB), nor in the rules on defective performance, *Mängelrecht*, §§459 BGB et seq. The *Bundesgerichtshof* (Federal Court, third instance) accepted the revision and discharged the previous decisions on the ground (among others) that as far as the contract involved building work it was to be construed as being a *Werkvertrag*. The court held that nothing in the contract excluded the employer's unqualified right to cancellation in §649 BGB. By employ-

---

[24] Legislation enacted on 26 November 2001 reforming parts of the BGB (*Gesetz zur Modernisierung des Schuldrechts*, BGBl I, 3138).

[25] L Olsen, 'The choice of the aggrieved party – An analysis of the remedies in the Principles of the European Contract Law' European Review of Private Law 1 (1999), 25.

[26] Grimme, op cit (n 9), 24.

[27] Now incorporated in the new §275 BGB (2002); see O Jauernig, *Bürgerliches Gesetzbuch* (2004) vor §275.

[28] WM 1972, 1025-1027.

[29] ZR 174/70.

ing the third party this right was exercised successfully. It was held that the cancellation could be expressed by a conclusive act by the employer, such as performing the agreed work himself.[30]

Another effect of the different classification of the contract concerned the maturity of the payment obligation; under a sales contract the defendant would have had to render performance first. Only on payment would the necessary steps towards a transfer of the property have been taken. Under a *Werkvertrag* the contractor has to perform first, §641 BGB. The defendant thus, was not delaying performance by withholding the DM25,000 and there was no breach.[31] The court did, however contemplate matters of delay and defective performance within the *Werkvertrag* context, §633 BGB.[32] This question concerns the distinction between breach of contract (*Vertragswidriges Verhalten*), and the 'extraordinary' right to cancellation 'on important grounds'.[33]

### 5.1.1 Standard terms: Do they offer a better solution than the UPICC?

In industry, standard terms are in use; there are hundreds of standard terms drafted by the various trade associations of specific branches and published by the *Bundeskartellamt*, the federal competition authority in Bonn, in its official organ, *Bundesanzeiger*. Weyers used a selection of about fifty of these standard terms in the course of his expertise on the *Werkvertrag* for the first reform project of the BGB.[34]

An example in the area of iron production ie, large-scale transactions, are the 1957 ECE (United Nations Commission for Economy) general terms relating to delivery and mounting for import and export of machinery and plant.[35] In practice, however, these seem to be mostly overruled by even more detailed contract drafts of negotiators.[36] In the field of construction contracts for plant building there are '*Allgemeine Beschaffungsbedingungen für Anlagen und Anlagenteile (Musterklauseln)*', (General conditions for acquisition of plants and parts thereof (sample clauses)).[37] These are drafted from the point of view of the employer / orderer regarding the wording and content.[38] In 1968, a working group of representatives from the iron producing (*Wirtschaftsvereinigung Eisen und Stahl*, ESI) and the iron manufacturing industry (*Arbeitsgemeinschaft verarbeitende Industrie*, AVI), agreed after negotiations to publish a paper containing clauses relating to the pur-

[30] See also BGH WM 1968, 847.

[31] BGH WM 1972, 1025-1027, 1026.

[32] Ibid.

[33] See 5.1.2 below.

[34] Weyers, op cit (n 8), 1115 et seq, titles and source listed in Anhang 4, 1201-1205.

[35] German and other language versions published by Maschinenbauverlag, Frankfurt/Main.

[36] Joussen, op cit (n 8), 397; Weyers, op cit (n 8), 1115, 1136.

[37] Text in Joussen, op cit, Anlage I, 402 et seq.

[38] Which differs from the practice in the UK: compare 4.2.2, above.

chase and order of plant and machinery, the '*Einkaufsbedingungen der eisenschaffenden Industrie*', ('conditions for purchase of the iron producing industry'),[39] the so-called AVI/ESI-conditions. These types of rules emerge as a consequence of balancing certain diverging interests between employer / orderer and contractor.

Standard terms in general however, do not seem – in terms of fairness and thoroughness – to be able to easily replace contract law.[40] Although, standard terms negotiated collectively among trade branches, which appear to provide an argument for the prevalence of this 'bilateral' and private kind of norms over traditional codification,[41] maintain a weakness in the sphere of effects on third parties and the problems of gaps in contractual agreements resulting from promoting individual interests through the negotiating process.[42]

### 5.1.2 The right of cancellation and the modified payment obligation in §649 BGB

In cases of cancellation, the payment obligation and maturity rule receive a unique treatment; §649 BGB grants a general right to cancellation. It gives the employer / orderer the freedom to cancel a building contract at any time before the completion of the work without having to give reasons. On cancellation, the contractor remains fully entitled to the agreed contract price, §649 S 2 BGB. The employer is still 'obliged to pay money' in the sense of Art 7.2.1 UPICC. Therefore, the full contract price can become due before the contractor has even started to carry out any building work. Cancellation replaces acceptance for the purposes of maturity. The employer's right to cancellation balances the contractor's right to require performance under a building contract. Primarily, it serves the interest of the employer not to be forced to proceed with a project. This provision represents a unique solution within the part of the BGB which deals with specific contract types.[43] Other ways of terminating the contract do, of course, exist besides the cancellation option, such as withdrawal (*Rücktritt*) and the general provisions discharging a contract. It is, therefore, often difficult to establish the appropriate way of interpreting the facts so as to decide about the contract's destiny.

The right to cancellation was introduced into the BGB with the express motivation for considering the orderer's interest in giving effect to changes in the employer's individual circumstances. At the same time, respect is given to the builder's (contractor's) interest; in that he does not remain unfairly exposed to this freedom of the employer in respect of his interest to obtain the contract price.

---

[39] For updates of the standard forms, contact the issuing institutions.

[40] Further discussion below; see also Weyers, op cit (n 8), eg, 1125, 1123 and 1124, pointing to the problem of effects of certain bilateral arrangements on third parties.

[41] This tendency is common in Nordic countries, especially in Sweden. See also Weyers, op cit (n 8), 1125.

[42] Nicklisch, op cit (n 9), 765.

[43] Weyers, op cit (n 8), 1134.

There are, of course, cases in which the contractor does have a specific interest in performing the contract rather than just receiving the agreed contract price. These are for example, prestigious 'pioneering projects' (*Pilotprojekte*) or the objective to maintain employment for the sub-contractors and workers involved.[44] However, with regard to the role of Art 7.2.1 UPICC, it has to be emphasised that the right to cancellation does not – even under German law – directly discharge the 'obligation to pay money'. If the employer is not 'obliged to pay money' under the contract in its original form, he may be obliged to do so under related provisions, namely due to the fact that the contractor does keep his right to require performance (§649 S.2 BGB), though in a modified form.[45]

The building contract might come to an end on cancellation, not so the payment obligation. This is one of the general dogmatic differences arising from the formulation of Art 7.2.1 UPICC and its position within the Principles.

Different from the German Civil Code, the payment obligation is positioned in isolation from the corresponding delivery obligation arising from a service contract. There is no synallagmatic (reciprocal) connection between the two obligations, at least not according to the text. The BGB formulates the two corresponding obligations in §631 I BGB, reinforcing its belief in any right to require performance in the context of a *Schuldverhältnis*, as a 'living entity',[46] as opposed to a concept of mere separate obligations as in the UPICC. The BGB provides for a set number of ways in which obligations can be discharged. They all operate within the framework of the contract.

The other aspect to be discussed comparing Art 7.2.1 UPICC is that of compelling performance against the unwilling employer. Cancellation is certainly a means to avoid this effect.

The parties are of course free to exclude any right to cancellation by agreement. Most construction contracts will in fact provide for such exclusion, due to the special nature of these complex and long term projects.[47] On such exclusion, a contractor can then actually force the employer to perform the contract. The *Oberlandesgericht* (OLG), Celle,[48] decided in a case where the plaintiff (an architect) claimed performance under a contract employing him to design and build property on a plot of land acquired by the defendants, which contained a clause obliging them to employ but the plaintiff in order to guarantee the successful development of the whole area. The defendants obviously feared a considerable delay in the performance of the contract because the architect had subsequently taken on several building projects and claimed a right to cancellation. The vendors of the land, however, had concluded a contract with the plaintiff to design and build property for them, as well as on a number of plots of land which were to be sold separately (by them) to third parties, such as the defendants, as part of a development project.

---

44 Ibid, 1136.

45 See 5.1.3 below.

46 See above, before 5.1.

47 Weyers, op cit (n 8), 1126, 1136: in almost half of the standard terms Weyers looked at, §649 BGB was excluded. These did not even relate to large scale projects.

48 OLG Celle, judgment of 1 November 1960, MDR 1961, 318/319.

The contracts were considered to be *Werkverträge*. The clause in the sales contract together with the fact that the parties agreed that the architect should provide for all necessary planning permissions, which he had done, was construed (§157 BGB) as expressing the parties' intention that the architect should not just be entitled to the contract price, his architect's fee, but also to the specific performance of the contract. The right to cancellation was thereby excluded and denied by the court. The anticipated delay in performance was not considered an 'important reason' which would have justified an 'extraordinary' cancellation. Here, the specific interest of the architect in the contract was protected.

An extraordinary right to cancellation is generally recognised with regard to contracts lasting over an extended period of time, such as contracts for employment or longstanding contracts for the supply of goods. This doctrinal development into a general principle of law[49] occurred after the enactment of the BGB, by the courts' practice derived from §242 BGB (the good faith provision), as well as from provisions of the *Handelsgesetzbuch* (HGB), the Commercial Code. This right cannot be excluded by contractual agreement. It is based on the assumption that long term contracts require an intact relationship between the parties in order to function well.[50] Contracts of this kind can therefore be cancelled 'on important grounds' by either party, even if no cancellation provision is contained in the agreement. The provisions in §§631 et seq BGB cover the whole range of *Werkverträge*, with short term ('discrete')[51] contracts with exchange character at one end, and large projects costing billions and stretching over several years, such as the construction of airports, nuclear power stations, tunnel systems or similar, at the other.

The highly abstract regulations of the law of standard terms are regularly supplemented by parties to construction contracts even from the rather small scale range of possible contracts such as TV repair orders or manufacturing of household appliances.[52] Most building contracts incorporate the VOB/B as standard terms. §8, Nos 2-6 VOB/B provide for special cases of cancellation which are admissible according to the 1976 law relating to standard contract terms (*Gesetz zur Regelung des Rechts der Allgemeinen Geschäftsbedingungen*, AGBG, now §§ 305

---

[49] Palandt and Heinrichs, *Bürgerliches Gesetzbuch* (2001) Ein l v §241, No 17.

[50] B Schmidt, '*Zur unberechtigten Kündigung aus wichtigem Grunde beim Werkvertrag*' NJW 20 (1995) 1314; RGZ 169, 203(206); BGHZ 50, 312(314); Otto von Gierke published his influential treatise on long term contracts ('*Dauernde Schuldverhältnisse'*, *Iherings Jahrbücher* (Ihering's Yearbooks) 1914, 355 et seq as early as 1914. In the US Jan R McNeil contributes to the discussion about long term contracts in modern contract law. He speaks of 'relational contracts' (*The New Social Contract: An Enquiry into Modern Contractual Relations* (New Haven and London, 1980), see 10-35.

[51] McNeil: see previous note.

[52] See examples of standard terms of different branches in Germany in Weyers, op cit (n 8), Anhang 4.

et seq BGB (2002))[53] because the building contract is a *Werkvertrag*, with characteristic elements of a long term contract (*Dauerschuldverhältnis*).[54]

### 5.1.3 The modified payment obligation as a disguised damages rule

The BGB creates a complicated relationship between cancellation and damages provisions regarding the nature of the payment obligation through the wording of §649 BGB. The payment obligation, although cannot be discharged by cancellation, is modified after the cancellation. The contractor can only claim the price reduced by the savings he makes as a consequence of the cancellation, which means that he does not have to perform.[55] Such a saving can be the opportunity of a compensating contract, and the contractor will have to deduct the gains from such a cover transaction from the price. If he maliciously refrains from taking up a compensating contract he will also not be able to rely on his right to require performance, §649 S 2 BGB. The burden of proof however, is carried by the employer, to establish the fact that the builder did take up a compensating alternative contract, or to prove that he maliciously and deliberately failed to take the opportunity to do so.[56] The employer's modified payment obligation does not differ much, effectively from a right to damages qualified by a duty to mitigate.[57] This view is supported by several decisions and provisions relating to the law of cancellation.[58]

The duty to mitigate is contained in §254 II S 1 BGB. It deals with cases of joint causation of damage and influence of the behaviour of the injured party on the amount of damages. Cover transactions in general, eg, in sales contracts, are not a regular duty of the aggrieved party,[59] but can be required as mitigation in certain cases.[60] If the market price of the rejected goods is falling, a cover transac-

[53] Now §§305-310 BGB (2002), '*BGB, Bürgerliches Gesetzbuch mit zugehörigen Gesetzen und Nebengesetzen*', Beck'sche Textausgaben (Munich 1999, C H Beck, 104th edn), 593 or later editions; or see BGB – Bürgerliches Gesetzbuch, annual edition, Beck-Texte im dtv (Munich, Deutscher Taschenbuchverlag).

[54] BGH BB 1962, 497; BGH WM 1984, 1375 (1376); NJW 1982, 2553 (2554); NJW 1993, 1972 (1973).

[55] Palandt and Heinrichs, *Bürgerliches Gesetzbuch* (2001 and 2006) §649, No 4; BGH, NJW 93, 1972. Compare Palandt and Heinrichs, Bürgerliches Gesetzbuch (2006) Einf v §631: new legislation is planned which seeks to clarify the extent of the contractor's right to the contract price on cancellation (*Forderungssicherungsgesetz).*

[56] Grimme, op cit (n 9), 255.

[57] See I Schwenzer. *Erfüllung und Schadensersatz nach den Unidroit — Prinzipien* (Basel, 1997) 5: a functional damages rule; Grimme, op cit (n 9), 248.

[58] BGH NJW 1973, 1190 (1191); P Neufang, '*Erfüllungszwang als* "remedy" *bei Nichterfüllung*' (1998), 313.

[59] Palandt and Heinrichs, *Bürgerliches Gesetzbuch* (2001) §325, No 17; OLG Frankfurt, NJW 77, 1015. Compare Palandt and Heinrichs, *Bürgerliches Gesetzbuch* (2006) §325.

[60] Palandt and Heinrichs, *Bürgerliches Gesetzbuch* (2001) §254, No 44; §325, No 17; BHG WM 65 102.

tion can amount to the seller's duty.[61] A shareholder can be expected to take advantage of subsequent positive stock market developments.[62]

The notion of damages also creeps into the cancellation system by way of the 'extraordinary' cancellation applicable to all long term contracts, *Dauerschuldverhältnisse*. In case of an extraordinary cancellation the contractor loses his entitlement to the modified contract price, as provided for in §649 S 2 BGB.[63] Only the work which has actually been performed at the time of cancellation has to be paid for, as agreed.[64] The detailed provisions of §8 Nos 2-4 VOB/B (which restate parts of the law relating to the 'extraordinary cancellation on important grounds') even provide for liability in damages of the contractor.

To demonstrate the complicated nature of the present[65] solution of the BGB the following may serve. The content of the payment obligation is sometimes disputed due to the interrelationship between the rules on the right to withhold, §273 and §320 BGB, defective performance in building contracts (§633 I and II (old) BGB), now §§633, 634 BGB (2002)), and delay in §§633 II (old; now §634 BGB (2002)) and §284 (old) BGB (now §286 BGB (2002)). So, in BGH WM 1972, 1025,[66] the parties litigated over the question as to whether the defendant had a right to damages arising out of a late performance by the plaintiff, and whether he could invoke this right successfully since he had not issued a reminder according to §633 II and §284 BGB. It was not clear, whether the defendant, the buyer of the house, was entitled to withhold payment, either on the basis of §641 BGB, or under §273 BGB, or, whether he had refused payment 'unlawfully' (breach) because he himself had to perform first under the contract of sale.[67] In that case the plaintiff (the vendor) would have had a right to withhold and claim under §273 and §320 BGB, and he would have been entitled to refuse to finish the building work under §326 S2 (old) BGB. It was discussed whether the defendant had a right to cancellation or whether he had committed a breach of contract by not paying. The court did not have to decide whether the manner in which the building work was done (the dissatisfaction of the buyer) was to be seen as defective performance and thus would have required a reminder prior to replacement performance by the builder (employer) himself under §633 III (old) BGB, or, whether the defendant did in fact have a right to cancellation under §649 BGB, in that case.

### 5.1.4 Law reform projects

Thoughts relating to a reform of this area of law have concentrated on the role of long term contracts. During the work of the reform commission (*Schul-*

[61] OLGZ 90, 341; BGH NJW 97, 1231.
[62] OLG Cologne, ZIP 90, 433.
[63] BGHZ 45, 372, 375; BGHZ 31, 224, 229.
[64] Palandt and Sprau, *Bürgerliches Gesetzbuch* (2001 and 2006) §649, No 4.
[65] Even after the enactment of the new law of obligations as far as old cases are concerned. Compare Chapter 8.
[66] Discussed above in 5.1.
[67] This was the view taken by the *Oberlandesgericht* Karlsruhe.

*drechtskommission*) numerous opinions on the quality of the existing norms have been published, especially on the forum of the *Deutsche Juristentag* (DJT).[68] These discussions and written opinions reveal a very contradictory and heterogeneous picture. As much as most commentators feel the need for more detailed regulations as to complex long term contracts,[69] they also seem to acknowledge and appreciate the workability of the norms in the BGB because of their 'high degree of abstractness'.[70] This however, is mainly emphasised in relation to the short term traditional contract for exchange, ie, the traditional type constellation which the code was originally drafted for,[71] where small scale business is carried out in the form of so-called on the spot transactions (*punktuelle Austauschverträge*)[72] or 'simple work contracts', *einfache Werkverträge*, such as plumbing services or the repair of shoes.[73]

There is a certain contradiction in the emphasis of the abstractness of the rules, which allows flexibility to adapt to modern practice on the one hand, and the allegation that the requirements of modern complex contracts – which form the majority of the trade volume as well as the biggest amount of litigation[74] – need new special regulations, on the other. Most suggestions result therefore, after thorough discussion, in the drafting of slightly modified rules to replace the old law, and some new rules relating to long term contracts and incorporating some of the usage in practice, eg, relating to payment practice. Nicklisch[75] and Weyers [76] both suggest that the 'extraordinary' cancellation be part of a new wording as well as a more detailed reference to the contractor's modified right to payment on cancellation. Weyers also includes the contractor's special interest in the performance of the contract in his draft proposal of a new §649 I BGB,[77] and makes this a reason for an exception to the employer's unqualified right to cancellation.

None of the authors, however, questions the system underlying the rules relating to the *Werkvertrag* in general; the mechanism of cancellation leading to modi-

---

68 See, eg, A Teichmann, '*Empfiehlt sich eine Neukonzeption des Werkvertragsrechts?*' Verhandlungen des 55 Deutschen Juristentages Hamburg 1994 1. Gutachten A (1984): A Soergel and Brandner published reports in the same volume. Other reports were commissioned by the *Schuldrechtskommission* and published, eg H-L Weyers, 'Welche Ergänzungen ...' 1115. Another analysis relating to the *Werkvertrag* is by Keilholz in the same work, second volume, 241 et seq. There were extensive discussions on the *Juristentag* itself as well as in the legal literature. The current version of § 649, however, is unchanged, hence those considerations are still valid, and questions unanswered. See 5.1.4. and 6.3.2 below for further discussion.

69 Nicklisch, op cit (n 9), 575, 759, 765; Grimme, op cit (n 9), 23; Joussen, op cit (n 8), 7; A Teichmann, op cit, A, A101; Weyers, op cit (n 8), eg, 1122.

70 Nicklisch, op cit (n 9), 757, 758, 759.

71 Weyers, op cit (n 8), 1115, 1122.

72 Nicklisch, op cit (n 9), eg, 757; see also 'Motive', II, 470.

73 Weyers, op cit (n 8), 1115, 1122.

74 90% of the disputed cases concerning *Werkverträge* are building contract cases and involve long term contracts, see Nicklisch, op cit (n 9), 758.

75 Nicklisch, op cit (n 9), 768.

76 Weyers, op cit (n 8), 1193.

77 Ibid, Anhang I, 1192.

fied payment obligation is not challenged at all. However, this section of the civil code contains a dogmatic weakness which could be rectified by recourse to a modern proposal such as the UPICC. The way the modified payment obligation in §649 BGB is formulated reminds one very much of the duty to mitigate contained in the damages provision of §254 II S 1 BGB. The party affected by a cancellation could be awarded the same amount of money, which would be calculated as an appropriate damages award in a case under §§249, 254 BGB. If a cover transaction can be required as duty to mitigate and can also be a condition for the entitlement to payment of the modified contract price as a contractual debt, the action has the same function in both cases; in the latter case, the rule establishing the modified payment obligation functions as a damages rule for dealing with the interest of the injured party, ie, the contractor who is affected by the cancellation. A functional damages rule is also contained in §324 I S 2 (old) BGB; just as the contractor can expect to be compensated for the work already carried out, the debtor of the non-monetary obligation, in cases of impossibility,[78] is entitled to compensation. This, under §324 I S 2 (old) BGB, is reduced by what the debtor saves due to the discharge of his obligation and by what he gains, or maliciously omits to gain, by investing his working power otherwise. There is a dispute in the literature as to how this provision is to be classified dogmatically. Some regard it as a right to performance,[79] some as a damages provision: 'However, the right is really an action for damages, an argument which is supported by the fact that compensation is reduced by investments which can be saved, and that there is a duty to mitigate.'[80] It is not the compensation itself which resembles the damages award directly, but rather the notion of the other (injured) party's contribution (by an act or omission) to the extent of the damage done by the defaulting party's initial act. This suggests that there is a factual damages situation to be dealt with by the law. The modified payment obligation in the current version of §649 BGB, is supposed to affect compensation for the contractor who, under the current regulation, bears the risk of the employer's unqualified right to cancellation.[81]

One extreme position under the *Werkvertrag* provision is the contractor's potentially unqualified right to performance which could lead to the employer having to accept work which is of no interest to him. The other is the free right to cancellation, which is only granted to the employer, and generally leaves the contractor with the risk of facing cancellation. Both risks are 'insured' under German law to a certain extent by §242 BGB, which would not allow any party to exercise a right maliciously (*rechtsmißbräuchlich*), ie, which is either of no interest to themselves or causes disproportionate losses to the other party. In this way, there is no 'unqualified right to performance' under German law, unless as we have seen, the parties know that the contractor has a special interest in carrying out the work.

---

78 Compare 5.3.2 below.

79 O Jauernig, *Bürgerliches Gesetzbuch* (2004) §649 Rz 4.

80 I Schwenzer, 'Specific Performance and Damages According to the 1994 UNIDROIT Principles of International Commercial Contracts' ELR 1 (1998/1999) 295.

81 Compare 5.1.2.

In order to observe the dogmatic stringency of the system of contract law however, a concept has to be found which fits into the pattern of contract law rather than tort. The closeness of the two areas of law is described by Professor Schwenzer:

> Contracts in commercial trade are usually reciprocal. For reciprocal contracts, the right to performance of the creditor of the monetary obligation is only justified if he or she has fully performed his or her own obligation to deliver goods or to do some work. In such a case there is practically no difference between the right to performance and the right to claim damages.[82]

The difficulty that the BGB faces here is that the concept of contract law does not know the notion of breach of contract in the wider sense in which it is understood under English law. There is only the occasional appearance of the term 'non-performance' (*Nichterfüllung*), triggering liability in damages; §325 I S 1 and S 2 BGB (impossibility) grant damages to the obligee in cases where the obligor has failed to perform and is responsible for the default. But this is not a paramount remedy.

The principal consequence of non-performance in cases of impossibility is the discharge of the corresponding obligation in reciprocal contracts. Non-performance is not a concept that German law generally supports. German law is rather concerned with balancing corresponding obligations in the network of obligations called contract. Contractual imbalances have to be resolved by disentangling the parties from this network rather than by 'termination' and subsequent damages awards. The contract has a strong cultural appeal to German lawyers and is treated as a piece of art by the BGB with its elaborate scientific structure. The proposals for a reform of the rules relating to building contracts do, accordingly, not challenge the boundaries of the system. They respect the basis of the BGB which contains the 'special law of obligations' (*Recht der Schuldverhältnisse*).

Recognising the changing needs of a modern world, almost every writer emphasises the lack of special rules for complex long term contracts, as well as their preference of the 'extraordinary cancellation' on special grounds, rather than the unqualified right to cancellation of §649 BGB. As a result, the draft proposals appear as restatements of the current judge-made law which really only reflects the current state of the existing law, rather than deserving the name 'reform'. In addition, sections of standard contract terms, frequently used by contracting parties, are suggested for implementation into the existing BGB regulations. The weakness of this approach lies in its often insufficient wording,[83] as well as a tendency to perpetuate the process of stifling the application of the law. Judge-made law based on underlying principles of the code – general rules, such as §242 BGB can be adapted to individual cases. The attempt to cast all these decisions into sections of paragraphs involves the risk of leaving cases unconsidered or, overrating certain details occurring in specialised areas of trade. The great appreciation of the

[82] Schwenzer, op cit (n 77), 293.
[83] Compare the draft proposal of Weyers: op cit (n 8), 1115 et seq, Anhang I, 1185, 1192.

'high degree of abstractness'[84] which makes for flexibility and openness of the rules, seems all the more convincing in the light of the existing reform proposals and certainly regarding the finished product, the new law of obligations.[85]

Regarding the right to cancellation it seems a common concern that the unqualified right to cancellation unduly ignores any specific interest the contractor might have in the performance of that specific contract.[86] Consequently, Weyers includes just this specific interest of the contractor into his draft of a new §649 I BGB, by excluding the right to cancellation, provided that the employer knew about this special interest at the time of the conclusion of the contract. This suggests that a verification of such a specific interest is regularly required which could effectively over-complicate exercising the right to cancellation. Weyers' subsequent mentioning of the right to cancel on special grounds ('remains untouched') creates confusion as to the relationship he suggests between the contractor's 'special interest' and the 'extraordinary cancellation'. His pointing to §626 I BGB (concerning contracts for services) in order to clarify the circumstances of an 'extraordinary cancellation' seems useful, though. These suggested changes are already in current usage and practice, are legally embedded in the VOB/B and do not require implementation into the BGB.

The dogmatic problem which the BGB poses is really the unqualified right to cancellation coupled with the modified payment obligation. Cancellation is the only appropriate mode of ending a contractual relationship given that this contract type of *Werkvertrag* was considered to require this special treatment when compared to the other contract types defined in the BGB. The fact that the creators of the BGB inserted the right to cancellation in just the way they did in the sections on *Dienstvertrag* (contract for services) and *Miet- / Pachtvertrag* (lease / tenancy), shows that they were in fact aware of the time factor which Nicklisch reminds us of in his article dealing with the requirements of modern complex building contracts.[87]

The oddity is really the contractor's initially fully remaining entitlement to the contract price on cancellation, ie, the right to performance. Normally a cancellation would lead to the termination of the contractual relationship *ex nunc* which means that all obligations come to an end.[88] In building contracts however, where the work has not been started, cancellation still leaves the full payment claim untouched which seems an overly rigid result. It grants an unqualified right to performance. This is systematically to be regarded as the basic rule, according to its

[84] Nicklisch, op cit (n 9), 757.

[85] Legislation enacted on 26 November 2001 reforming parts of the BGB (*Gesetz zur Modernisierung des Schuldrechts*, BGBl I, 3138). Compare Chapter 6 (6.3.2) and Chapter 8 for further discussion, and see J Kohler, *'Rechtssetzung im demokratischen Rechtsstaat und Rechtswissenschaft – Anmerkungen zu Stil und Bedeutung neuerer Gesetzgebung' Kritische Vierteljahresschrift für Gesetzgebung und Rechtswissenschaft* KritV 4 (2002) 369-391.

[86] Compare 5.3.2 below.

[87] Nicklisch, op cit (n 9), 768, 757, et seq.

[88] Just as the effect of termination in the sense of Art 7.3.1 UPICC.

wording.[89] The modification of the contractual debt in the special case of *Werkverträge*, by way of discounting any savings made or maliciously missed on cancellation, is justified by the special circumstances in building contracts where the payment obligation only becomes due on completion of the work. The modification by subsequent savings is then practically applied as the normal rule, so that the builder/contractor has to prove savings, together with his claim of the contract debt.[90] In practice, he can therefore never claim the full amount originally granted by the rule in §649 S 2 first half, but he may come out with the full contract price if there are no savings (ie, in cases where a unique piece of work is commissioned, eg, a car made to match the needs of a disabled person, a special musical instrument, etc). The employer then has to prove further savings as a defence requiring further factual investigation and expense.[91]

The theoretical system of the BGB does not allow a solution establishing the notion of breach of contract followed by a damages claim as it is to be found in the Anglo-American tradition. This would, however, be a much more simple and convincing model in these cases, and as far as international contracts are concerned, the UPICC should serve as a model which can help to justify the introduction of this solution. Unfortunately, the reform of 2001 has introduced another hybrid[92] called *Pflichtverletzung* (breach of duty) obviously trying to merge different worlds together, ie, the law of obligations and the seemingly international hybrid law of conventions like the CISG.[93] The intention of the reformers was to simplify the law, to modernise it and to assimilate it to 'international standards',[94] but in my view the new solution has led to more incongruity and isolation as far as the notion of *Pflichtverletzung* is concerned, not to mention the fact that §649 BGB has remained untouched and still poses the same problems as before. The work of the parliamentary reform commission is clearly flawed by a superficial understanding of the international law which they were trying to implement:

*Die Anknüpfung an den Begriff der 'Pflichtverletzung' entspricht dem UN-Kaufrecht. Zwar verwendet es in Artikel 45 Abs 1, 61 Abs 1 den Begriff der 'Nichterfüllung' der vertraglichen Pflichten. Aber daring liegt nur ein verbaler, kein sachlicher Unterschied.* [95]
(Drawing on the notion of *Pflichtverletzung* corresponds to the UN sales law. This, however, uses the expression of non-performance of contractual liabilities in its article 45(1) and 61(1). In fact this is only an editorial difference, not a different meaning.)

---

89 Neufang, op cit (n 55), 313.

90 BGH, 131, 362; Palandt and Sprau, Bürgerliches Gesetzbuch (2001) §649, No 6 and Palandt and Sprau, Bürgerliches Gesetzbuch (2006) §649, No 8.

91 See previous note.

92 Ie, a derivative from the notion of breach of contract, non-performance and the uniquely German expression *Leistungsstörung*.

93 *Deutscher Bundestag, 'Entwurf eines Gesetzes zur Modernisierung des Schuldrechts'* 14 May 2001, 89.

94 Bundesministerium der Justiz, *'Einführung in den Entwurf der Bundesregierung und der Koalitionsfraktionen für ein Gesetz zur Modernisierung des Schuldrechts, BR-Drs 338-01, BT-Drs 14-6040'* 15 June 2001, 3 and 4, (II and II.2) of the 'Einführung'.

95 See *Deutscher Bundestag*, op cit (n 86), 92.

This understanding is incorrect and the inference very superficial. It ignores the whole background of the UN sales convention and its intention to blend legal systems of different origins, hence its international spirit. This understanding is not in line with the interpretation maxim of Article 7 CISG. The notion of non-performance itself draws on the more holistic concept of contract of common law systems and is based on the notion of breach of contract as a basis for claims. It would have been a better idea to reform areas of German law in keeping with these already existing models. It is also disappointing to see that the UPICC or indeed the PECL have not been taken into account at all in the process of this reform, despite their wider scope and actual use in international practice.

In fact, the reform was brought about in haste,[96] and instead of clearly deciding to change existing structures of the law for the right reasons and with regard to specific areas, these concepts and structures of the BGB are generally said to be flawed and incapable of accommodating new developments especially in European law.[97] This is an unnecessary pretext for patching up the law of obligations with incidental new ideas. Reforms should be either correctly integrated into existing concepts to provide clarity and consistency or they should expressly create separate new and consistent structures and clearly state the aims and objectives of the new concepts.

A comprehensive and systematically different concept would match the factual requirements of the parties involved in disputes, especially in modern complex international building contracts, better. If another reform of domestic law is welcomed in this area of law the UPICC might be an appropriate model. They can, however, *de lege lata* be applied as *lex specialis* to international commercial contracts.

One example might illustrate the significance of systematic compliance for German lawyers. Although the oscillating nature of the modified payment obligation in §649 S 2 BGB and in §324 I S 2 (old) BGB – appearing formally as a contract debt, but functioning and operating as a damages rule – is recognised by the courts and many writers,[98] its functional role as a duty to mitigate is rejected in connection with the right to performance, which is a purely contractual right belonging into the law of obligations.[99] Accordingly, the mere consideration that the

---

[96] See, for a brief summary of its creation, D Medicus in *Neues Schuldrecht: Genegnüberstellung BGB neu-alt mit Nebemgesetzen* (2002), X.

[97] B d Justiz, '*Einführung in den Entwurf der Bundesregierung und der Koalitionsfraktionen für ein Gesetz zur Modernisierung des Schuldrechts, BR-Drs 338-01, BT-Drs 14-6040*', 15 June 2001, p 2 (fig A); compare also FAZ, 2 June 2001, p 17 and see the concern of Medicus, op cit (n 96), XII, that the BGB, without the reform, might have become a monument for the sake of it, incapable of providing solutions, even to simple cases.

[98] See BGH NJW 1973, 1190, 1191; v Caemmerer, Schlechtriem, and Huber, '*Kommentar zum Einheitlichen UN-Kaufrecht*', 1995, Art 28 No 38.

[99] See eg, F Peters, '*Die Stornierung von Verträgen*' JZ (1996) 73, 74 where he was seduced into using the term 'compensation' (*Entschädigung*) despite his outspoken preference for the formal and dogmatic clarity in regarding the claim in §649 S2 BGB as a modified right to performance.

right to performance in Art 7.2.1 UPICC could be limited by a duty to mitigate, evokes strong opposition:

> But how can these thoughts be harmonised with the unlimited right to performance (of the creditor) of the monetary obligation as stated in Art 7.2.1 of the UNIDROIT Principles? A first possible interpretation would seek to apply the duty to mitigate as stated in Article 7.4.8 paragraph 1 of the UNIDROIT Principles to the right to performance as well. However, in that context there are dogmatic hurdles which cannot easily be overcome. Virtually all legal systems apply the duty to mitigate only to damages but not to the right to performance.[100]

Having previously stated that the modified right to performance eg, in §324 I S 2 BGB, is really a disguised duty to mitigate, and the provision a functional damages rule,[101] this appears to be a contradiction. It only shows, however, that dogmatic compliance has to be maintained within the legal systems, but that nevertheless there is room for an alternative regulation, drawing on the factual situation and offering a solution similar to the common law solution of breach of contract sanctioned by liability in damages.

The proposals for domestic reform of the law relating to complex building contracts cannot offer such a step. An alternative set of rules to apply to international contracts might therefore be a favourable solution for parties to international building contracts. The UPICC can be such a system, a different mode of law to suit special cases:

> Hardly any national judge would therefore limit the right to performance by a duty to mitigate.[102]

This statement, relating to national legal systems, provides an argument for the use of the UPICC instead of national law from the point of view of German law. It seems that the legislator does, in fact, practically apply the duty to mitigate to the right to performance, however in a well adapted manner by using the modified payment obligation. Due to the above discussed dogmatic difficulties, the judiciary would therefore possibly tolerate and recognise an alternative solution, replacing the cancellation and subsequent modified right to performance, by a system of termination and damages. There are good reasons for integrating such a concept into the existing legal situation.[103]

---

[100] Schwenzer, op cit (n 77), 295.
[101] See 4.2.3, above.
[102] Schwenzer, op cit (n 77), 295 compare the situation in common law jurisdictions, 4.1.3-4.1.5.
[103] This involves questions of conflict of laws which are to be discussed in Part 3.

## 5.2 Compatibility of the solution provided by the UPICC with German law

The previous section, 5.1, demonstrated the problems arising under current German contract law and made some comparative reference to the UPICC. This section asks what the solutions of the UPICC are with regard to the German position and whether these would be tolerated within the German doctrinal system – possibly offering a welcome alternative to law reform.

Under Art 7.4.2 UPICC the aggrieved party has a right to damages for non-performance. The refusal of an employer in a building contract to proceed with the contract and pay for the work would be regarded as non-performance since this is the employer's main obligation in a building contract. The contractor can, under Art 7.4.2 (1) UPICC, claim full compensation for his loss. Full compensation is described as:

> ...harm sustained as a result of the non-performance. Such harm includes both any loss which it [the party] suffered and any gain of which it was deprived, taking into account any gain to the aggrieved party resulting from the avoidance of cost or harm.

Coupled with the duty to mitigate provided for in Art 7.4.8 UPICC the contractor would be entitled to claim a sum of very much the same size as he would get under German law in a case of non-performance by the employer, under German cancellation or impossibility provisions.

### 5.2.1 The contractor's right to terminate

Termination of the contract would however, be up to the contractor. After taking notice of the intention of the employer not to proceed with the contract, the employer can choose to terminate the contract under Art 7.3.3 UPICC. The rules to restitution, which apply under the UPICC after termination, take special account of long term contracts such as international building contracts for large projects; Art 7.3.6(2) UPICC provides that 'restitution can only be claimed for the period after termination has taken effect', 'if performance of the contract has extended over a period of time and the contract is divisible'. In large projects contracts usually are divisible since payment is often made in instalments on completion of certain sections of the work. This provision takes the place of the contractor's right to performance under the German law of the *Werkvertrag*. It means that the contractor is only entitled to payment under the contract for the work actually carried out, just as he would be under §649 BGB. Further losses are to be compensated by way of damages under the UPICC. The employer's liability in damages arising from any (anticipatory) non-performance corresponds, in the pecuniary sense, effectively to the German right of cancellation and its consequential remaining modified payment obligation.

### 5.2.2 The employer's right to terminate

The right to termination can be exercised by the employer in cases where the contractor fails to perform in the contractually agreed way. This right is comparable to the 'extraordinary cancellation' under German law. The grounds for termination contained in Art 7.3.1 UPICC include termination on undue delay (Art 7.3.1(3) UPICC). The guidelines for determining whether a non-performance amounts to a fundamental one allowing for termination, provide a limitation of the use of the right to terminate the contract; the criterion of the potential occurrence of any 'disproportionate loss as a result of the preparation or performance if the contract is terminated', takes the contractor's interests[104] into account.

### 5.2.3 The rules on termination in the UPICC as a suitable substitute for cancellation

Termination cannot be invoked by either party without special reason. It is a remedy for non-performance, rather than a regular option for the employer. Termination is not a contractual right as is cancellation. The UPICC do not contain such an option which puts the contractual relationship at the disposal of one party only. The parties can nevertheless agree a right to cancellation in their contract. In practice this is rarely the case.[105] The parties regularly exclude the unqualified right of cancellation in their contracts under domestic law. Cancellation on special grounds however, remains a common provision which as we have seen, is at the same time, a common principle of the German law relating to long term agreements.[106] This right is, in effect, sufficiently reflected by the provisions on non-performance by the UPICC. This particularly includes the legal mechanism of compensation and restitution corresponding to the German modified right to performance.[107]

Problems arise in cases where the employer, for motivations not related to any act or omission of the contractor, announces his intention not to proceed with the contract and not to pay the contract price. This is the area giving rise to general doubts as to the workability and acceptability of the UPICC, from the perspective of the civil law systems recognising a general right to cancellation.[108] Where the employer wants to get rid of the contract for reasons other than those the contractor gives rise to, he cannot rely on termination; his intention not to pay could be regarded as amounting to a fundamental non-performance under Art 7.3.1 UPICC, especially where it is 'intentional or reckless' (Art 7.3.1(2)(a) UPICC). Because the contractor will always have to perform first however, the non-performance can only be anticipatory except for intermediate payments of completed sections. Can-

[104] Compare 5.3.2, below.
[105] See above, 5.3.2.
[106] See especially 5.1.3.
[107] See 4.1.2-4.1.3.
[108] See German law (§649 BGB etc), Swiss law (Art 377 OR); French law (Art 1794 CC).

cellation provisions only allow for cancellation before completion of the work. Under the UPICC, the employer would still depend on the contractor's decision to exercise his right to termination. The question remains whether the contractor can force the employer to proceed with the contract by way of his right to performance under Art 7.2.1 UPICC.

There are two ways of resolving this conflict. One way is to consider, by way of inherent interpretation, an underlying principle in the UPICC which would amount to a duty of the contractor to exercise his right to termination if the work is of no interest to the employer following special changed circumstances. This would be an inherent limitation to the right to performance of the contractor. Such a limitation could be based on the application of Art 1.7 UPICC, the duty to 'observe good faith and fair dealing in international trade'. This has been discussed in the context of Art 77 CISG; 'Art 77 would mean, in other words, that the aggrieved party must mitigate loss through the choice of remedy'.[109] Kastely denies this duty for systematic reasons within the Convention. Such a duty to mitigate as a limitation of the right to performance in Articles 46 and 62 CISG, was expressly rejected at the 1980 Vienna Conference. This solution is also discussed by Professor Schwenzer,[110] who observes a disadvantage in the prospects of uniformity in application of the UPICC.

## 5.3 Specific performance in German law: The civil law position

This section asks how historic development helps in understanding the present significance of aspects of specific performance in German contract law and also in a common law system. With regard to the idea of written law as such, it analyses the attitude taken in civil law jurisdictions towards the notion. This also serves to confirm and further explain the findings stated in Chapter 4 regarding the situation under English law. It helps to explain how the two spheres from different viewpoints can relate the uniform law approach to specific performance which is suggested in the UPICC.

Dawson observes that the main differences in perceiving specific performance are those between the attitudes typically held by common law as opposed to civil law jurisdictions:

> The contrast between the French and the German treatment of specific performance is one among many demonstrations of the great differences between the 'civil law' systems. Despite their long exposure to ideas derived from Roman law, each of the 'civil law' systems

[109] A H Kastely, 'The Right to Require Performance in International Sales: Towards an International Interpretation of the Vienna Convention' Washington Law Review 63 (1988) 607-651, 622.

[110] Schwenzer, op cit (n 77), 295.

is the product of independent, conscious choices. Each has drawn important values and objectives from the society it purports to regulate. [111]

German law provides a rather unqualified support for the keeping of promises; specific performance is the paramount remedy. Despite the fact that the Code Civil was already in force in some German states,[112] when it came to the drafting of the 1877 Code of Civil Procedure (*Zivilprozeßordnung*, ZPO, effective from 1879), a suggestion to adopt Art 1142 CC was rejected by a governmental opinion, 'that this rule of French law … "does not correspond to the German legal conscience"'.[113] In fact, the rules concerning enforcement of judgments are part of the law relating to civil procedure and thereby totally separate from substantive law. There is no doubt that any obligation can be required to be performed specifically, but this does not mean at the same time that there are harsh methods of enforcement at hand without due consideration by the courts. The courts can grant a remedy under the law of contract and they still have to decide in a second step if and how, this right conferred onto the plaintiff is to be enforced. Again the attitudes of scholars in the nineteenth century have to be seen in a political context, similar to the debate on the views of Pothier during the years around 1789, the year of the climax of the French Revolution.[114] The first constitutions arose, limiting the powers of the feudal system,[115] and thereby granting more political influence to the 'bourgeoisie'.[116] The protection of personal freedom became a value worth considering when deciding about the importance that enforcement of contracts should have. From 1868 imprisonment for debt was forbidden by statute.

Nevertheless, the BGB should not be conceived as reflecting a compromise between the 'bourgeoisie' and the crown and aristocracy. After the defeat of liberalism in 1848 when the proclamation of the republic in the Paulskirche in Frankfurt had failed, and despite the absence of a great revolution, the aristocratic part of society did not seem to see a challenge in the legislative efforts of the drafting commissions.[117] The code is now regarded as the result of a struggle between the German federal states.[118] The fact that Germany was not, like France, a centralised

---

[111] J Dawson, 'Specific Performance in France and Germany' Michigan Law Review 57 (1959) 495, 525.

[112] French law, brought to Germany by Napoleon, lived on as 'Rhenish Law', much valued by its subjects, and sought after even by other German states, namely Bavaria and Hessen-Darmstadt and Würzburg: see U Eisenhardt, *Deutsche Rechtsgeschichte* (2004) §55.

[113] *Protokolle der Kommission des Reichstags* 413-414 (1875); Dawson, op cit (n 107), 527.

[114] Compare F Wieacker, *A History of Private Law in Europe*, 364 and 365.

[115] Constitutions of the German states evolved from 1818 (Bavaria); Württemberg (1819), Baden (1818), Hessen (1820), Kur-Hessen (1831), Saxony (1831), Hannover (1833) and Braunschweig (1832).

[116] U Eisenhardt, *Deutsche Rechtsgeschichte* (2004) §56.

[117] K Kroeschell, '*Rechtsgeschichte Deutschlands im 20 Jahrhundert*' Vol 1681, 1992, 19.

[118] Bavaria supported the strict form of transfer of land as notary deeds successfully against Prussia while the requirement of personal authorship of a testament supported by Baden and Bavaria had to wait for the last stage of the creation of the BGB, the approval of the

state has to be borne in mind. Only in 1873 was the Reich conferred legislative power to regulate the complete 'civil' (private) law, ie, the law relating to private individuals,[119] comprehensively.[120] This happened after years of resistance by the kingdoms of Bavaria, Württemberg and Saxony.[121] The BGB was not commanded by an emperor at his best, but it was the result of a joint political decision, as well as the common effort of various individuals representing a remarkable range of different areas of society, in the course of the drafting history of the BGB. The First Commission prepared the first draft (published in 1888) and consisted of ten members and its president H E Pape, a judge and president of the supreme commercial court of the Reich. The members were five judges, three civil servants and two Professors. One of them was the famous pandectist Bernhard Windscheid (the only legal scholar in the group) and whose name today is closely related to the creation and theoretical background of the Code. Although Gottlieb Planck, general reporter of the Second Commission (consisting of up to 24 persons)[122] was probably more of an influential personality involved in the drafting work than Windscheid, the BGB was later criticised by those who favoured the more 'Germanic' approach and the German legal tradition as being a compendium of pandects cast in legal paragraphs (Otto Gierke).[123] They saw a more 'socialistic' attitude represented by this order, for example, in the way they conceived of property rights; Gierke[124] postulated a limitation to the 'absolute' right to private property (excluding everyone else), intrinsic to this right and formed by, paramount public interests which could justify disowning property. Anton Menger, professor of civil procedure in Vienna and the other most noteworthy critic of the First Draft saw a threat to the *besitzlosen Klassen*, the underprivileged classes, in the great abstractness and the demanding linguistic and scientific approach of the BGB, namely in the structure of land law which was indeed based on traditional German laws.[125] These critics were mostly 'left wing conservative academics' (*Kathedersozialisten*, attacked by Friedrich Engels),[126] who hoped to influence the outcome of the codification project. They had however, only little influence at least during the codification period. Although regard was, in general, made to social aspects of

Reichstag; Bavaria and Mecklenburg contended each other's preference relating to mortgages, see Kroeschell, op cit (n 113), 19.

119 For the development and meaning of the word 'civil' see Wieacker, op cit (n 110), 365.

120 By the '*Lex Lasker*', an Act of 20 December 1873, promoted by the members of the Reichstag Miquel and Lasker; see Eisenhardt, op cit, §67 II 1; Kroeschell, op cit (n 113), 12.

121 Kroeschell, op cit (n 113), 12.

122 Ibid, 14.

123 See Hattenhauer and Buschmann, *Textbuch zur Privatrechtsgeschichte der Neuzeit* (1967), 279 et seq.

124 See Otto Gierke, *Der Entwurf eines BGB und das deutsche Recht* (1888); *Die sociale Aufgabe des Privatrechts* (1889); see also S Pfeiffer-Munz, *Soziales Recht ist deutsches Recht. Otto v Gierkes Theorie des sozialen Rechts, untersucht anhand seiner Stellungnahme zur deutschen und schweizerischen Privatrechtskodifikation* (Zürich, 1979).

125 Anton Menger, *Das bürgerliche Recht und die besitzlosen Klassen* (1899).

126 Kroeschell, op cit (n 113), 15.

legislation at that time, the discussion was not fully appreciated by Menger's and Gierke's contemporaries.[127]

The role of Roman law in German legal scholarship and practice was different from that in France, since it remained some kind of underlying last resort in relation to the *Partikularrechte*, the scattered laws of the numerous German states (*ius commune, Gemeinrecht*), throughout the lifetime of the Holy Roman Empire. As such it had been subject to continuous research and criticism. The Pandectists finally initiated a development that lead to the scientific movement in legal science,[128] which eventually produced the 1900 Civil Code (*Bürgerliches Gesetzbuch*, BGB). This codification with its five 'Books'[129] was created according to the *Pandektensystem* (system of pandects) which was a common principle in legal science in the nineteenth century, especially after the writings of Georg Arnold Heise.[130] This system did not directly copy the pandects in 50 books containing the digests, but was developed on the basis of Roman law as well as the 'common' German law – the *Naturrecht*. This, for example, adhered to the distinction between the law of obligations and the law relating to 'things' (movables, *Fahrnisrecht*, and immovables Liegenschaftsrecht, comprising possession, proprietary and related rights),[131] thereby creating the *Abstraktionsprinzip*; the principle of abstraction which contributes so much to the specific scientific appearance of the system of the BGB.

Due to the scientific approach and aspiration of the BGB, another feature of the treatment of specific performance arises. This is the paramount significance of the contract as an object with a life of its own, and one of special qualities within the system and network of the BGB, which gives the notion of specific performance its paramount appearance. Particularly the First and Second Book of the BGB (*Allgemeiner Teil*, general part, §§1-240 BGB and *Recht der Schuldverhältnisse*, law of obligations, §§241-853 BGB), are derived from the pandectist findings. Thus, this notion plays a vital role for the interpretation of the UPICC because these are to be conceived a 'general part' for international contract law. The pandectists' heritage means that the BGB follows in its structure, a pattern progressing from the general to the specific, visible in the consecutive appearance of the notions of *Willenserklärung – Rechtsgeschäft – Vertrag – Schuldvertrag – Kaufvertrag* within the first two 'Books'.

The high degree of systematic coherence and consistency of the provisions, as well as their terminological precision and strictness, trying to achieve a kind of 'scientific' logic and accurateness, makes for the character of the BGB. It is the abstractness in the detailed formulation of the concrete provision which gives

[127] Ibid, 16, pointing to Planck's sharp reaction towards Gierke's proposals. Compare 8.2.2.7 and 8.3.3, below.

[128] H Brox, '*Allgemeiner Teil des Bürgerlichen Gesetzbuchs*', 2005, Nos 22 and 23.

[129] *Allgemeiner Teil – Recht der Schuldverhältnisse – Sachenrecht – Familienrecht – Erbrecht* (General Part – law of obligations – law relating to objects/things – family law – heritage law).

[130] *Grundriß eines Systems* (1807).

[131] J F Baur and R Stürner, *Lehrbuch des Sachenrechts* (1999) §2.

great flexibility to the Code;[132] the abstract formulation is seemingly unsuitable for real life in a changing world but still today, catalogue or self-service sales (§151, S 2 BGB), computerised banking transactions, ticket sales via machines on railway platforms are tackled with the tools of the BGB just because the law does not speak of '*Kolonialwarenhändler*', '*Pferdebahn*' or '*Contorgehülfe*', which would be inhabitants of a vanished world. The law describes the legal conceptions behind the concrete objects.[133]

Today, the rules relating to specific performance or, better, the enforcement of specific obligations, have to be seen in the light of the strict rule of law within the constitutional framework of the separation of powers.[134] Courts will not apply measures of enforcement which would cause disproportionate harm or disadvantage to a judgment defendant. This corrective belongs to the procedural world rather than to the world of substantive contract law.[135] The division between the spheres of 'private' and 'public' law in Germany[136] contributes to this structure which allows a restriction of unwanted effects of specific performance outside contract law.[137] Specific performance occurs in two stages; in the prejudgment or trial stage of an action and, after the rendering of the judgment, the stage of execution, formally distinct and governed by the code of civil procedure.[138] It is the latter stage that causes the worries within the common law world. There are not many cases in which specific performance has been excessively used; '... the court entrusted with execution will normally be ready, without hesitation, to order specific enforcement when requested by the judgment plaintiff. Doubts can only concern cases where, specific relief is impossible, would involve disproportionate cost, would introduce compulsion into personal relationships or compel the expression of special forms of artistic or intellectual creativity.'[139] The latter restric-

---

[132] See, for building contracts in particular, Nicklisch, op cit (n 9), eg, 757.

[133] See Karsten Schmidt, *Die Zukunft der Kodifikationsidee* (1985); Kroeschell, op cit (n 113), 20; also below 'Building contracts under German law', 10.

[134] See H Brox, '*Allgemeiner Teil des Bürgerlichen Gesetzbuchs*', 2005, No 29; Art 20 III GG (*Grundgesetz für die Bundesrepublik Deutschland* of 23 May 1949 (BGBl 49 S.1, in: *Grundgesetz - Staats- und Verwaltungsrecht Bundesrepublik Deutschland, Reihe Textbuch deutsches Recht*, 41st edn, Heidelberg 2006, C F Müller ).

[135] H Brox, '*Allgemeiner Teil des Bürgerlichen Gesetzbuchs*', 2005, No 12.

[136] Compare above 1.1.2.

[137] Some corrective measures became necessary and were carried out sometimes even before the publication of the BGB: the *Abzahlungsgesetz* (18 May 1894) concerning payments for purchase of goods in instalments as well as the Gesetz zur Regelung der Miethöhe (18 December 1974) regulating the increase of rent between landlord and tenant.

[138] Compare above 1.1.3.2.

[139] Dawson, op cit (n 107), 530. He quotes a decision of the Reichsgericht, RGZ 39, 420 where a chemist was required to turn over his own previous invention of a process for manufacturing mirrors. The court said that it would not have granted an order to invent against the chemist. This case, however, had a famous predecessor: August 'the Strong', the king of Saxony, imprisoned the pharmacist Johann Friedrich Böttger (1682-1719) in order to force him to invent a process to turn a substance into gold. He invented Meissen porcelain, the 'white gold'.

tion is expressed by §888 ZPO. Arrest and fines are limited and cannot be ordered in certain cases, §888 II ZPO.

However, specific performance is not a compulsory remedy. In practice the remedy of damages is resorted to in a large number of cases, particularly in commercial law and sales of goods.[140] This shows how legal systems may differ much in theory but less in practice.

### 5.3.1 Specific performance in the language and system of the BGB

The basic provision of the BGB establishing the supremacy of specific performance is §241:

By virtue of an obligation the obligee is entitled to demand performance from the obligor. The performance may also consist of an abstention.

The provision takes its force from its position in the BGB (general law of obligations) given the formal and systematic structure of the code. It also shows an important aspect to be considered:

'Obligation' is more than just 'being obliged'. This legal expression and concept rather denotes a 'relationship of obligation' (*Schuldverhältnis*). This is the source of the entire legal relationship between the parties.[141] This mechanism applies to the whole code; *Schuldverhältnisse*[142] create (single) obligations and rights that are interrelated. Whatever affects one obligation, affects the whole relationship – the network of obligations form the *Schuldverhältnis*, the contract as a specific kind of 'obligation', often a mutual or 'synallagmatic', 'reciprocal' one.[143] (The contract types are listed in the seventh section of the BGB, contracts for sales, tenancy, lease, services, exchange, etc.) *Schuldverhältnisse* are regarded as living things ('organisms')[144] in that they are a complex entity, a 'meaningful network' ('*sinnhaftes Gefüge*')[145] or a 'chronologically progressing process' ('*finaler Prozeß*').[146]

---

[140] Dawson, op cit (n 107), 530.

[141] Palandt and Heinrichs, *Bürgerliches Gesetzbuch* (2001), Einl v §241, No 1.

[142] Neufang states for the US that the term 'debt' is used today to describe a wide range of legal relationships, and that the term 'indebtedness' serves to specifically describe a debt in the traditional strict sense. It seems to me that the expression indebtedness corresponds very much to the German expression *Schuldverhätnis*. See for the use of 'debt' and 'indebtedness' in American law: A L Corbin, *Corbin on Contracts* Vol 1, 1963, §117, 508; 11 USC. § 101 (12) and §105 (5) Restatement (Second), Contracts, §82 and Comment b ('indebtedness').

[143] The principle of *do ut des*.

[144] Palandt and Heinrichs, *Bürgerliches Gesetzbuch* (1998), Einl vz §241, No 2; Bruns in *Festschrift für Zepos*, 1973, 69.

[145] K Larenz, *Lehrbuch des Schuldrechts. Erster Band: Allgemeiner Teil*, 1982, §2 V, 27.

[146] Ibid, pp 27 and 28.

One difficulty in applying and interpreting the UPICC arises from this mechanism and special 'scientific' character of the BGB, as has been explained above.[147]

German lawyers, just as common lawyers,[148] distinguish as to whether an action to obtain a sum of money is based on a damages provision (secondary claim) or on specific performance of a contract debt (primary claim). Both awards would grant money, they are not, however, the same type of money judgment.

The rule in §241 BGB does not literally read 'demand performance', but demand *Leistung*. This word is not identical with *Erfüllung*, another form of legal performance,[149] which would literally mean fulfilment or completion and would be used in connection with a concrete contractual obligation, which can be described specifically. *Leistung*, [150] in this provision is used to describe a very general form of performance applying to any contractual agreement.

Not every aspect of the occurrence of specific performance in German law can be discussed here. It does not purport to the aim of this study to describe the details of procedural law relating to the enforcement of specific performance.[151] The degree of tolerance of substantive German law towards the UPICC is of interest here.

### 5.3.2 The notion of legitimate interest limiting performance claims

The solutions pursued in the BGB and also in modern German jurisprudence and court practice often try to give as much effect as possible to the interests of the parties in a specific situation, as far as they are protected by the law and subject to the specific legal rule.[152] In respect of contracts and specific performance of single obligations, the attitude of the obligee can have different focuses. They are well described and classified by Lena Olsen:

His (the creditor's) interest could be directed specifically to the contracted performance, ie, because it is rare on the market or because of the special qualities of the debtor himself,

---

[147] Eg, 4.1.4.

[148] Compare above, Chapter 4.

[149] Performance would literally have to be translated as '*Durchführung*', a very neutral expression. Specific performance is therefore closer to the meaning of *Erfüllung* than *Leistung*.

[150] The literal meaning being achievement or effort.

[151] A good overview is given by Dawson, op cit (n 107), 527/528; see also Neufang, op cit (n 55), and A-C Zweiter Hauptteil, 273-328.

[152] *Interessenjurisprudenz* (interest jurisprudence). This expression was first used by Philipp Heck (P Heck, *Begriffsbildung und Interessenjurisprudenz*, 1932). Since the 1950s the predominant practice of legal reasoning is called *Wertungsjurisprudenz* (valuing jurisprudence). The essence of this doctrine is to extend legal reasoning beyond the black letter text of the rule and beyond the documented intention of the legislator by considering certain factual circumstances in which interests and values of the parties involved in a legal transactions manifest. See Kroeschell, op cit (n 113), 51 and K Larenz and M Wolf, *Allgemeiner Teil des Deutschen Bürgerlichen Rechts* (2004) §4 for further reference on interpretation techniques in German law.

specific interest. His need could also be functional so that he needs the performance because of the use he can make out of it, functional interest. Finally, he could be interested in the performance solely because of the profit he intends to make, profitable interest. Even if there is no sharp distinction between these three interests it is important to realise the distinction to be able to fully acknowledge the needs of the parties.[153]

These specific interests are given effect, and protected by, the rules relating to the assessment of damages under German law, eg, in cases of pre-contractual liability, 'cic' (*culpa in contrahendo*) or cases of injury or damage caused in the course of a transaction, positive *Vertragsverletzung*, covering consequential damage. They would determine whether a plaintiff can claim *Erfüllungsinteresse* ('positive interest' in the consummation of the contract) or just claim the *Vertrauensschaden*, the damage incurred in reliance on the contract, a 'negative interest', §249 BGB.

The exact degree to which German law supports the unqualified right to specific performance by giving effect to a creditor's interest in a contract can only be derived by taking the whole of the contractual rules, including all remedies and defences, into account. See, for example, how the system of rules dealing with all kinds of *Leistungsstörungen* (§§320-327 (old) BGB),[154] operates. These are irregularities, 'disturbances' occurring in the course of the performance and consummation of contractual transactions.[155] They correspond to the system of remedies for breach of contract and excused non-performance in the UPICC. But 'breach of contract' is not a *terminus technicus* (a technical term) in the BGB and not a pre-requisite[156] for a remedy. §320 BGB only gives the right to withhold a party's own performance as a defence against non-performance in a synallagmatic/reciprocal contract. It does not discharge the debtor's obligation to perform.

### 5.3.3 Direct limitations to the right to performance

A general direct limitation to the general right to require performance is contained in §275 BGB, for cases of subsequent impossibility or incapability (§275 II (old) BGB, §276 BGB (2002)) for the innocent debtor, ie, if no failure on the debtor's part can be established. In these cases, the debtor becomes free from his obligation to perform, §275 I BGB.

An obligor of a payment obligation, however, can rarely rely on these exceptions to the rule of §241 BGB, because there are some fundamental differences between monetary and non-monetary obligations. Payment cannot become 'impossible in law or fact', 'unreasonably burdensome or expensive'; the party entitled to

[153] Olsen, op cit (n 23), 24.

[154] This rather sophisticated term was first introduced by Heinrich Stoll in his work *Die Lehre von den Leistungsstörungen* ('The doctrine of the *Leistungsstörungen*'), 1936, now published as Heinrich Stoll, '*Die Lehre von den Leistungsstörungen*' in *Interessenjurisprudenz*, ed Günther Ellscheid. Wege der Forschung (Darmstadt, Wissenschaftliche Buchgesellschaft, 1974) Vol 345 pp 153-216.

[155] See Palandt and Heinrichs, *Bürgerliches Gesetzbuch* (2001 and 2006) Vorb z §275.

[156] Olsen, op cit (n 23), 24-25.

it cannot be expected to 'obtain performance from another source', it is not of 'an exclusively personal character' (Art 7.2.2 (a) to (d) UPICC).[157] Money is never short as goods can be in times of shortage, or where they are made to match special specifications or similar. Money is never 'ascertained'.

The rules relating to impossibility do not apply to debts.[158] It is thought to be an axiom of the legal order that economic incapability cannot be an excuse for non-payment.[159] Money represents, 'abstract economic power by virtue of wealth represented in units of a specific currency';[160] it is a 'quantum (quantity) of purchasing power', although the debtor does not have to guarantee the inner value, the exact value of a currency on its market within its economy; the debtor owes the nominal, not the economic value of the money.[161]

The five express limitations listed in Art 7.2.2 UPICC are thus specifically designed to fit non-monetary obligations. Art 7.2.2 UPICC grants a right to specific performance due to the special interests a party can have in the performance by one specific debtor. These interests are however, protected to the degree expressed in Art 7.2.2(a) to (e) UPICC. The Erfüllungsinteresse, the specific interest in performance, ends where these limiting circumstances occur. The absence of express limitations of the right to require performance of monetary obligations thus arises out of the need for special treatment. But since German law does not know any isolated limitation of the right to require performance, the question arises; if, and why, this limitation is being missed and desired by German lawyers? [162] The only case of an isolated limitation of the enforceability of a right to require performance is the defence of time limit (*Verjährung*) (§§194-225 (old) BGB, §§194-218 BGB (2002)).

Apart from this, express limitations of the right to require performance itself are unknown to German law. It is therefore a doctrinal inconsistency to demand such a technique to reach a result which might be inherent to the UPICC anyway, and can be realised by due application and interpretation. Express limitations, such as those in Art 7.2.2 UPICC, are alien to German law, and therefore consideration has to be made as to whether these can be integrated into domestic law, and if they are compatible with, and acceptable to, German legal theory and practice.

---

157 See I Schwenzer, *Erfüllung und Schadensersatz nach den Unidroit – Prinzipien* (1997, unpublished), 4.

158 Palandt and Heinrichs, *Bürgerliches Gesetzbuch* (2006) §245 No 14; K Schmidt, '*Geldrecht: Geld, Zins und Währung im deutschen Recht*' Vol XXXIII, 1983, C 29.

159 Palandt and Heinrichs, *Bürgerliches Gesetzbuch* (2006) §245, No 14; K Larenz, *Lehrbuch des Schuldrechts. Erster Band: Allgemeiner Teil* (1982) §12 III.

160 Palandt and Heinrichs, *Bürgerliches Gesetzbuch* (2006), §245 No 2; Schmidt, op cit (n 154), A 14 et seq.

161 Larenz, op cit (n 155), §12 III; BGH 61, 38; 79,194; BVerfG 50, 57.

162 See Schwenzer, n 153 above.

## 5.4 Conclusion

The discussion in Chapter 5 has revealed that there is no clash in the substantive law between the UPICC and German law. A thorough analysis of the Principles helps to reveal their full potential. Since legal science plays a formative role in the German legal system, this analysis itself can contribute to the integration of the UPICC into domestic German law and can form a method of applying uniform contract law rules successfully.

The UPICC are particularly interesting for German law under the aspect of law reform with regard to international building contracts (sections 5.1 and 5.2). They could contribute considerably to creating improved legal solutions in this area even after the recent reform enacted in the form of the revised BGB (*Schuldrechtsmodernisierungsgesetz*, the reform of the law of obligations with effect from 2001).

The flawed method of applying uniform law by unwittingly applying double standards as described in Chapter 3 can be explained as follows with a view to German contract law: The right of cancellation which Professor Schwenzer says is lacking in the UPICC and potentially serving as a limitation to Art 7.2.1 UPICC, does by no means discharge the employer/orderer from his payment obligation arising out of the synallagmatical contract under German law. Consequently, such a legal effect cannot be demanded from the UPICC by invoking standards of German contract law, thereby accusing the Principles of lacking a right to cancellation and supporting an overly rigid right to performance. The neutral formulation of §649 BGB, disregarding any further subjective or objective requirements, corresponds to the generous concept of non-performance and termination in the Principles. Under German law relating to building contracts, the orderer's unqualified right of cancellation leaves him with the generally unqualified, though potentially modified, payment obligation. This result has already been criticised in German legal science and legal profession.[163] The way this payment obligation is subsequently to be settled according to German law corresponds to a great extent with the way the Principles tackle the situation, yet, from a different angle; under the UPICC the orderer has the opportunity to be discharged from his obligations or be liable in damages as specific factual circumstances arise under the provisions on termination and non-performance. Overall, the outcome, in terms of the actual sum of money to be paid under the various factual circumstances, is almost identical relying on either the domestic or the international legal provisions. The rule of Art 7.2.1 UPICC is therefore compatible with German law and also offers an excellent model for law reform, incorporating a simplified formulation and method, as well as an international background.

The traditional understanding and use of specific performance in German law implies sufficient limitations to the right to performance to prevent coerced performance, and at the same time recognises a special and distinct treatment of pay-

[163] See Grimme, op cit (n 9), 247.

ment obligations (section 5.3). Therefore, this understanding ought to be applied to Art 7.2.1 UPICC in order to justify its content.

# Conclusion (Part 2)

Part 2 has proven that Art 7.2.1 UPICC is compatible with domestic law on the level of substantive national contract law. Chapters 3, 4 and 5 have demonstrated a comprehensive method of interpretation allowing for the successful application of the UPICC within each domestic legal system and thus, their integration into the domestic legal process. This method consisted of reviewing and analysing underlying concepts of current legislation and case law, and also taking recourse to legal history using standard domestic methods of application and interpretation to the uniform contract law, treating those as an independent comprehensive body of law rules. This technique resulted in the removal of obstacles in the area of substantive law by revealing preconceived expectations towards uniform law which are owed to a superficial understanding. By reviewing positions which assume limitations that are in fact not there, it is possible to remove those limitations by assuming a non-static view on national legal concepts. This is an extended autonomous interpretation technique and forms a novel methodology of international contract law.

# Part 3 The UNIDROIT principles in the conflict of laws

## Introduction

The previous sections, Parts 1 and 2, identified two barriers against an easy application of contemporary transnational uniform contract law within domestic legal systems. These barriers arise in connection with general contract doctrine (Chapters 1 and 2) and in the course of specific application of individual rules within domestic legal systems (Chapters 3, 4 and 5). Parts 1 and 2 suggested ways of removing these barriers in traditional contract doctrine and in legal practice, by applying familiar concepts according to an extended autonomous methodology of international contract law.

This concluding section, Part 3 now asks how uniform contract law is treated in the conflict of laws. The issues are; what is the status quo in English and German conflict of laws (Chapter 6), how do the conflict rules of each national law act as a gateway for the application of uniform rules, do they hinder or facilitate the application of the UPICC in practice, particularly in arbitration (Chapter 7), and what can be done to remove difficulties to make it easy and desirable for international contractors to apply the UPICC to their contracts? The core questions therefore consider whether such law rules are regarded as a source of law (Chapter 6), and whether the UPICC – as an example of uniform law – can be applied as the law governing the contract via choice of law rules (*kollisionsrechtliche Verweisung*), rather than merely as contract terms (*materiellrechtliche Verweisung*). This section also examines how these questions can be answered by a state court as opposed to an arbitration tribunal (Chapters 7 and 8).

# 6 Status quo of transnational law in the conflict of laws

This chapter debates the current status quo of current conflict of laws legislation, case law and doctrine in English and German legal systems, with regard to the source of law function of uniform contract law. It also asks what solutions can be derived from this *lege lata* as it presently is and thereby what can be suggested for advancing the integration and applicability of uniform contract law, such as the UPICC, which are designed to facilitate international contracts and trade.

In order to provide a basis for discussion, this chapter commences with a summary, recapitulating the relevant law relating to the conflict of laws in England and Germany. This allows for the highlight of the relevant considerations, which can lead to a suggested method of integrating application of national conflict law in order to use the UPICC in international commerce (6.1). The chapter then discusses the question as to whether the UPICC can be a source of law, so as to make for a governing law, *lex contractus*, under current conflict rules (sections 6.2 and 6.3).

## 6.1 Choice of law under English and German law – and the Rome Convention

This section asks what the current status quo of the *lex lata*, the existing law in the area of choice of law, is. It encapsulates the role of the Rome Convention and traditional conflict law looking at the choice of law aspects in contract law matters. This helps to investigate the attitude of current national conflict law towards introducing uniform law in order to deal with matters of commercial contracts.

Both the United Kingdom and Germany have adopted the 1980 Rome Convention on the Law Applicable to Contractual Obligations.[1] Although 'harmonisation' of the domestic conflict of law rules was the aim of this Convention, there are still differences between the legal systems, which lead to different observations regarding the potential of the UPICC to be recognised as governing law.

---

[1] The Rome Convention of the European Economic Community on the Law Applicable to Contractual Obligations of 19 June 1980 first came into force, as regards the United Kingdom and Germany, on 1 April 1991, and has been amended by the Third Brussels Accession Protocol of 29 November 1996. For the German text see E Jayme and R Hausmann, eds, *Internationales Privat-und Verfahrensrecht* 12th edn, 2004.

### 6.1.1 The scope of the RC in the UK and traditional English choice of law

Despite the adaptation of the 1980 Rome Convention and its implementation by the Contracts (Applicable Law) Act 1990, common law still plays a role and has to be discussed here.

The time factor, as well as the scope of, and certain exclusion clauses in the Rome Convention still leave room for the traditional rules for the choice of law in English law. The scope of the Rome Convention as set out in Art 1(2)(b) excludes arbitration agreements from its application. The United Kingdom did exercise the right to exclude Art 7(1) (concerning mandatory laws) and 10(1)(e) (effect on nullity of contracts) under Art 22(1)(a) and (b) of the Rome Convention. Section 2(3) of the Contracts (Applicable Law) Act provides that the Rome Convention does not apply to cases of 'conflicts of different parts of the United Kingdom', following Art 19(2) of the Rome Convention.

### 6.1.2 The scope of the RC in Germany and traditional choice of law rules

German choice of law rules are regulated in the *Einführungsgesetz zum Bürgerlichen Gesetzbuch.*[2] This codification was thoroughly reformed in 1986[3] in order to incorporate the Rome Convention. The rule stating the method to determine the applicable law regarding contracts is contained in Art 27 and 28. Art 28 (1) EGBGB states that the contract is subject to the law of the state with which 'the contract is most closely connected' ('... *unterliegt dem Recht des Staates, mit dem er die engsten Verbindungen aufweist*'). Art 28(2) EGBGB then establishes a guideline for the application of section (1) in that, 'The contract is deemed to have the closest connection with the state in which the party, who is to perform the characteristic performance, is resident at the time of the conclusion of the contract ...', ('*Es wird vermutet, daß der Vertrag die engsten Verbindungen mit dem Staat aufweist, in dem die Partei, welche die charakteristische Leistung zu erbringen hat, im Zeitpunkt des Vertragsschlusses ihren gewöhnlichen Aufenthalt hat ...*').

---

[2] Abbreviated EGBGB, 'Introductory Law to the BGB', first enacted on 18 August 1896. For a German text of the relevant provisions see E Jayme and R Hausmann, eds, *Internationales Privat-und Verfahrensrecht*, 9th edn, 1998. Full German text see, eg, BGB – *Bürgerliches Gesetzbuch mit zugehörigen Gesetzen und EG – Richtlinien,* 105th edn, Beck'sche Textausgaben (Munich: C H Beck, 1999) 503 et seq or later editions, or *BGB - Bürgerliches Gesetzbuch*, annual edition, Beck – *Texte im dtv* (Munich: Deutscher Taschenbuchverlag).

[3] By the *Gesetz zur Neuregelung des internationalen Privatrechts* of 25 July 1986. German text of the relevant provisions of the current version in E Jayme and R Hausmann, eds, *Internationales Privat-und Verfahrensrecht*, 9th edn (1998) No 1, 1-19; full text in BGBl 1994 I, 2494 and in Palandt and Heldrich, *Bürgerliches Gesetzbuch*, 1998 or later editions; J Pirrung, *Internationales Privat-und Verfahrensrecht nach dem Inkrafttreten der Neuregelung des IPR. Texte, Materialien, Hinweise* (1987).

This general rule is, however, accompanied by a provision applying to cases where the characteristic performance in a contract cannot be established (Art 28(2), second phrase); the rule is not to be applied in those instances (*'Dieser Absatz ist nicht anzuwenden, wenn sich die charakteristische Leistung nicht bestimmen läßt'*). This will often be the case in modern international commercial contracts.

The rules preceding this version of Art 27 and 28 EGBGB – the law as it was in force before the enactment of the Rome Convention – still applies to cases which arose before 1 September 1986 (Art 220(1) EGBGB). This law consists of customary and judge-made law to a great extent.[4] It still applies to contracts concluded before 1 September 1986.[5] The original EGBGB contained but a few express provisions mainly regulating family and inheritance matters.[6] The law of obligations and other contractual conflict of laws was unregulated by statutes and thus only manifested in case law.

### 6.1.3 Traditional English and German choice of law rules

#### *6.1.3.1 The role of contractual obligations as a criterion to determine the applicable law*

Traditional English choice of law rules are governed by the doctrine of the proper law of the contract. This doctrine can lead to results which are quite different from the ones based on the rules of the Rome Convention itself, as well as on pre-Rome Convention German conflict law. As a general rule, German traditional law used the test of the closest connection of the 'typical obligation' arising in a contract. The legal system which this is most closely related to is to govern the contract. This method of determining the governing law was often criticised by scholars. It also conflicts with fundamental English views on contract. Just as English law does not conceive a contract as being a network of individual and potentially separate obligations[7] it will not determine the proper law of the contract by relying on a single obligation, but rather, by looking at the contract as a whole. The distinction between 'typical' or 'essential', from not so typical or less essential, obligations in a contract thus seems somewhat artificial, especially, when looking at a variety of types of international commercial contracts.[8]

---

4 See Palandt and Heldrich, *Bürgerliches Gesetzbuch* (1998) EGBGB Einl Art 3, No 5; Palandt and Heldrich, *Bürgerliches Gesetzbuch* (2006) EGBGB 220, No 2; G Kegel and K Schurig, *Internationales Privatrecht* (2004) §4 I.

5 See Palandt and Heldrich, *Bürgerliches Gesetzbuch* (2006) EGBGB Art 220, No 4; BGH NJW-RR 90, 249.

6 See Kegel and Schurig, op cit (n 4), §4I, for an account of the history of the 1896 conflict of laws legislation.

7 See above Chapter 4, eg, 4.1 and 4.1.1.

8 See above Chapter 1 and 4.1.4. See also S Shackleton, 'The Applicable Law in International Arbitration Under the New English Arbitration Act 1996' Arbitration Interna-

#### *6.1.3.2 Finding a legal system for the contract*

Traditionally, under English law the test applied to establish the proper law of contract is:

If no system of law has been expressly selected and it is not possible to infer one, the court will look for the system with which the contract has its closest and most real connection. [9]

In *Amin Rasheed Shipping Corporation* v *Kuwait Insurance Co*[10] this led to the application of English law by establishing that the contract 'was redolent of English law'[11] although it had nothing to do with England. This means that it not only selected English law as a system of law, rather than a country whose law was to apply, but that English judges looked at the contract in a more comprehensive way – seeing the contract as a complex entity.

### 6.1.4 Finding a state for the contract under the scope of the Rome Convention

Following Swiss law, the Rome Convention adopted and brought about the civilian approach of 'characteristic performance' (Art 4(2) RC) which determines the country with which the contract is 'most closely connected'; Art 4(1) RC. This means that after the enactment of the Contracts (Applicable Law) Act 1990, there is a change of view in English law to the extent that there is a 'country' to be determined rather than a 'system of law'.

The underlying confession that law is very much a 'state owned' thing and that law is national seems thus to be emphasised by the RC. From the point of view of the RC, can there then be any support for the UPICC being the proper law of the contract?

The concept of the 'characteristic performance', or better the habitual residence of the party who has to perform the characteristic performance in a contract, Art 4(2) RC, is at the same time the limit of the scope of the RC and the main argument for the application of a set of rules such as the UPICC.

In international commercial contracts it is sometimes difficult to establish which obligation is the 'characteristic' one. They can be delocalised in nature. Their performance may spread over many countries and legal systems[12] (whose

---

tional 13.4 (1997) 375: '…recognition of the specificity of international transactions as distinct from purely domestic contracts…'.

9 J G Collier, *Conflict of laws* (2001) 193.

10 [1984] AC 50.

11 Collier, *Conflict of laws* (1987) 161 and see J G Collier, *Conflict of laws* (2001) 194, n 19.

12 Compare R Goode, 'Usage and its Reception in Transnational Commercial Law' International and Comparative Law Quarterly 46 (1997) 1-36, 30-31, who gives the example of a pipeline running through six different countries. See also the example of string sales as described above in Chapter 4.

existence cannot be denied even if ignored by the RC). Parties to a contract change frequently and the actual performance of such a contract may not even be its main purpose.[13] What is the argument in these cases to insist on establishing a characteristic performance? It appears very likely that this argument serves to determine a country by hook or by crook, so that state, jurisdiction and law coincide. The emphasis is on state governance rather than on dispute settlement. The parties' intention and the nature of their contract, is not given first priority. The decision to allocate the contract is made before the parties set up their contract with its specific characteristics and its potential specific requirements. The determination of a states' dispute settlement procedure reflects therefore, not only the intention to serve the parties' need to reach a solution or an agreement regarding their problem, but also to bring state jurisdiction into play. This attitude can however, in a large number of cases, especially in modern international trade, create quite a considerable gap and incongruence between the nature and requirements of the matter to be dealt with and the 'tools' at hand.

As has been demonstrated above[14] domestic law does in some areas not meet the requirements of international trade because its rules are designed for domestic use. Also domestic rules necessarily involve matters of public policy and incorporate a general social component in order to fulfil any state's general task to provide an order for people's lives in their community. Matters of consumer protection for example, nowadays play a role in almost every area of private law. The judge is part of the state's order and bound to protect this order, be it by way of strict constitutional order (Art 20 GG) or by legal tradition.[15]

Parties to international commercial contracts, however, very often cannot be said to be part of the 'social sphere' (*Sozialsphäre*) of a particular state; in this particular context they act in a way which cannot be allocated to a specific country in the traditional way. This resembles very much the situation of the mediaeval *Hanse*, where merchants travelled far and wide setting up residences and trading posts in distant countries and could hardly be 'protected' by their country of origin.[16] Generally they were also strictly separated from the local community. They required their own legal cosmos since their domestic law could not be enforced where they required it. This led to the original development of *lex mercatoria* which was recognised by local governments who often mutually granted privileges to foreigners within their own territory, regardless of any strict jurisdiction claims.[17]

---

13 See above, Chapter 4, regarding string sales where the typical obligations of the sales contract – traditionally delivery of the goods – is of minuscule interest compared to the payment of the price (unless, of course, the goods are lost or damaged).

14 See above, Chapter 1, at 1.2.1.1.

15 See below for further discussion, eg, Chapter 7.

16 Compare U Ziegler, *Die Hanse – Aufstieg, Blütezeit und Niedergang der ersten europäischen Wirtschaftsgemeinschaft* (1996). The term *Hanse* was actually derived from an old English word for merchant.

17 Compare Goode, op cit (n 12) 27; see also Ziegler, op cit; L J Mustill, 'The New Lex Mercatoria: The First Twenty-Five Years', in Martin Bos and Ian Brownlie (eds), *Liber Amicorum for Lord Wilberforce*.

The determination of the 'characteristic performance' in a modern international commercial contract can hardly be established in a convincing way, anyway, looking at the various obligations created by such an agreement it is hard to justify giving priority to one of them. Why should the place of business of the seller regularly determine the law governing the contract rather than the seat of the buyer? In many commercial contracts there is a chain of buyers and sellers and the common purpose of commodities contracts may be its assignment, so that the actual delivery of goods might not be the 'characteristic' performance eventually. In barter contracts, joint ventures and financial services, this operation of establishing the 'characteristic performance' and localising the contract loses its attractiveness completely. It is worth considering, therefore, the recommendation of the application of a set of rules like the UPICC which are designed to meet the requirements of international trade and even addresses some special problems domestic law does not refer to.[18]

A certain 'advantage' regarding potential flexibility in dealing with international commercial contracts did exist in the German conflict law before the incorporation of the Rome Convention into German law in 1986. The law applicable to contractual obligations was to be determined by finding the 'hypothetical intention' of the parties. There was a rich and complicated system in use to determine this intention, which was not expressed in the contract, but to be derived from it by the judge.[19] The criterion of the closest connection was at least to be investigated by looking at different aspects of the contract. Under the Rome Convention the criterion is now pre-selected ('characteristic performance') although it allows exceptions in Art 4(5). Art 4(5) RC resembles the common law solution for establishing the 'most real' connection by granting discretionary room for deviation from the rule in Art 4(2) RC in case 'it appears from the circumstances as a whole that the contract is more closely connected with another country'. The emphasis is, however, on the country rather than on the system of law as at common law.

Overall, therefore, the wording of Art 4 RC gives so much room for exceptions from the 'characteristic performance' rule, that the question arises whether it would allow the original German, or the common law solution, to be applied.[20] Traditional German law used the seat or residence of the party performing the 'typical' obligation in a contract as an appropriate criterion for determining the law applicable to the contract, thus letting the parties' interests determine the applicable law, rather than a pre-defined legal policy. The common law solution seems to try to establish a more 'objective', ie, a fact orientated rather than intention orientated procedure to find the proper law. It seems that the wording of Art 4(5) RC comes closer to this common law approach.

---

[18] Frank Vischer recommends especially Art 6.1.14 and 2.22 UPICC: F Vischer, *Die Relevanz der UNIDROIT Principles für die richterliche und schiedsrichterliche Beurteilung von Streitigkeiten aus internationalen Verträgen* (1997) 16.

[19] See G Kegel and K Schurig, *Internationales Privatrecht* (2004) §18 I d.

[20] See below for further discussion and compare J Basedow, *German National Report on the UNIDROIT Principles of International Commercial Contracts* 125-150, 146-147.

The following section will discuss the ways in which the two domestic legal systems would allow the UPICC to be applied as being the proper law of the contract, in addition to being implied into the contract as part of contractual stipulations.

## 6.2 Current use of the UPICC: Experience in practice

The previous section, 6.1, looked at the *lex lata* and current scholarly positions in a general sense. This section explores the *lex lata* and current scholarly positions, ie, the attitude of national lawyers, in more detail. It asks specifically what the current position is regarding the source of law function of the UPICC and similar uniform law models for the use of the UPICC as governing law in cases involving commercial contracts.

On the XVth Congress on Comparative Law, held in Bristol, a broad account was given by the national reporters on the current use of the UPICC worldwide and on instances of their application in practice.[21] In January 1999 a symposium took place in Hamburg at the Max-Planck Institute for International and Foreign Law where the latest developments in the area of uniform law rules, and especially the UPICC, were discussed.[22] This should serve as a first reference for an investigation into the conflict of laws aspects of the UPICC in Germany and England. Another source of guidance is a review of selected cases which have been resolved using the UPICC either in a state court or in arbitration.

### 6.2.1 Source of law function of the UPICC in general legal doctrine

The paper delivered to the Hamburg symposium by C-W Canaris [23] on the legal nature of the UPICC and the PECL is of special interest in the context of this book. Canaris comments on the source of law function of the UPICC from within the German forum of discussion and gives account of recent developments. His contribution reflects the traditional and currently prevailing position under German law regarding the status of the UPICC from a conflict of laws perspective.[24]

---

[21] All available national reports and the General Report are published in M J Bonell, ed, *A New Approach to International Commercial Contracts* (1999).

[22] Contributions published in J Basedow, ed, *Europaeische Vertragsrechtsvereinheitlichung und deutsches Recht* (2000).

[23] C-W Canaris, *Die Stellung der 'UNIDROIT Principles' und 'Principles of European Contract Law' im System der Rechtsquellen* 5-31.

[24] Compare C v Bar and P Mankowski, *Internationales Privatrecht* 1 Allgemeine Lehren, 2003, §2 III, especially Nos 2 and 75: the authors emphasise their traditional position but concede that the UPICC might 'strengthen' into a source of law; G Kegel and K Schurig, *Internationales Privatrecht* (2000) §1 IX (d); Palandt and Heldrich, *Bürgerliches Gesetzbuch* (1998) Art 27 EGBGB No 3, fig 2(a); Palandt and Heldrich, *Bürgerliches Gesetzbuch* (2006) Art 27 EGBGB, No 3; R Goode et al, *Transnational Commer-*

His article draws on the views of a number of influential writers on the subject and can therefore serve as a vehicle to explore the status quo, as well as the possibilities for further development of the German legal position in this respect. Furthermore, the position described in this article is to a great extent representative, not only of civil law jurisdictions, but also overlaps in parts with common law positions so that useful contributions for the development of a suitable doctrine of a-national law can be derived from it.

Along with most legal writers in Germany,[25] Canaris rejects the idea of the UPICC serving as the governing law under conflict rules (*kollisionsrechtliche Verweisung*/vocation). He recognises three different categories of sources of law (*Rechtsquellen*): *Rechtsgeltungsquellen*, *Rechtserkenntnisquellen* and *Rechtsgewinnungsquellen*. All of these form the law within a jurisdiction.

This catalogue of terms corresponds to English legal theory according to Professor Goode, who comments on the 'elements' (meaning sources of law in the context) forming the *lex mercatoria*:

> Some create law, some declare law, some are not themselves law but are sources of rights and some are evidence of law … This is the theory of the common law but it is recognised that in reality the existing law represents a framework within which the judge has a limited power to create law. [26]

Only formal rules of law however, which create law, can form the first category of sources of law mentioned by Canaris, *Rechtsgeltungsquellen*, because they have passed through the parliamentary legislation procedures according to constitutional rules. These sources possess direct authority in a strict 'specifically juridical' sense '*spezifisch juristisch*',[27] meaning that they are presupposed in any discussion about the law, not derived from any other concept.[28]

Because the UPICC are clearly not of this nature, they cannot serve as the proper law of the contract in Canaris' view.[29] They fail the 'test of pedigree' as Canaris puts it, quoting Dworkin.[30] The authority, which a legal norm has to have to qualify for this category of source of law, must be derived from an institutional organ competent to issue legal norms, so that the norm follows the maxim *auctoritas non veritas facit legem* which Canaris quotes after Hobbes' 'Leviathan'.[31] In Germany specifically, norms of this formal nature must necessarily be part of the

---

*cial Law: International Instruments and Commentary* (2004) 40; see also U Drobnig, 'The UNIDROIT Principles in the Conflict of Laws' Uniform Law Review 2/3 (1998) 385-295, 387, n 7 for further references.

25 See previous note.

26 R Goode, 'Usage and its Reception in Transnational Commercial Law' International and Comparative Law Quarterly 46 (1997) 1-36, 4 and n 7.

27 C-W Canaris, '*Die Stellung der 'UNIDROIT Principles' und 'Principles of European Contract Law' im System der Rechtsquellen*', 9.

28 Ibid.

29 Ibid, 13 and 17

30 Ibid, 13.

31 (1651) Chapter XXVI; see Canaris, op cit (n 27), 13.

whole of the 'hierarchy of norms', the *Stufenbau der Rechtsordnung*. This hierarchy is formed by the constitution at the top of the hierarchy and the institutions of legislative, judicial and administrative powers shaped under its provisions.

Although Canaris accepts the existence and legitimacy of other sources of law, which do 'not originate from formal legislation but are nevertheless of a legal nature' ('*nicht gesetzlicher Herkunft, gleichwohl aber rechtlicher Natur*'),[32] he does not see that any of these norms or legal rules qualify for their being considered the law applicable to a contract under Art 27 and 28 EGBGB and Art 3 and 4 of the Rome Convention. German law doubtlessly recognises sources of law which are not expressly laid down in formal legislation and does therefore not adhere to a strict positivistic concept. This is reflected in the constitution, in Art 20 III GG, which states that the courts are to observe '*Gesetz und Recht*', legislation and the law. Thus, there must be an 'extra-legislative' legal order, an *außergesetzliche Rechtsordnung* which has already been described by Wieacker.[33]

The term *Rechtsquelle* – literally translated as source of law – does not have a precisely defined meaning in German legal doctrine or legislation. Larenz makes it clear that *Rechtsquelle* is not the law itself but rather, describes its origins – the source conferring its normative function onto it; this normative function being the force of law, which is equally and objectively binding for everyone.[34] In this sense Larenz considers the term *Rechtsquelle* a misnomer. The real source of the law would be the act of formal legislation or, in the case of customary law, the manifesting common conviction of the validity of specific rules.[35] Nevertheless, the use of the term *Rechtsquelle* refers to all types of legal norms and other law rules in German legal discourse. There is legal discourse about the precise extent of the normative function of different forms of law[36] using inconsistent terminology and very differing results.[37] Hübner, for instance, distinguishes 'formal' and 'substantive' legal norms.[38] The prevailing view, however, distinguishes the effect of binding force of law of formal legislation from the non-binding quality of other legal notions, which may well be creating law as a practical effect (*Rechtsfortbildung*), such as usages of trade, judgments, different kinds of agreements or self-

32 Canaris, op cit (n 27), 10.

33 Franz Wieacker, *Gesetz und Richterkunst, Zum Problem der außergesetzlichen Rechtsordnung* (1957).

34 Compare K Larenz, *Allgemeiner Teil des Deutschen Bürgerlichen Rechts* (1983) 7: '*...Erscheinungsformen des...für alle geltenden objektiven Rechts...*'.

35 Ibid, 7 (I§1), note 13; see also Goode, op cit (n 26) for a comprehensive account of the development of trade usages into customary law.

36 See, for an introduction, Larenz, op cit (n 34) 7-14.

37 See for example the view of Meyer-Cording about voluntary submission of individuals under a legal regime and that of Fikentscher regarding the binding force of supreme court decisions, *Fallnormtheorie*, which effectively does make judgments a directly binding legal norm, meaning that they create law, while they are merely *Rechtserkenntnisquellen* Canaris' system, see W Fikentscher, *Methoden des Rechts* Vol IV 336 et seq, and Meyer-Cording, *Die Rechtsnormen* (1971) 70 et seq.

38 '*Gesetz im formellen und materiellen Sinn*', see H Hübner, *Allgemeiner Teil des Bürgerlichen Gesetzbuches* (1996) 16.

governing rules. Under this system only *Rechtsgeltungsquellen* are law, the other two types introduced by Canaris, *Rechtserkenntnisquellen* and *Rechtsgewinnungsquellen*, would not be law but could be called potential sources of law (if and when their substantive content materialise into the first category of sources of law).

### 6.2.2 Significance of the doctrines of sources of laws in practice

Admittedly this discussion introduces very abstract concepts and might at first sight appear confusing, rather than clarifying the legal nature of the UPICC. Indeed, German legal science undertakes great efforts to set up and distinguish clear cut categories in this field of legal theory. It seems an important foundation for the operation of law rules. A careful analysis of the practical side of the legal profession has shown, however, that the theoretical concept does not consistently reflect the practice of the application of the law.[39] Indeed, the theoretical concept as described by Canaris and others, may not be followed in practice because it might not live up to, or might completely ignore, the mechanisms of judicial practice and the complexity of the human decisions prior to the eventual delivery of a judgment. Court decisions sometimes amount to *Rechtgeltungsquellen* even in German law according to their practical impact,[40] rather than confining themselves to *Rechterkenntnisquellen.* After all, these instances are then called judge-made law, or *richterliche Rechtsfortbildung* in German. Although there is extensive reasoning and discourse about the borderlines between interpretation and creation of the law by the judges,[41] German court practice does not differ very much from that of other legal systems in that there is necessarily the creative determination of human individuals, the *homines judicantes*, behind each decision.[42] The *Rechtserkenntnisquelle* might therefore be but a confession. Judges do in fact strive to merely 'find' the law and not to create it themselves:

> A Common Law judge will say that he applies a principle already existing in the Common Law to the case ... A Continental judge will assert that he applies existing legal values which are to be found in the law ... The legal values are not invented: they are already there. [43]

[39] See O Lando, '*Homo judicans*' Uniform Law Review 2/3 (1998) 535-544, who draws on his own insights but also refers to both the Cornell project and the work of the Trento group under U Mattei and M Bussano; see also Chapter 2 (2.2.2.1).

[40] For example, the case law developed under §242 BGB with its numerous findings regarding pre-contractual liability, change of underlying circumstances, protection of the weaker party and consumers.

[41] See for an introductory account K Larenz, *Methodenlehre der Rechtswissenschaft* (1991) Chapter 5.

[42] See Lando, op cit (n 39) 541 and 542.

[43] Ibid, 542.

But this is not the entire reality of judicial decision-making. The ideal situation might in fact be but a convention; the fact that law rules sometimes exist over long periods of time and that they are sometimes quite general or vague in their wording ('open-textured') requires a considerable amount of interpretation. This can even be the purpose of the wording of statutes, especially in Germany and in the BGB, so as to make them adaptable to changing times.

In some cases there is no statute to guide [the judges]. They cannot refuse to decide, so they have to establish the rules and change them later as needed. The same applies when the statutes are unclear. Their true meaning will not emerge until the courts have spoken. Some statutory provisions are general clauses which expressly leave it to the courts to fill them in. And when the ancient statutes are interpreted to mean something quite different from what they actually say, this does not provoke the legislator. He sees it and tolerates it. [44]

This is a very useful account of the reality and practice of judicial decision making. It demonstrates the conflict between legal theory and practice. This insight devalues the category of *Rechtserkenntnisquelle* due to its lack of precise definition and practical relevance.

Continental Europe boasts a hierarchy of sources. Doctrines on this hierarchy as established by legal writers abound, but the judges have seen to it that no hierarchy can be rigidly maintained.[45]

This weakness of doctrine might provide the necessary space for the development of a method for the integration of rules like the UPICC, into domestic legal theory and practice.

It shows that there is no final and convincing determination or definition of the sources of law and that there is room for discussion. Due to the strong significance of doctrine in German law, it is therefore possible to attribute an appropriate space and position for the UPICC within German legal theory and practice by providing a convincing theoretical conception.[46]

The further discussion in this section therefore continues to follow the line of Canaris' considerations on the special occasion of the Hamburg symposium, and discusses the nature of the UPICC *de lege lata*, before discussing possible ways of integrating the UPICC into the theoretical conceptions of the German and English conflict of laws.

### 6.2.3 The UPICC in the traditional doctrine of sources of law

The non-legislative legal order to which Canaris refers, is formed by rules which derive authority from their persuasive force; *veritas non auctoritas facit legem.*

---

[44] Ibid.
[45] Ibid, 539.
[46] See Chapter 8 for further discussion.

These can also be *Rechtsgeltungsquellen* in Canaris' system[47] and would therefore also qualify as *Vertragsstatut*. The required degree of persuasive force, however, is only recognised in single individual norms within the UPICC (and the PECL) by Canaris; he does not attribute this quality to the whole set of rules.[48]

Other than Basedow,[49] Canaris purports to the view that only state legislation – the law of a country rather than 'a legal system' – can form the *Vertragsstatut*; the law applicable to the contract, because exclusively the law of a state can be employed by virtue of the conflict of law rules. Particular instances, where parties to a contract seek clarification before a state court, provide an argument for Canaris to require state law to be applied to an international contract under the conflict of law rules.[50]

The admission of the UPICC as a mere private set of rules would mean allowing the parties to escape from the law of any state and submit their affairs exclusively to a private set of rules. Canaris reminds us that to accept such a solution would mean to apply Art 27 I EGBGB to any other potentially lesser kind of 'soft law', which could be much less of a masterpiece, which is what he sees in the UPICC and PECL.[51]

Canaris does, however, recognise the UPICC to be applied directly in arbitration under §1051 III ZPO. This provision allows the arbitrator to stipulate the applicable law under considerations of reasonableness (*Billigkeitsentscheidung*).[52] Canaris rejects the view that the UPICC could be applied directly to a contract under §1051 I ZPO mentioning *Rechtsnormen*, legal norms, because he does not regard the UPICC as formal legal norms.

The other two categories of legal sources, *Rechtserkenntnisquelle* and *Rechtsgewinnungsquelle* are both attributed to the UPICC by Canaris. The first category comprises judgments, as they confirm what the law is. Restatements would also fall into this category. The latter category is a more contour-less one. It describes legal reasoning and legal theory. 'General principles of law' would certainly fall within it, also comparative legal argumentation.[53] Canaris sees elements of both types of sources of law in the UPICC. Where the UPICC are more than just the strict 'common core' of the legal systems which served as a basis for the Principles, they should be regarded as a *Rechtsgewinnungsquelle*.[54]

The recognition of the UPICC as a source of law, however, does not make them automatically a suitable legal instrument to govern international contractual disputes before national courts. The option of including the UPICC by the parties as contractual terms does not necessarily lead to an unqualified application of the

---

47 C-W Canaris, '*Die Stellung der 'UNIDROIT Principles' und 'Principles of European Contract Law' im System der Rechtsquellen*', 12

48 Ibid, 14: Canaris does not mention any particular rules of the UPICC expressly.

49 See 6.6.3.1 and 6.7.1.2, below.

50 C-W Canaris, '*Die Stellung der 'UNIDROIT Principles' und 'Principles of European Contract Law' im System der Rechtsquellen*', 17.

51 Ibid, 19, 26 and 28.

52 See Chapters 7 and 8 for further discussion.

53 Canaris, op cit (n 50), 17.

54 Ibid.

whole comprehensive set of rules, according to Canaris, but might rather, subject the UPICC to the AGBG,[55] the law protecting against unfair contractual terms.[56]

## 6.3 Consequences under the prevailing view regarding the UPICC as governing law

The previous sections, 6.1 and 6.2, mainly recapitulated in a descriptive way the current positions in current legislation, case law and doctrine regarding the source of law function of the UPICC. The following section 6.3 asks what consequences can be derived from these observations and the given set up in modern national conflict of laws. It investigates possible solutions from a doctrinal point of view in general conflict doctrine.

Overall, Canaris explains that under the current status quo of the theoretical foundations relating to sources of law, the UPICC definitely fulfil the criteria of legal norms in Germany, but that they cannot *de lege lata* be applied to international contracts as the governing law of the contract, as *Vertragsstatut, kollisionsrechtliche Verweisung* or vocation. As contractual stipulations they would be subject to mandatory German law and could therefore not necessarily apply as a whole comprehensive set of rules. As a result, Canaris seems to assume that in certain instances individual rules within the UPICC can serve as a source of law in the extra-legislative sense, as a so-called *Rechtsgewinnungsquelle*, where legal argumentation and further reasoning is sought perhaps based on a gap-filling function of the UPICC.[57] The other instance would be where the Principles doubtlessly restate the 'common core', of a number of (national) legal systems, rather than adding any novel notions or ideas of their creators; a group of scientists who lack legislative competence.[58] Here, the UPICC would qualify as a *Rechtserkenntnisquelle*.

### 6.3.1 Considerations permitting further evolution of the UPICC towards sources of law

Although this results in a very restricted role of the UPICC as sources of law before national courts, Canaris nevertheless emphasises the superior qualification of

[55] AGBG: *AGB-Gesetz – Gesetz zur Regelung des Rechts der Allgemeinen Geschäftsbedingungen* (Law regulating Standard Terms) of 9 December 1976, now integrated into the BGB (§§305-310), incorporating EC Directive 93/13/EWG of 5 April 1993, regulating Unfair Contract Terms. For text, see Palandt and Heinrichs, *Bürgerliches Gesetzbuch* (2001); for new BGB provisions, see *Aktuelle Wirtschaftsgesetze* 2002, 55-62.

[56] In case the UPICC were only stipulated by one party unilaterally, which is unlikely, compare Canaris, op cit (n 50), 21-23.

[57] Ideally, the national law should have a gap-filling function. See Chapters 7 and 8 for examples in practice and theory.

[58] Canaris, op cit (n 50), 19.

the creators of the UPICC and thus their 'persuasive force', so that certainly *veritas non auctoritas facit legem* in this case, or following Kötz and Drobnig, they derive validity '*imperio rationis*' rather than '*ratione imperii*'.[59]

Canaris does refer to the UPICC as a *Regelwerk*, a set of rules, but still only seems to conceive of individual legal rules within this set, which can be and sometimes have to be, assessed and applied regardless of their comprehensive context, eg, in instances where either the attributes of 'restatement' or 'alternative legal solution' are identified. He discusses instances of conflicting substantive solutions under German national law and the UPICC, and concludes that the UPICC might be considered to offer novel solutions to specific areas in German law where the *lex lata* is too vague and lacking uniformity.[60] He accepts a potential beneficial influence through the persuasive force of some of the solutions offered in the UPICC on German national law, and even recognises that this question has as yet attracted very little attention within scientific discussion.[61]

Basedow, on the other hand, recognises that the UPICC require a genuinely new approach in legal doctrine, and comments in his National Report for the XVth International Congress of Comparative Law:

> The traditional approach in German law ... would be to characterise the Principles as forming part of a certain group of norms – statutes, conventions, customary law, commercial usages and practices – and to draw conclusions from the respective place in the hierarchy of legal norms. Such an investigation would be of little avail, however, since it would be clear from the very beginning that the UNIDROIT Principles do not fit into any of the traditional categories. Their normative quality can only be assessed by a new theoretical reflection. It has to cross the traditional borderline between law and fact, and it must overcome the positivistic concept that law making is an exclusive prerogative of the state to the effect that normative texts can only produce a binding effect if they have been approved in the proper constitutional way.' [62]

The legitimation of the UPICC functioning as a potential novel source of law must be derived from their broad acceptance:

> '... it should be clear that the constitutional enactment can only be dispensed with if a certain text is supported by the broad approval of those applying the law and of those who are subject to it.'[63]

---

59 Heinrich Kötz, '*Gemeineuropäisches Zivilrecht*' in *Festschrift für Zweigert* (1981) 492; Ulrich Drobnig, '*Ein Vertragsrecht für Europa' in Festschrift für Steindorf* 1990) 1151.

60 Canaris, op cit (n 50), 27 and 31. The examples concerned question the extent of the liability for *culpa in contrahendo*, the breach of pre-contractual duties and its relationship to §123BGB, the avoidance of the contract for reasons of mistake and fraud.

61 Ibid, 27. A similar contradictory attitude is taken by P Manowski, 'Rechtswahl für Verträge des internationalen Wirtschaftverkehrs' RIW 1 (2003) 11 and 12; see Chapter 8 for further discussion, eg, 8.2.3.4.

62 J Basedow, 'The UNIDROIT Principles of International Commercial Contracts and German Law' (1998 Conference Paper), published as J Basedow, *German National Report on the UNIDROIT Principles of International Commercial Contracts* 128.

63 Ibid.

This seems to be a different condition than that postulated by Canaris, who accepts only those rules of the UPICC which can be said to be a pure essence of a variety of legal systems.[64] Basedow's idea is to derive legitimacy from the consensus among legal subjects, rather than from the origin of the legal norms. The UPICC would gain acceptance to the degree of normative effect from their use, and 'general approval by commercial circles and their lawyers'.[65] This again refers to the persuasive force of the UPICC which appear to be the most prominent category of a formative aspect, for sources of law in respect of the UPICC.

### 6.3.2 Suggested focus of research to establish the origin of source of law function of the UPICC

In my view the main novelty and important formative part of the persuasive force of the UPICC is the fact that they are designed as a comprehensive set of rules. These rules can be applied in a consistent way, which has been shown in Part 2 of this study in one specific instance.[66]

The legitimation of their application should be derived from the specific nature of their subject; international commercial contracts. Even though the UPICC might not serve to find, and establish, the gap in the legislation as Canaris criticises,[67] they certainly should have a gap-filling role. The gap in the law seems to be the lack of recognition of specific needs of parties to international commercial contracts, and the failure of legislators to refer to international commercial contracts as an emerging species of legal concept.[68] The gap originates from the factual sphere, not from the sphere of substantive law.

The result of the recent German reform of the law of obligations has shown that international model laws, or restatements such as the UPICC, have still not had a convincing influence on the process of drafting modern rules. Although the German legislator was prepared (and probably forced), to implement the novel notion of 'consumer' into the BGB, no need was seen for the introduction of the international contract as special type of contract. This reform therefore was in fact pursued *ratione imperii,*[69] since it was effected following EU Directives and thus institutional law rather than an adaptation to modern trade developments. The longstanding Anglo-American influence on uniform laws such as the CISG, and sub-

---

64 'Quantitative method'; compare F D Ly, 'Dutch National Report', 232 and see below.

65 Ibid. This is in line with Professor Goode's view in Goode, op cit (n 12), 4 and 8 et seq. Also see Chapter 7.

66 See also Chapter 7 for an example in arbitration.

67 Canaris, op cit (n 50), 7.

68 Compare 7.3, 7.3.2, and 8.4, below.

69 Especially taking the pragmatic view of Prof Dieter Medicus into account, who, in his preface to the 2002 edition of *Neues Schuldrecht: Genegnüberstellung BGB neu-alt mit Nebemgesetzen* at p XI, remarks that there is a legitimate interest of the rulers to finish what they have begun ('*ein legitimes Intersses der jeweils Herrschenden ... das Begonnene zu Ende zu führen*').

sequently the PECL and the UPICC, by way of the notion of breach of contract, which has led to the development of the notion of 'non-performance' in uniform law, has now resulted in the creation of the notion of '*Pflichtverletzung*', breach of 'duty' or 'obligation' in the BGB. This concept might, or might not, be an adaptation to, or integration of, 'international' standards. It seems to be at best an attempt to combine the idea of a network of obligations in the tradition of the civil law with the Anglo-American conception of the contract as a more wholesome entity, which offers more simplicity as regards its 'breach'.

At worst it might be a misunderstanding of these models, or a confusing *aliud*, hence another peculiarity and certainly no assimilation to and not inspired by current international drafts of contract law.[70]

It is submitted that there is a need for reform and updating of existing legal solutions. A set of rules such as the UPICC should be considered as a legitimate source of law where there is no legal environment provided by national law, even before national courts. A draft provided by an independent study group, as is the case with the UPICC and the PECL, certainly has a novel persuasive force *imperio rationis*.

Certainly, the model of the UPICC should not suggest that assimilation of national contract law to 'international standards' is a goal in its own right.[71] But it ought to be, or rather has always been, a goal to provide for specific rules relating to specific circumstances, and following globalisation of trade there should be the recognition of 'globalised' commercial contracts in national legislation and legal proceedings.[72]

It is therefore my submission that a gap in national law exists where national contract law fails to recognise specific requirements of parties to international contracts, and that the UPICC should serve as a source of law complete as a comprehensive set of rules in those instances. This source of law has the quality of a lex specialis applying to the special contract type of international commercial contract. The effort of establishing legal categories should focus on developing the category of international commercial contracts, in addition to that of the nature of the UPICC as a (national) source of law. Definitions can be developed starting from the ones provided by Art 1 CISG and, eg, the collection of transactions listed by Labes and Lörcher in their edition of the 1985 UNCITRAL Model Law on In-

[70] See J Kohler, '*Rechtsezung im demokratischen Rechtsstaat und Rechtswissenschaft – Anmerkungen zu Stil und Bedeutung neuerer Gesetzgebung*' in *Kritische Vierteljahresschrift für Gesetzgebung und Rechtswissenschaft* 4 (2002) 381. Giving examples of further flaws in style in recent German legislation and explaining the importance of consistency due to the significance of the systemic form and position of a rule within the German method of statutory interpretation: '*Systemgenauigkeit ist daher nicht nur eine Angelegenheit des Stils, sondern der Rechtessubstanz*'. ('Systematic correctness is therefore a matter not only of style but of legal substance.')

[71] And should certainly not merely serve to promote new marketing strategies in academic carriers as is criticised by Manowski, '*Rechtswahl für Verträge des internationalen Wirtschaftverkehrs*' RIW 1 (2003) 13, col 1.

[72] See Chapter 8 for discussion of the law merchant in Germany.

ternational Arbitration.[73] National law should then serve to fill the gaps of the more specific rules of the UPICC.

This method does not mean to suggest a hierarchy of norms where the international set of rules prevail, but to assume a qualitative ranking, a logical order on the substantive level.

The main problem corrupting the persuasive force of the UPICC is actually the habit of using them as a quarry for legal solutions and answers where national laws, including conflict rules do not offer a convincing solution. The tendency is to use only individual rules rather than applying the whole set.[74] Canaris seems to adhere to this method by attaching two different categories of source of law to different parts of the UPICC, depending on when the UPICC are definitely purely a restatement, and when they might be the product of original 'legislation' by their creators.[75]

Perhaps Basedow's view is similar to that of Lookofsky, expressed in the National Report presented by Denmark on the reception of the UPICC to the XVth International Congress of Comparative Law; that the UPICC can contribute to a process of:

> progressive (rule-improving) harmonisation by consent, a clearly stated alternative to the more wooden, lowest-common-denominator kind of unification …[76]

It seems that the more traditional view expressed by Canaris does not consider the possibility of the emergence of a novel process of law-making, a modern type of 'legal formant' in the sense of Rodolfo Sacco.[77] Modern legal science and doctrine should observe and analyse this process open-mindedly and ought to help to prepare the ground for a successful outcome of this process by optimising the theoretical foundations in the interest of the commercial community.

The basic properties of the UPICC are nevertheless well acknowledged even by the more traditional view in German legal science, of which Canaris can certainly be taken as a suitable representative; he does see the persuasive force of the Principles, especially in terms of quality of the legal material, its consistency and its creators. Although he attributes a source-of-law-function to the UPICC, he still cannot prepare the ground for a sphere of application within national law. This is

---

[73] H W Labes and T Lörcher, ed, *Nationales und Internationales Schiedsverfahrensrecht* (1998) 185, n 3.

[74] This is the case in most court decisions referring to the UPICC, for example in order to confirm that good faith is a general rule of international law, although usually this technique is inevitable due to the facts of the case, compare Part 2, especially Chapter 3.

[75] Compare Canaris, op cit (n 50), 16 and 31. This corresponds to the treatment the UPICC received from the ICC tribunal in case No 7110 (see Chapter 7, 7.2).

[76] J Lookofsky, *Danish National Report on the UNIDROIT Principles of International Commercial Contracts*, 77.

[77] See R Sacco, 'Legal Formants: a dynamic approach to comparative law: Instalment I of II', American Journal of Comparative Law 39 (1991) 1 and R Sacco, 'Legal Formants: a dynamic approach to comparative law: (Instalment II)', American Journal of Comparative Law 29 (1991) 343.

because there is a missing link to bridge the gap between the *Rechtsgeltungsquelle*, ie, formal legislation and customary law, and the other two types of sources of law, the *Rechtserkenntnisquelle* and the *Rechtsgewinnungsquelle*.

This missing link has to be developed by an active complementary research-based doctrine and practice.

## 6.4 Conclusion

Although not clearly admitted in conflict of laws legislation, the UPICC are attached to a source of law function even under traditional legal doctrine. This applies especially due to their high degree of consistency and comprehensiveness as well as the high quality of the drafting technique. A gap in national law exists where national contract law fails to address specific requirements of parties to international contracts. The UPICC should serve as a source of law complete, as a comprehensive set of rules, in those instances. This source of law has the quality of a lex specialis applying to the special contract type of international commercial contracts. The effort of establishing legal categories should be focused on developing the category of international commercial contracts, in addition to that of the nature of the UPICC as a (national) source of law. Definitions can be based on Art 1 CISG and the 1985 UNCITRAL Model Law on International Arbitration.[78]

[78] H W Labes and T Lörcher, eds, *Nationales und Internationales Schiedsverfahrensrecht* (1998) 185, n 3.

# 7 Methods of integration in the general conflict of laws

While the previous chapter reviewed the status quo of current national conflict law regarding the position of uniform contract law, this chapter asks what suggestions have been made by scholars and in legal practice that would allow the UPICC to be applied to international contracts and disputes, as the law governing the contract – applying as a whole set of rules.

The chapter first reviews suggestions and theories taken from current legislation, by scholars who support the view that the UPICC have a source of law quality (section 7.1). It then looks at what answers can be found in arbitration to the question of the UPICC' source of law function (section 7.2). The last section (7.3) looks at those suggested choice of law methods which are based on traditional conflict law doctrine, such as complementary choice of national laws and the theory of gaps in uniform law, and asks whether these can succeed in introducing uniform law. The chapter concludes with the author's suggestions on how to achieve a more successful legal environment for the use of uniform law, within the national conflict of law rules (section 7.4).

## 7.1 Review of the current discussion regarding the status of transnational law

This section asks what has been put forward by scholars in order to overcome the traditional rejection of the UPICC as a source of law and as serving as governing law for international commercial contracts. This question is more specifically pointed towards the use of the UPICC as *lex contractus* compared to the investigations of the previous chapter (Chapter 6). The chapter investigates theoretical suggestions supporting the use of uniform law as governing law, which are based on the traditional approach described above (also, Chapter 6).

A number of suggestions have been put forward regarding giving effect to the UPICC as the law governing international contracts before state courts, by way of '*kollisionsrechtliche Verweisung*' or vocation (according a to choice of law clause by the parties) as '*Vertragsstatut*' (absent choice of law and by choice of the judge or arbitrator).

The UPICC have of course, received widespread interest and recognition in international legal science. Merely taking into account that 17 National Reports were received from all over the world in response to the questionnaire preparing the 1998 Congress of Comparative Law, demonstrates that the UPICC receive attention virtually worldwide.[1] Out of these, a few comments by civil lawyers on legal theory and practice might contribute to the formation of a modern approach to handling international contractual disputes by employing transnational rules.

### 7.1.1 Art 3 RC

Katharina Boele-Woelki[2] suggested allowing parties to stipulate the UPICC as the law governing their contract by extending an argument used by the Dutch Supreme Court; parties to a contract were allowed under the Rome Convention to submit their contract to the 1956 CMR Convention,[3] and a general rule was derived from this decision saying that parties to a contract can choose any international uniform law convention to govern their contract regardless of whether this convention would otherwise be applicable according to its scope. Boele-Woelki suggests that this choice be extended to other uniform law rules. Even under the regime of the Rome Convention, Dutch legal writers maintain that parties can choose any international uniform law convention as the law governing their contract.[4]

> Uniform rules that are both coherent and indicate ways of filling possible lacunae – and the Principles meet both these requirements – may be chosen by the parties as the law governing the contract, in the sense that that system of law which would have been applicable had no choice been made, is substituted in its entirety, including the mandatory rules it may encompass, by the designated uniform law.[5]

Boele-Woelki conceives this argument as a 'broad interpretation of Art 3 of the 1980 Rome Convention'.[6] Such a broad interpretation is supported by another Dutch author who comments that if parties can choose a national law which is completely unrelated to their contract or their own places of business or residence, they must be allowed to choose conventions covering the substance of their contract.[7] This idea seems to bridge the gap between the narrower interpretation of Art 3 RC (that only state law can be the governing law) and the view that a-national law should be an option to choice of law by the parties before a state

---

[1] See M J Bonell, 'General Report', 1-17, 2.

[2] K Boele-Woelki, 'Principles and Private International Law' Uniform Law Review 4 (1996) 652-678.

[3] Decision of 26 May 1989, published in NJ 1990, 105. The Netherlands have been a party to this Convention since 1961.

[4] Boele-Woelki, op cit (n 2), 665.

[5] Ibid, 666.

[6] Ibid.

[7] Ibid, 666, quoting L Strikwerda in '*Kroniek van het internationaal privaatrecht*' NJ 1996, 411-412

court. This view draws on the formal and official qualities of conventions, regardless of whether or not they are in force in the state of the forum in any given case.

This view has been criticised by Professor Goode[8] who remarks that because not every draft convention gets ratified by any particular state and eventually enters into force, the application of its provisions might indeed contravene the intentions of these states and thus not at all carry the required formal legal authority. Goode however, distinguishes between national judges and arbitrators, the latter having the liberty to try a case with convention rules forming the governing law of the contract. One such example is an ICC case, decided in 1989,[9] where the Tribunal applied the Vienna Sales Convention, although at the time of the conclusion of the contract this had not been published and not long ratified. This served to establish a trade usage relating to examination of the goods in due time in international sales.

Professor Basedow supports the view that the UPICC can be chosen as governing law under Art 3 RC, because party autonomy is of such fundamental importance under the RC that it cannot be limited by a restricting interpretation of Art 3(1) RC. Such an interpretation is often based on Art 7 RC which strengthens the application of certain mandatory rules of individual signatory states. This would however, according to Basedow, be sufficiently guaranteed by an appropriate interpretation of Art 7(1) RC in conjunction with Art 1.4 UPICC, which confirm the application of domestic mandatory rules.

### 7.1.2 No source of law function without state legislation

Basedow implicitly ignores in his argumentation the conventional understanding of the term 'law' – referring to formal legislation and state law, as opposed to 'rules of law', which allow for including 'other', a-national law such as the UPICC. Indeed, this understanding of 'law' ought to be subject to re-discussion. There is, however, a high degree of 'consent' within legal writings on the use of this terminology.

The UPICC however, are not vested with any more authority by Basedow's argument based on Art 3 RC, than the persuasive force of their quality and comprehensiveness which they entail. The lack of legitimation through state legislation cannot be overcome by this argumentation.

Most authors therefore accept that the UPICC cannot be the law governing the contract in countries where the RC is in force and that this is the generally accepted prevailing and traditional approach. [10]

[8] R Goode, 'Usage and its Reception in Transnational Commercial Law' International and Comparative Law Quarterly 46 (1997) 1-36, 24.

[9] ICC case No 5713, partly reported in (1990) XX ICC A Y B 70, in Jarvin et al, 'Collection of ICC Arbitral Awards', Vol II, 223.

[10] U Drobnig, 'The UNIDROIT Principles in the Conflict of Laws' Uniform Law Review 2/3 (1998) 385-295, 391; Boele-Woelki, op cit (n 2) 664; M J Bonell, 'The UNIDROIT Principles of International Contracts and CISG – Alternatives or Complementary Instruments?' Uniform Law Review 1 (1996) 26-39, 38; M J Bonell, 'The UNIDROIT

There are a few German authors, however, who contest this interpretation of Art 3 and 4 of the Rome Convention and who attribute source of law functions to the UPICC which make them a suitable option for governing international commercial contracts.

### 7.1.3 Party autonomy as source of law

J C Wichard[11] bases his argument on the motivations behind the traditional conception in German choice of law rules. These manifest in two theses: 1. Only a state can create a law which protects equally and fairly the interests of parties to a contract and which provides legal certainty and is comprehensive enough; 2. Only state law rules are 'law' in the sense incorporated in Art 3 RC and Art 28 EGBGB because only law rules – as recognised by a sovereign state – can be enforced by a state. Other law rules are applied by way of equitable and arbitrary decisions which state courts are not allowed to do. Regarding the second statement, Wichard also reminds us that party autonomy itself is conferred and guaranteed by the state through Art 27 I EGBGB. The state is free to grant the choice of a-national law, and rules of a-national law are in fact enforced by state courts indirectly by way of arbitral awards based on a-national law rules such as the *lex mercatoria*, including the UPICC.[12] With regard to the first statement, Wichard refers to the substantive quality of the UPICC, namely their comprehensiveness and the fact that they can derive authority from a thoroughly prepared draft in a similar way to that in which the *ius commune* used to operate for a long time in European jurisdictions, as *ratio scripta*.[13]

More important than the formal observation of actual enforcement of a-national law in a state, is Wichard's argument that the purpose of choice of law rules is not the protection of the interest of a state to apply its own law, but rather the idea of letting the parties find the best law to govern their contract according to subjective considerations.[14] The idea behind this 'political' choice is that the parties know the best way of regulating their own affairs and that they will find the correct balance between competing interests. This argument is supported by the fact that parties are free to choose the law of any country, even if it is totally unrelated to themselves and their contract, and even if their contract is purely domestic.

---

principles of international commercial contracts: Why? What? How?' Tulane Law Review 69.5 (1995) 1121-1147, 1144; F Ferrari: 'Defining the sphere of application of the 1994 "UNIDROIT principles of international commercial contracts"' Tulane Law Review 69 (1995) 1225-1237, 1231, 1232; Goode, op cit (n 8), 28.

11 J C Wichard, '*Die Anwendung der UNIDROIT– Prinzipien für internationale Handelsverträge durch Schiedsgerichte und nationale Gerichte*' *Rabels Zeitschrift für ausländisches und internationales Privatrecht* 60 (1996) 269-301.

12 See Chapters 7 and 8, below.

13 Wichard, op cit (n 11), 283.

14 Compare the discussion referred to above at 1.2.1.2 and note the similarity of this opinion to the one expressed by Collier in J G Collier, *Conflict of laws* (2001) 385.

### 7.1.4 Substantive argument

It is obvious that law rules such as the UPICC should be regarded as the preferable choice of law when compared with the law of a country which none of the parties knows anything about and which is usually chosen simply for reasons of neutrality. This is true from the point of view of protection of the parties' interests, such as fairness and balance of rights.[15] To the extent that a state doctrine sets out to protect these interests by way of exclusively admitting state law to govern the contract, the UPICC must prevail on the ground of the quality of their substantive solutions.

The question of the doctrine behind private law rules as such, and the relationship between the state and the private individual as a contracting party, is dealt with above in Chapter 1.

## 7.2 Arbitration awards as source of law: ICC case No 7110

The previous section, 7.1, introduced scholarly opinions which suggest ways of using the UPICC as governing law in conflict cases. This section asks how case law, and specifically arbitration disputes, can provide an answer to the question of uniform law as a source of law in matters of international commercial contracts. Specific tension is added to this discussion in the context of absence of choice of law. The traditional view exclusively applies conflict of law rules in order to find the applicable (state) law. Other views want to derive an implicit choice of a-national rules of law. An intermediate case occurs where the parties choose 'general principles of law', the *lex mercatoria* or the like, to govern their contract. This choice of law might not lead to the acceptance of a-national law as *Vertragsstatut*, or the law applicable to the contract, but it can be conceived as a deliberate exclusion of national laws ('negative choice of law') for reasons of neutrality.

A rewarding example for the treatment of such a choice of law and the subsequent successful application of the UPICC takes the form of a sequence of two partial arbitration awards which were introduced and analysed at the 1998 Bristol Comparative Law Congress by Professor de Ly, from Rotterdam.[16] De Ly comments on ICC case No 7110, Partial Award of 13 July 1995 and Partial Final Award No 2 rendered on 4 May 1998 in The Hague. At the time of de Ly's report, the quantum stage of the case was still pending.[17]

---

[15] In a substantive sense, not in terms of procedural fairness and guarantees, see Chapter 8 below, eg, 8.2.3.6.

[16] Filip de Ly, 'Dutch National Report on the UPICC', published in M J Bonell (ed), *A New Approach to International Commercial Contracts* (1999) 203-235.

[17] The cases are unpublished and Professor de Ly reported the issues in his capacity as counsel and expert witness for the parties.

The case concerned a series of contracts between an English company and a Middle Eastern State party, a trading agency. The terms of the contract, or rather several (nine) contracts, contained no express stipulation of any municipal law but instead referred to 'natural justice' and 'laws of natural justice'.[18] The conflict of laws issues were discussed extensively by the parties, so that useful considerations could be recorded.

### 7.2.1 Application of the UPICC and general principles of law under procedural aspects

The important aspect in the reasoning of the Arbitral Tribunal in these proceedings is the treatment of the choice of law clauses in the contracts.

The prevailing domestic legal doctrine relating to the choice of law and party autonomy does not accept general principles of law to govern the contract absent choice of law for the reasons explained above so far. Also, the assumption that the parties want to deliberately exclude municipal laws from governing their contract, by either not mentioning any national law, or by referring to general principles of law, the *lex mercatoria* or similar, is not accepted in legal science and practice because of the general rejection of the criterion of 'the implicit, implied, presumed or hypothetical intention of the parties'.[19] Such a choice would not lead to the appropriate law with enough certainty, so that prevailing conflict of laws doctrines – at least after the enactment of the RC in various countries – try to follow 'objective' criteria, such as the closest connection or characteristic performance test.[20]

Therefore, the Preamble of the UPICC does not contain the express option that the Principles should apply in the absence of an express choice of law by the parties, but does state that they are to apply if the parties have so chosen. This was a deliberate decision taken by the Unidroit Governing Council taking controversial positions in various legal systems into account.

### 7.2.2 Construction of choice of law clause

In this award, however, the Tribunal interpreted the contract clauses by also referring to the negotiation process, and managed to arrive at the conclusion that the parties deliberately wanted to exclude national laws from their contract settlement procedures by also deliberately opting for arbitral adjudication. Since the facts of the case provided enough reasons to conclude that general principles of law were to govern the contracts, the Tribunal overall presented the following two propositions as formulated by de Ly:

---

[18] de Ly, op cit (n 16), 217.

[19] Ibid, 219.

[20] Compare 6.1.4, above.

1. Natural justice – language in choice of law clauses without references to municipal law is a strong indication that the parties wanted a neutral non-national law to apply. Thus, general principles and Unidroit Principles may be applied.
2. Absent a choice of law clause, the law governing State Contracts is general principles of law and the Unidroit Principles.[21]

Arbitrators may follow these maxims on two grounds; the state law allowing them to apply general principles of law regardless of municipal conflict rules[22] (*voie directe*), and the general authorisation of the parties submitting their dispute to arbitration. As is shown exemplarily in this award, the arbitrators base their argument on the 'consensual starting point of arbitration'[23] and can therefore specifically derive their argument from the construction contract clauses in conjunction with the negotiation process. The subjective component which is employed is thereby better shielded against the criticism it has received in the traditional and modern (ie, post RC) conflict doctrine. The argument takes into account the need for the award to persuade the parties so that they accept it and neither challenge nor subject it to setting aside procedures afterwards.

The general acceptance and success of Arbitral Awards demonstrates that this effect is legitimate, very typical for and an important factor of, arbitral adjudication. It is obvious that such a solution is justified in cases of a contract clause referring to general principles which de Ly describes convincingly as 'natural justice language', but less so in cases where no choice of law and no such clause is present at all. An important factor is of course also the involvement of a State party, where the requirement of neutrality of the applicable law, as well as the concern that one State does not want to submit itself to the law of another state, is an obvious criterion of contract drafting.[24]

### 7.2.2.1 Scope of the UPICC according to their Preamble

Another more procedural aspect of the application of the UPICC to the substance of the contract is the interpretation of their Preamble. It seems to be common ground that although the Preamble does not mention this *voie directe*, absent choice of law, the Principles cannot determine their own scope of application:

> As a non-binding instrument, the intention of the drafters can be helpful to determine the objectives of their venture but cannot by itself determine its scope of application.[25]

Thus the final procedural stepping stone on the way to a direct and comprehensive application of the UPICC as law governing the contract can be formulated as follows:

---

21 de Ly, op cit (n 16), 225. Compare also 8.2.3.8, below.
22 See Chapter 8 for further discussion.
23 de Ly, op cit (n 16), 219.
24 Compare also Chapter 8.
25 de Ly, op cit (n 16), 224.

[2.] The Unidroit Principles cannot decisively determine their own criteria for application. The Preamble of the Unidroit Principles (as amended by the Unidroit Council) does not control and does not prevent arbitrators to make their own determinations on the basis of the arbitration agreement and the application rules. [26]

#### *7.2.2.2 Substantive aspects supporting application of UPICC*

On the substantive side, the Tribunal took into account that criticism is often made regarding the potential clash of the UPICC (or any other a-national law) with national laws, in particular with so-called mandatory rules of law. For German law this could be certain provisions of the AGBG (now incorporated into the BGB). For the UK it could be provisions of the Unfair Contract Terms Act. Although the UPICC contain mandatory rules themselves (eg, Art 1.7(2)), and they expressly refrain from excluding municipal mandatory rules of law (Art 1.4), the possibility of their being subject to modification by national law is generally considered enough reason for abstaining from employing them in contract conflicts.[27] In addition, national mandatory rules are deemed to provide a superior quality of protection within their intended scope compared to the UPICC.[28] The Tribunal reasoned as follows in the case discussed here, as reported by Professor de Ly:

[1.] A clash between the Unidroit Principles and municipal legal systems is unlikely because the parties did not want municipal laws to apply. For that reason, the Unidroit Principles can be applied in the absence of a choice of law provision in the contract without this being a threat to municipal legal systems; … [29]

The second substantive reason for the application of the UPICC is, of course their comprehensiveness, accessibility and the quality of the solutions they offer:

[5.] The Unidroit Principles are clearly articulated and are organised in a coherent and systematic way. Thus, rather than providing vague rules and general guidelines, their very nature makes them well fit for application to concrete cases.

[1.] … They were made by a distinguished group of international experts coming from the most important legal systems of the world who are independent from states or governments. Thus, the Unidroit Principles are characterised by high quality and neutrality. Furthermore, the Unidroit Principles reflect the present stage of consensus regarding international legal rules and principles with respect to contracts and particularly express fairness and provide appropriate solutions for international contractual problems. [30]

---

[26] Ibid, 225.

[27] See C-W Canaris, *'Die Stellung der 'UNIDROIT Principles' und 'Principles of European Contract Law' im System der Rechtsquellen'*, 21-27.

[28] Ibid, 26. Canaris' concern is, of course, related to the case that the UPICC could be incorporated into the contract by only one party. This is quite unlikely within the present context, and certainly following the construction method used by the Arbitral Tribunal in ICC case No 7110. See also below.

[29] de Ly, op cit (n 16), 225.

[30] Ibid, 223.

### 7.2.3 Application to the substance of the dispute

In particular, specific provisions of the UPICC were employed in the following way in the arbitral procedure. After the applicability of the UPICC was first decided by rendering the Partial Award on 13 July 1995, a second stage of the proceedings lead to Partial Final Award No 2 of 4 May 1998 upon a hearing in September 1997. In the course of this hearing the UPICC were orally discussed on nine counts, but only seven of them were discussed and reported in the Award. These drew on Arts 1.7, 2.18, 2.4, 7.1.3, 7.4.5, 7.4.8, and Chapter 4 on termination.

The discussions are included in this section because they demonstrate another example of how to apply the UPICC consistently and successfully to the substance of a dispute. The award also contains considerations relating to the source of law function and the legal nature of the UPICC on the part of the Arbitration Tribunal.

The considerations relating to the scope and value as source of law, which the Tribunal attributed to the UPICC in this instance, may amount to a contribution to the development of an integrated doctrine of the application of a-national law rules in Germany and England.[31]

#### *7.2.3.1 Primary or secondary sources of law? Ambiguous situation*

The Tribunal seemed to take quite an ambiguous view. One option was to regard the Principles as restatements rather than primary law. This means that the Principles would have only 'secondary authority' and would simply help to find general principles of law. The other option, attributing primary source of law qualities to the UPICC, is to be seen in the so called better law approach which is based on qualitative criteria. Rather than merely 'collecting' the views on a particular question of law in several jurisdictions and deriving general principles of law from them only if these are recognised in a number of them[32] (the so-called quantitative method), the latter method gives effect to the formulation of a rule of law which is drafted to achieve the best solution. Some of the rules in the UPICC are in fact of this nature according to the express report of its creators. Following the former approach the quantitative method, and considering the legitimacy of the UPICC as stemming from their being a restatement, means deciding individually for every single rule, whether or not it is a restatement or a conscious determination by its creators. According to this method the UPICC can obviously not be applied as a whole without more discussion, even in arbitration procedures where the arbitrators are *amiables compositeurs*, ie, ruling *ex aequo et bono*. It seems that even in these instances a very cautious approach prevails.

The Tribunal in ICC Case No 7110 took different views in single instances while deciding different questions of the dispute. There were instances where a

---

31 See Chapter 8 for further discussion of the role of arbitral awards as 'sources of law' in England.

32 And how would one select the relevant amount of jurisdictions and select which ones count?

contradiction was seen between rules of the UPICC and general principles of law, and there were other instances in which the Tribunal favoured one particular legal solution in fact as the better law.

### *7.2.3.2 Four counts of analysis of UPICC provisions*

The first question was one of limitation issue which was decisive for the further course of the proceedings. It was therefore discussed intensely. Had the decision to apply the UPICC to the facts of the case not been made in the preceding Partial Award, the Tribunal[33] – dealing with this next stage of the proceedings, the hearing in September 1997 – would perhaps have rather not taken this decision since the UPICC now faced the arbitrators with a gap.[34] It was resolved to be common ground that the UPICC do not deal with limitation issues, so that general principles of law had to be found. The Tribunal then dismissed the idea that a general principle of the application of time-limits was to be derived from a comparative view on a number of national laws. It also rejected the idea of deriving such a general principle from the 1974 New York Limitation Convention.[35] Another general principle, the one of an obligation to bring an action within a reasonable time span, was considered and the issue resolved relying on the facts of the case.[36] Whether this principle is backed by Art 1.7(2) UPICC, was not decided.

The next issue was decided by relying on Art 7.1.3 of the UPICC, stating that this provision reflected a general principle of law, namely the civil law concept of *exceptio non adimpleti contractus*. The formulation to be noted is: 'as confirmed by Art 7.1.3 of the UPICC'.[37] The discussion of this point continued with the defendant raising concerns about the seller having sold the (tailor-made) goods on, invoking his rights as unpaid seller and claiming to comply with his duty to mitigate damages.

The sale of the goods was discussed under the head of Art 7.4.8 and 7.4.5. UPICC. This discussion as reported by de Ly demonstrates that the UPICC do provide a basis for legal reasoning and argumentation even in a case where 'gaps' seem to arise within the application process.[38] It shows that the UPICC are a suitable basis for legal reasoning if only the parties draw on the full potential of the provisions, ie, undertake to apply them exhaustively just in the way they would do if they were in fact municipal law. The UPICC can technically be handled like a statute.

Dealing with the fourth issue, the Tribunal avoided discussing questions of contractual interpretation under the rules spelled out in Chapter 4 of the UPICC. Instead, it was resolved that the conclusive evidence clauses contained in the con-

---

33 The Chairman of the Tribunal had changed subsequently.

34 Gaps in international uniform laws will be dealt with below.

35 New York UN- Convention on the limitation in contracts for international sales of 13 June 1974.

36 By stating that there was no reason to assume an inexcusable delay.

37 As reported in the formulation of Professor de Ly, op cit (n 16), 229.

38 Compare de Ly, op cit (n 16), 229.

tracts were not successfully challenged because the claimant failed to bring any evidence. De Ly sees a tendency of the Tribunal to reinforce the prevalence of contractual terms over general principles and the UPICC by this manoeuvre,[39] and thereby an emphasis of the principle *pacta sunt servanda*. This implies that the application of the interpretation rules contained in Chapter 4 of the UPICC might be conceived to exercise a correcting function and could result in modifications of the contractual contents by way of interpretation. This understanding probably favours the interests of contracting parties, in that it wants to see parties vested with the authority to create their own legal cosmos and thereby a kind of sovereignty, with the contract taking the highest rank in the hierarchy of private law rules. I do not believe, however, that the Tribunal saw a conflict here between contract clauses and general principles which would have required a deliberate choice between *pacta sunt servanda* and contractual interpretation (governed by the good faith principle under the UPICC). The Tribunal merely wished to optimise their role in the dispute resolution sought by the parties, and therefore preferred to decide according to factual analysis and close application of the contract terms,[40] in order to achieve a persuasive effect for the parties which is an important factor in arbitration:

> ... in tackling the many substantive issues, the Tribunal found that many issues could be solved in a way convincing to the parties and in a generally acceptable way by applying factual analysis and contract terms rather than standards such as general principles and the Unidroit Principles. Given the State contract nature of the disputes, these pragmatic solutions do have important redeeming virtues.[41]

#### *7.2.3.3 First conclusion: Questionable role of arbitration tribunals as pioneers of integrating a-national law rules into domestic doctrine*

This constellation and relationship between the Tribunal and the disputing parties is important to note in comparison to the role of state courts and litigants there. The source of law function of any rule must be analysed in the context of its application. It is however worth discussing whether the attitude of state courts and state law as it generally is, serves to resolve disputes in international trade satisfactorily. This also involves the question of the nature of private law as discussed in Chapter 1. As a matter of fact, arbitration tribunals do achieve high levels of successful dispute resolution with only a small percentage of awards being challenged in state courts. This aspect of economy is not the highest priority in state litigation and in state legislation. This situation should be reviewed, however, in light of the existence of the UPICC.

Arbitral tribunals could be conceived as pioneers in applying the UPICC. This practice could then be introduced into state law by way of giving effect to the

[39] Ibid, 230, n 67.

[40] Thereby complying with Art 17(1) and (2) of the ICC arbitration rules of 1 January 1998.

[41] de Ly, op cit (n 16), 234.

findings of the Tribunals through enforcement or upholding awards in state litigation.[42] The gateway through which the UPICC could be introduced into national law would then be the standard of the applicable municipal arbitration law. The way the UPICC are dealt with and classified in arbitration would then form a model character for state litigation. However, due to the special circumstances of arbitration procedures, as set out above, it is questionable as to whether this can be accepted without further analysis. The way in which arbitrators apply rules of law of formal or informal nature differs in important aspects from the way in which state judges have to work. The need to comply with a given framework of legal rules is much greater for state courts as well as the requirement to comply with traditional standards of reasoning. The impact of a state judgment on the formation of the entire legal system is greater than an arbitration award which only binds the parties to the dispute.[43] This applies especially to legal systems based on precedent. This factor is also reinforced in state litigation by the appeal system and its standards of judicial review.

With a view to the need to improve and develop the qualitative aspect of applying the UPICC, creating a high standard for their reception, it seems therefore, that arbitration is not the prime gateway for the UPICC to enter the traditional world of the conflict of laws.[44]

Professor de Ly's report in conjunction with ICC case No 7110, however, contributes to the shaping of the legal nature of the UPICC with regard to their source of law function and their compatibility with municipal law.

#### 7.2.3.4 Fifth and sixth count of reference to UPICC and analytical evaluation

The way of applying Art 7.4.8 UPICC to resolve the fifth issue reported by de Ly again leaves it open as to whether the Tribunal regarded this rule as 'confirming' the general principle of *exceptio non adimpleti contractus* and thereby applied this general principle (the mitigation of harm maxim) to the facts of the case, or whether it decided the case 'under Art 7.4.8 UPICC', ie, applied the UPICC as a

---

42 'This approach has been adopted in case law' (R Goode, 'Usage and its Reception in Transnational Commercial Law' International and Comparative Law Quarterly 46 (1997) 1-36, 29); compare *Deutsche Schachtbau- und Tiefbohrgesellschaft mbH V* R as *al-Khaimah National Oil Co* [1987] 3 WLR 1023. 'The courts increasingly accept arbitral awards as sources of law and the arbitral process and independent of the courts.' (S Shackleton, 'Challenging Arbitration Awards – Part III: Appeals on Questions of Law' New Law Journal 6 December 2002, 1834-1835; see also J C Wichard, '*Die Anwendung der UNIDROIT – Prinzipien für internationale Handelsverträge durch Schiedsgerichte und nationale Gerichte*' *Rabels Zeitschrift für ausländisches und internationales Privatrecht* 60 (1996) 269-301, 283, who believes that the UPICC become positive law rules by choice of law and subsequent enforcement under national law, they receive 'state blessings through enforcement' ('*Staatliche Weihe ... im Wege der Vollstreckung...*'). Compare Chapter 8.

43 Compare 7.2.3.5, below.

44 Compare 7.2.3.5, below.

positive rule of law. The latter formulation is employed by de Ly dealing with the sixth instance of referring to the UPICC in this Award.[45] It could be called 'law language', describing a primary source of law whereas the former, ie, the UPICC 'expressing' or 'confirming' a general principle of law could be called 'restatement language' – describing the UPICC as being a restatement. This language of law and restatement is actually mixed within the award. The fifth issue discussed therein relating to the selling of unpaid goods by the Defendant was resolved by relying on the principle of *exceptio non adimpleti contractus*, as adopted by Article 7.1.3 UPICC.[46] While the Tribunal accepted Art 7.4.8 UPICC as a 'generally accepted principle of mitigation of harm',[47] the arbitrators dismissed Art 6.2.1 to 6.2.3 as expressing general principles of law. They did expressly reject the idea that the theory of changed circumstances form 'part of widely recognised and generally accepted legal principles, as referred to in the 13 July 1995 award'.[48] De Ly, however, still seems to classify Arts 6.2.1-6.2.3 UPICC, which restate the law on hardship, as in line with general principles of law. This clearly means that there is no general acceptance of the UPICC as the law governing the contract absent choice of law without further analysis. The UPICC seem only in parts to coincide with the general principles of law pointed to by the 'natural justice language' of a certain type of international commercial contract. This is at least, the view taken by the Tribunal in ICC case No 7110. For the application of the UPICC, this obviously means that every single rule has to be analysed as to its quality as a restatement which obviously even includes the option of differing results regarding individual rules. The better law approach thereby seems to be dismissed for the purposes of offering a genuinely neutral ground for settling a dispute absent choice of (municipal) law and choosing 'natural justice language', as is typically favoured in state contracts (contracts involving a state party). This attitude at least gives the utmost priority to the parties' intentions to settle their dispute according to 'neutral' principles of law, ie, to party autonomy. This benefit is clearly not conferred to the same extent by state legislation which refuses to give effect to this interest unconditionally and thereby possibly at the same time refuses to recognise the existence of such typical contractual relationships.

The Tribunal also named the general principles of law by their Latin origin rather than quoting the wording of the UPICC rules which had been deemed to restate ('confirmed' or 'expressed') these principles. This clearly illustrates the superior position of the general principles as the law governing the contract rather than the written rules of the UPICC.

This choice made by the Tribunal in this reported case may however, not have been intended to make general (and binding) assumptions relating to the UPICC. It is more likely that above all the Tribunal followed the purpose of rendering a convincing award in the way described above. This pragmatic approach seems to be the appropriate attitude in this instance. However, the proficient use of factual

[45] de Ly, op cit (n 16), 231.
[46] Ibid.
[47] Ibid, 231.
[48] Ibid.

analysis and application of contractual terms in this case does not necessarily diminish the merits of the UPICC here.

The fact that such a large number of issues were intensely discussed under their headings (although on the part of the defendants counsel) indicates that the written quality, comprehensiveness, and practical manageability of the UPICC are welcomed by litigants, and have a convincing force notwithstanding the parallel existence of general principles of law.

More concern should arise from the arbitrary manner in which the Tribunal employed the UPICC on the basis of vague and sometimes even contradictory explanations or motivations. The rules on hardship in the UPICC were rejected because they do not reflect a general principle of law since they are, for instance, not recognised in French, Belgian and English law. 'In case of a conflict between these general principles and the Unidroit Principles, the former should control.'[49] This attitude towards a hierarchy seems to be deliberately and consciously taken by the Tribunal.[50] The conclusion to be derived there from is not, however, that the UPICC are 'secondary' sources of law in terms of suitability for disputes of this kind, but rather that the Tribunal did not feel authorised to apply the UPICC instead of general principles of law. The problem, ie, the flaw in consistency of the argument in this specific case is induced by the fact that the Final Partial Award was rendered by a different panel than the preceding Partial Award, stating that the UPICC were to govern the contract. A contradictory use of the a-national law results into this inconsistency. This is a weakness which is typical, yet legitimate and acceptable in commercial arbitration but not in state litigation. This methodological flaw is the reason for the lack of recognition of rules like the UPICC in national legal systems. The discussion about the hierarchy of norms and subsequent authority derived from general principles of law on one hand, and the UPICC on the other, is not aimed at their legal nature but at the underlying choice of law argument. In ICC case No 7110 a shift from one underlying decision (the UPICC to govern the contract) to another (general principles law to govern the contract) took place on the part of the arbitral tribunal, but not on the part of the litigating parties, especially the Claimant, without being expressly discussed.

The underlying decision of the arbitral tribunal as to the legal nature of the UPICC can be described as follows:

- The UPICC are an *aliud* from general principles of law.
- The UPICC contain restatements of general principles in individual rules but not as a whole.
- The application of general principles of law does not authorise the arbitrator automatically to apply the UPICC exclusively.

This qualification seems to be justified. A common criticism is that arbitral tribunals jump to the application of a-national law too readily whenever no choice of

[49] Ibid, 232.

[50] The issue was explicitly discussed within the hearing.

law clause is contained in an international commercial contract.[51] The reasons behind this absence are not always the intention of the parties to exclude any national law but often the parties want to leave it to arbitration to find the applicable law. The application of a-national law can therefore lead to the award being set aside if it is found that the arbitrator exceeded the authority conferred to them by the parties and disregarded their party autonomy.[52] Such an analysis was carefully undertaken in ICC case No 7110, however. There were good reasons to assume that the parties wanted to exclude national laws due to the state contract nature of the venture as well as the 'natural justice language' in the contracts. The second panel did obviously place the utmost priority on the selection of the appropriate law rules and therefore resorted to 'general principles of law' as the ultimate authority. They did not seem to be insecure in terms of the contents of these principles, and in particular seemed quite proficient in the use of the comparative method to establish the substantive law within the general principles.

### 7.2.3.5 Second conclusion

De Ly reports the overall treatment of individual issues by the Tribunal in the following way:

> ... two conclusions may be drawn. One is that the Tribunal's view that the Unidroit Principles are not primary law governing the contract but only may help the Tribunal to find general principles of law. Secondly, the Tribunal seems to suggest that a quantitative approach should be taken to general principles of law. Hardship for instance is not such a general principle since it is unknown in a number of countries such as France (for civil and commercial contracts), Belgium and England. Thus, the better law approach based on qualitative criteria and implying a judgment regarding the merits of a particular solution is implicitly rejected ... One may note, however, that the Tribunal rejected the quantitative comparative survey approach in relation to limitation which deems to be contradictory to the approach taken here with respect to hardship.[53]

However, this inconsistent approach suggests that arbitral awards are not a prime source of a novel international doctrine of conflict law. Commercial arbitration can therefore not serve as the main gateway for the UPICC to be introduced into domestic litigation and to be integrated into municipal legal systems. The transformation of arbitration awards based on the UPICC by way of enforcement can be regarded as admittance through the back door, but due to the methodological flaws in the application of a-national law this technique will not open the front gates of the fortress of domestic law.

Advocating the integration of the UPICC into national law does not necessarily involve the postulation of the use of a-national law at any expense. Reservations against the 'premature' use of a-national law can only be met by the development of a more clear-cut doctrine of international private law. It is questionable how-

[51] Compare K P Berger, *The Creeping Codification of the* Lex Mercatoria (1999) at 81 and n 333 quoting a number of relevant awards.

[52] See below.

[53] de Ly, op cit (n 16), 232.

ever, whether this doctrine, judging by the current prevailing views in legal science and practice, is elaborate enough at present to support Berger's view that a decision of arbitrators to apply the *lex mercatoria* absent choice of law is not actually a decision *ex aequo et bono* (needing special authorisation in the arbitration agreement) since the *lex mercatoria* is not part of 'equity' any more, due to the high degree of codification and other standards in international legal doctrine.[54]

As much as arbitration tribunals provide a testing ground [55] for the UPICC, the chances for the outcome of the use in arbitration to infiltrate domestic legal doctrine directly are small, due to the characteristic irrelevance of doctrine and analysis for arbitration proceedings.

More analysis is therefore undertaken in the following in order to establish and arrange the relevant material which might form such a new approach to a-national law in the conflict of laws and domestic legal theory.

## 7.3 Reconciliation of UPICC with domestic conflict of laws

This section asks which tools are needed to build up an appropriate doctrine of choice of law allowing the use of uniform law to govern international commercial contracts. It investigates a way forward using concepts of current conflict of laws in an integrating way, contributing to a modern methodology of international contracts.

### 7.3.1 Combination solution in choice of law clauses

Paving the way for international uniform law instruments within municipal systems of law can only be achieved by reconciling them with domestic law.

This view is supported by Spellenberg in his commentary of the German conflict law.[56] He suggests 'tolerating' a-national law as lex contractus if 'combined with the subsidiary choice of a national legal system'.[57] As much as such a restriction would be unacceptable for parties wanting to exclude municipal laws from their dispute resolution, this statement positively suggests combining the two sets of law rules in exactly the opposite way to that traditionally suggested. This technique was actually employed by an arbitral tribunal in a case which was decided

[54] Compare Berger, op cit (n 51), 86: '...a decision based on the *lex mercatoria* may not be equated with a decision based on equity'; see also 85. Under the present English conflict of laws and arbitration law, this question does not even arise since there is no distinction made between these two notions, see, eg, Arbitration Act 1996 s 46(1)(b) and see below for further discussion.

[55] Drobnig, op cit (n 10), 395.

[56] *Spellenberg in Münchener Kommentar*, No 24 preceding (vor) §11 EGBGB.

[57] Drobnig, op cit (n 10), 392.

before the 'Hamburger Freundschaftliche Arbitrage' on 29 December 1998.[58] The tribunal reasoned:

*Nur soweit Fragen weder im CISG geregelt noch nach den Grundsätzen des CISG lösbar sind, ist gemäß Art 7 Abs. 2 CISG ergänzend das nach dem internationalen Privatrecht bestimmte innerstaatliche Recht anzuwenden, d.h. das gewählte deutsche Recht.* [59]
(Only as far as questions are neither regulated in the CISG nor answerable under the general principles of the CISG, Art 7(4) CISG provides that the domestic law applicable under private international law is to be applied supplementary, ie, the chosen German law.)

This is not in keeping with the analytical position adopted in domestic legal science.[60] But it indicates that this technique appears to its 'users' to be the natural way of applying uniform private law.

The gap-filling role is not attributed to the international rules anymore but to the domestic law rules. This technique requires two conditions to be accepted; the national law must provide the procedural and doctrinal space for the UPICC to apply legitimately, and the combination of the UPICC with the substantive law rules must actually work. The latter problem has been discussed above in Part Two, where examples from construction contract law have been successfully resolved under both regimes. The former issue is under consideration here.

### 7.3.2 The doctrine of gaps in international uniform laws and supplementary application of domestic law

The actual transition from one sphere to the other is supposed to take place when a gap arises in solving a case under the international uniform law instrument, in this context, the UPICC. Following the results of the analysis in Part Two, a gap can only arise after thorough interpretation and application of the whole of the UPICC as a comprehensive set of rules. This technique has also been successfully demonstrated by the discussion of various Articles of the UPICC in ICC case No 7110,[61] between the Tribunal and namely the defendant's counsel.

In relation to international uniform conventions such as CISG and the Ottawa Conventions on international factoring and leasing contracts, gaps are assumed under two headings.

*Lacunae intra legem*, internal gaps, are to be distinguished from matters which are not covered by the conventions, as for example described by Art 4 and 5 CISG, formation of contracts or the transfer of ownership. The former are gaps arising in the course of the application of international law when an issue, generally within the scope of the convention, turns out to be unanswered by its rules. In

[58] *'Schiedsverfahren der "Hamburger Freundschaftliche Arbitrage" – anwendbares Recht: Schiedsspruch vom 29.12. 1998'* RIW 5 (1998) 394-396.

[59] Ibid, 395 (IV 3).

[60] See below; compare Mankowski, *'Rechtswahl für Verträge des internationalen Wirtschaftsverkehrs'* RIW 1 (2003) 10, col 2.

[61] Compare de Ly, op cit (n 16), 229 and 230.

this case, most conventions provide for a gap filling role of the underlying general principles of law,[62] to which the text of the conventions usually refer.[63] The domestic law applicable under conflict rules is then another default standard for finding the appropriate solution under the international convention, as expressly provided for in Art 7(2) CISG and Art 4(2) of the 1988 Factoring Convention.

Both under domestic law and under international conventions it is common practice to fill gaps by analogous application of the relevant rules to comparable cases.[64] There is an established practice of dealing with gaps once they have been specified. More problems will arise from the definition of a 'gap' in an international convention or uniform non-binding instrument. Before a gap can be assumed, all possibilities of interpretation under the applicable rules of the relevant codification should be exhausted,[65] as has been demonstrated above in Part Two and also in ICC case No 7110 as reported by de Ly. The mere 'silence' of a set of rules regarding a specific question is not necessarily a sign for a missing link or incompleteness. Under domestic German legal theory, a gap should only be assumed where completeness was an express objective of a codification in the first place.[66] Matters can be left unregulated deliberately though for the sake of specific legal policies. In dealing with international uniform law rules such as the UPICC it will be important, therefore, to guard against an attitude which considers the presence of 'gaps' as deficiencies. The treatment of Art 7.2.1 UPICC by Professor Schwenzer, as discussed in Part 2, is an example of this regrettable but frequently taken attitude towards uniform law, which results in an inappropriate application of the UPICC and other uniform law instruments.

The importance of highlighting this flaw in the treatment of uniform law cannot be emphasised enough. Why should a legal phenomenon, which is characteristic for the law in general and commonly dealt with in domestic law,[67] give rise to substantial criticism on the level of uniform codifications?

One reason might be that the objective of exhaustive regulation of a specific matter (eg, the whole of contract law) is not present in international conventions or other uniform law. This might be regarded as a deficiency which seems to justify a

---

62 See F Ferrari, '*Das Verhältnis zwischen den Unidroit-Grundsätzen und den allgemeinen Grundsätzen internationaler Einheitsprivatrechtskonventionen*' *Juristenzeitung* 1 (1998) 9-17, 10 and 11.

63 Eg, Art 7(2) CISG.

64 Ferrari, op cit, 11; K Larenz, *Methodenlehre der Rechtswissenschaft* (1991) 381 et seq.

65 For an account of the definition of gaps in domestic (German) law see Larenz, op cit, 370 et seq. Larenz emphasises that the 'silence' of the law relating to a specific question is not necessarily a gap in terms of an incomplete regulation.

66 Compare Larenz, op cit (n 64), 371.

67 Compare *Münchener Kommentar, Einleitung*, No 64 quoting Heck, *Gesetzesauslegung und Interessenjurisprudenz* (1914): '*dass ein sehr großer Teil, vielleicht weitaus der größte Teil der zweifelhaften Rechtsfragen, auf dem Vorhandensein von Gesetzeslücken beruht*' ('the biggest part of doubtful legal questions of law arises from the presence of gaps in the law'). See also S Shackleton, 'The Applicable Law in International Arbitration Under the New English Arbitration Act 1996' Arbitration International 13.4 (1997): 375-389, 387: 'In reality, however, all legal systems are incomplete…'.

lesser standard of methodology. The filling of gaps is therefore an important tool for working with international uniform private law rules, particularly due to the limited scope of most international instruments.

### 7.3.3 Suggested method for an integrating conflict of laws doctrine

Regardless of the technique used to arrive at a complementary law, be it the underlying general principles of law or the *lex fori* or the law applicable by virtue of conflict rules, the combination of the uniform law with the complementary (municipal) law must be performed in a consistent way. For this technique a high standard should be applied based on thorough international legal research and practice.

National legislators might aid this process by providing supporting conflict of law rules. Therefore, law reform might be required to update existing rules relating to choice of law for international commercial contracts. In the area of judicial review transnational commercial law might be integrated into domestic legal systems by decisions confirming its application and interpreting statutory law accordingly. Doctrine, specifically in Germany, can prepare the ground for such case law.

The following specific issues are to be realised in order to achieve a method of applying the UPICC appropriately:

1 The complementary application of municipal law as suggested here requires the awareness that it is not intended to switch from the application of uniform law to domestic law entirely. The uniform law instrument still remains the law governing the contract. The assumption of a gap takes place on the level of substantive law and therefore does not represent a conflict rule appointing domestic law for the entire dispute.
2 The underlying theoretical foundations (the legal nature) of municipal law must be made conscious. Municipal law is for providing solutions for specific, possibly partial aspects of a dispute, in addition to the solutions provided by the uniform law. Any assumption of a superior degree of legitimacy and superseding force of law should be eliminated from methodology in those instances. Therefore, mandatory rules of the domestic law should only apply where the mandatory rules of the uniform law leave room for their application. The scope of the uniform law should prevail. Domestic law can take different meanings and be subject to different interpretations in the light of the uniform law. There might be instances in which terminology has to be assigned a new meaning different from the familiar one in the domestic context.

These two aspects are in fact much specialised postulations made from the point of view of an international forum of legal research and practice. In a purely domestic context they require a very high degree of adaptation, acceptance and education on all levels of legal research and practice. It is an important task to accomplish a higher standard of international legal practice, however, in the interest of modern developments of internationalisation of trade both on a small and large scale.[68]

## 7.4 Conclusion

This chapter has recapitulated different suggestions in legal theory of how to reach a position where the UPICC could be granted a source of law function. Contributions by German scholars have been put forward (7.1), examples of case law taken from arbitration (7.2), and traditional methods in international private law which are established in respect of other uniform law such as the CISG and other international conventions and model laws (7.3), have been considered. All of these, however, do not seem to provide a consistent solution to the question of the UPICC as source of law, and none of these theories are as yet accepted by traditional prevailing views in legal science neither in England nor Germany, and not by the courts in respect of the UPICC. They have also not as yet led to express provisions in legislation relating to the choice of law, neither in international arbitration, nor in domestic conflict law and the relevant procedural rules.

The aim of integrating uniform contract law into domestic law can, however, be achieved even under the prevailing doctrine by applying certain standards to its application. These are set out in the concluding section (7.4) of this chapter. Common mistakes in the use of current domestic law must be made obvious and eliminated, such as the misinterpretation of substantive rules of uniform law as being conflict rules. The preservation of the international character of the uniform law has to be emphasised and the correct application of such rules needs to be postulated. In the course of this method, irrational ideas about the general superior quality of domestic law in relation to international uniform law have to be identified and dropped because they are unfounded in the context of contract law. This eventually allows for the correct use of existing methods of applying uniform law, such as the theory of gaps and that of complementary law. These already exist and are acknowledged methods which can be used successfully if uncluttered by prejudice and preconceived limitations.

Further support and justification for the advancement of the standing of international uniform contract law can be derived from the efforts already made in doctrine and case law, as set out in sections 7.1 and 7.2, above.

[68] Contrary to the view taken by Mankowski, '*Rechtswahl für Verträge des internationalen Wirtschaftsverkehrs*' RIW 1 (2003) 2-15, 13, col 1, there is no general disadvantage within the transnational commercial law sphere for smaller enterprises. Taking part in cross-border trade and commerce is by no means an exclusive experience of 'global players', 'repeat players' or otherwise giant businesses. The UPICC provide progress especially in the area where no trade associations and branch specific agencies operate, thereby counteracting any potential discrimination arising from the dominating position of these bodies.

Then uniform law can be successfully integrated into domestic law and rules like the UPICC can be easily and reliably used by international contractors, lawyers and arbitrators.

# 8 Methods of integration through commercial arbitration

The previous section, Chapter 7, demonstrated how uniform contract law can have a source of law function in the general conflict of laws and thereby make the law governing the contract to the exclusion of national contract laws. Chapter 7 analysed the position under current doctrine of conflict law in domestic legal systems and in arbitration and suggested ways to integrate the findings into national laws in order to use the UPICC more easily and more securely as the governing law of an international commercial contract.

This chapter looks at procedural aspects of the integration of transnational uniform law. It investigates the way in which decisions, which have been reached by employing a-national rules of law such as the UPICC, are dealt with in national legal systems. Such decisions are frequently arbitration awards. The chapter therefore focuses on the question of whether arbitration awards can be based on the UPICC as the law governing the contract (*lex contractus* or *kollisionsrechtlice Verweisung*) and whether they can be upheld and enforced under domestic laws, or whether they are likely to be overturned by the national courts in England and Germany.

Current scholarly discussion on this issue is discussed in this chapter in addition to a suggested approach for facilitating the use and successful application of uniform contract law in the context of both contract and procedural laws of modern nation states, particularly arbitration law.

The chapter also asks if practitioners and merchants are likely to actually include a-national law into their contract rather than domestic law, this time from an empirical and forensic viewpoint.[1]

Due to the significance of doctrine within the German legal system, legal science has to prepare the ground for future court decisions in this area.[2] Analytical considerations are therefore central regarding German law. English law is subject to different formative aspects; the Courts play the leading role, and are much less influenced by doctrine and analytical writing. A different pattern therefore applies to the treatment of a-national law in commercial arbitration.

The first section of the chapter (8.1) therefore sets out the current English and German law regulating choice of law in arbitration proceedings. It particularly addresses doctrinal questions of recently reformed law in Germany and compares

[1] Compare Chapter 2.

[2] See for an example of recourse to legal science in decisions of the Federal Court BGH in NJW 1986, 1436 and 1437, jurisdiction on the law of arbitration proceedings.

other national, specifically English, legislation on the subject to prepare further discussion. The second section (8.2) asks if and how arbitration awards can be overturned under national laws on the grounds that they are based on a-national contract law such as the UPICC and what the prospects of development in this area are.

The third section (8.3) asks what the desirable standard of arbitration law ought to be and reflects on what could be done to overcome existing difficulties and obstacles to employ the UPICC more securely and easily in international arbitration, or even state litigation and certainly other alternative dispute resolution. The concluding section (8.4) refers especially to the German national legal system because of the significance of doctrine there, as mentioned above.

## 8.1 Choice of law in commercial arbitration

This first section of Chapter 8 asks what the current English and German national law on arbitration (8.1.1 and 8.1.5) stipulates with regard to choice of law questions. It investigates the current opinion of legislators (8.1.1 and 8.1.4), courts (8.3), and scholars (8.2) expressed in the written law as well as in doctrine and case law, about choice of law in arbitration under the heading of enforcing and upholding awards in nation states. This review includes some comparative analysis looking at other European jurisdictions (8.1.5).

### 8.1.1 Current German law of arbitration

The new German law regulating arbitration procedures and the enforcement of awards is regulated in the Code of Civil Procedure, the ZPO, in §§1025-1066 (10th book), reformed 22 December 1997 and in force since 1 January 1998.[3] Regarding questions of law, there is no case law applying the new provisions in the area of recourse against arbitration awards, as yet. A number of documents, however, contribute to the shaping of an understanding of the new legislation; namely, the report of the reform commission,[4] and the official reasons published by the government (ministry of justice),[5] as well as some recently published comments by academic teachers.

---

3 For a text of just the 10th book see H W Labes and T Lörcher, eds, *Nationales und Internationales Schiedsverfahrensrecht* (1998) 53-70 or later editions. For a full text of the ZPO and other procedural law see H Thomas and H Putzo, *Zivilprozeßordnung* (2003) or later editions.

4 *Kommission zur Neuordnung des Schiedsverfahrensrechts: Bericht mit einem Diskussionsentwurf zur Neufassung des Zehnten Buchs der ZPO* (1994).

5 'Bundestags-Drucksache (BT-Drucks) 13/5374' published by Deutscher Bundestag, available via internet.

The new law does not import the formulation of Art 28 (2) of the UNCITRAL Model Law on arbitration into the new legislation but incorporates a different wording into §1051 (2) ZPO:

*Haben die Parteien die anzuwendenden Rechtsvorschriften nicht bestimmt, so hat das Schiedsgericht das Recht des Staates anzuwenden, mit dem der Gegenstand des Verfahrens die engsten Verbindungen aufweist.* (§1051 (2) ZPO)
(If the parties have not chosen the applicable rules of law the arbitration tribunal has to apply the law of the country with which the subject matter of the procedure has its closest connections.)

This rule is mandatory; the tribunal has to apply the law of a state absent choice of law. There is no room for any ex officio considerations by the arbitrator as to the application of a-national law, the *lex mercatoria* or similar unless chosen by the parties. Even though the expression '*Rechtsvorschriften*' (rules of law) in §1051(1) ZPO can be construed to include a-national rules,[6] it seems that in the absence of a choice of law clause the options of the applicable law are thereby narrowed so that only the law of a state can apply.

### 8.1.2 Doctrinal requirements disregarded by legislator

It is unclear why the legislator left §1051(2) ZPO without the further provisions and guidelines following the otherwise identical Art 28(1) first sentence EGBGB. This seems inconsequential given that the legislator intended to both integrate the UNCITRAL Model Law, as well as comply with Articles 3 and 4 of the RC.[7] This wording poses interpretation problems. From the official records accompanying the draft ZPO[8] no clear answer can be derived.[9] It remains open as to why the further provisions of both the EGBGB and the Rome Convention were not included into the new paragraph, and to what exactly the intention of the legislator was, regarding the treatment of choice of law matters. The legislator seems to have suggested that a choice of a-national law is possible under Art 28 EGBGB,[10] but leaves the important question of status[11] un-discussed. The official reasons also state that the solution incorporated into the new draft §1051(2) ZPO corresponds

6 Although possibly not as governing law but merely as contractual terms, see below.
7 Compare *BT-Drucksache* 13/5274.
8 *BT-Drucksache* 13/5274 contains the reasons of the government published with the draft, and the report of the law reform commission contains their recommendations, see *Kommission zur Neuordnung des Schiedsverfahrensrechts: Bericht mit einem Diskussionsentwurf zur Neufassung des Zehnten Buchs der ZPO* (1994). The draft provisions were later enacted without any further changes to their wording.
9 For a full discussion of the wording of §1051 ZPO-E and a detailed analysis of its relationship to the EGBGB, the Rome Convention and the UNCITRAL Model Law see D Solomon, '*Das vom Schiedsgericht in der Sache anzuwendende Recht nach dem Entwurf eines Gesetzes zur Neuregelung des Schiedsverfahrensrechts*' RIW 12 (1997) 981-990.
10 '*Bundestags-Drucksache (BT-Drucks)* 13/5374', published by Deutscher Bundestag, 52.
11 Contractual term or governing law.

and harmonises with Art 27(1) first sentence EGBGB.[12] This is clearly not the case according to the prevailing view in German legal science and case law. Especially in conjunction with the limits of choice of law contained in Art 27(3), Art 29 and 30 EGBGB; additional explanation on the part of the legislator would clearly have been advisable.[13] The official reasons thus create more confusion than clarification. There is no answer to the question as to whether or not any limits to the choice of law were intended to apply by recourse to the general conflict rules of German law and to what extent. The reasons merely present the vague explanation that it was self-evident that 'unlimited choice of law' was certainly not admissible.[14] This does not only avoid the question of the limits but also clearly differs from the common understanding of the UNCITRAL Model Law provision of its Art 28.[15]

Most possibly the legal background of the matter to be regulated and the impact of their reform on it was not familiar to the legislator in its depth or at least to the legal team who drafted the official reasons.

A lack of understanding of the role of the conflict law in arbitration as compared to general contract conflict law also shows in the official reasons relating to the scope of the new §1051(2) ZPO. Subject matter of choice of law in arbitration disputes can actually not only be contracts, but also certain related and preceding questions of family matters, inheritance, movables or indeed, questions of tort and restitution where a choice of law is generally accepted.[16] These questions are not per se and entirely excluded from arbitration. It is therefore doubtful whether the unqualified reference to Art 28 EGBGB, which regulates contract conflicts of laws, is appropriate and sufficient to regulate the entire conflict of laws in arbitration.

---

12 '*Bundestags-Drucksache (BT-Drucks)* 13/5374', published by Deutscher Bundestag, 52.

13 Especially since there had already been case law relating to arbitration clauses in consumer contracts. See OLG Düsseldorf, RIW 1994, 420; OLG Düsseldorf RIW 1996, 681, 683, BGH in NJW 1987, 3193, 3195.

14 'Unlimited choice of law' is a favourite enemy of traditional legal science: '*Ein von den Parteien ad libitum aus den verschiedensten Rechtsordnungen zusammengestelltes Schuldstatut, so eine Art rechtlichen Potpourris oder Mosaiks, ist nicht zu dulden.*' ('A governing law compiled *ad libitum* by the parties like a potpourri or mosaic is not to be tolerated.'): Raape, *Internationales Privatrecht*, 5th edn (1961) 472. Another opinion sees signs of immaturity in potential users of unlimited choice of law: '*Die Lehre von der Teilrechtswahl bedeutet nicht, daß sich die Parteien Gesetze wie Kinder die Rosinen aus dem Teig herauspicken dürfen.*' ('The doctrine of a cumulative choice of law does not mean that the parties are allowed to pick the raisins from the dough like children do.'): C v Bar, *Internationales Privatrecht: Besondere Lehren* Vol 2, No 426.

15 It also differs from the view taken by the reform commission who delivered preparatory work preceding the draft ZPO: '*Kommission zur Neuordnung des Schiedsverfahrensrechts: Bericht mit einem Diskussionsentwurf zur Neufassung des Zehnten Buchs der ZPO*' (1994) 167.

16 Compare Art 40 EGBGB (1999), Palandt and Heldrich, *Bürgerliches Gesetzbuch* (2001) Art 38 EGBGB (old), No 13; Palandt and Heldrich, *Bürgerliches Gesetzbuch* (2006) Art 40 EGBGB, No 7; J Kropholler, *Internationales Privatrecht* (2001) §53 IV 5; G Kegel, and K Schurig, *Internationales Privatrecht* (2004) §8 III, IV d, §4 I.

Reference to the practice of Swiss law, made by the government in the official reasons, is misleading; under Swiss law the rules relating to conflict of laws in arbitration are regarded as *lex specialis* and apply exclusively and superseding the general provisions of the IPRG on conflict of laws in contracts.[17] The wording of these applicable rules is identical to the new §1051(2) ZPO, but is consciously and deliberately not qualified by the further provisions of Art 117 IPRG, which contains similar guidelines to Art 28 EGBGB. Reference to Swiss law therefore, results into a self-contradiction in respect of the aforementioned opinion expressed by the legislator – that Art 28 EGBGB applies self-evidently to arbitration.

The picture of the legislator's attitude gets more and more blurred. Art 28 EGBGB might apply by way of the law of the forum if one were to assume that the arbitration tribunal is subject to the lex fori and its conflict law. In this case §1051(2) ZPO would have to be construed as of a purely declaratory nature so that a reference to Art 28(2)-(5) EGBGB would indeed be 'self-evident'.

The reform commission at least supported the view that arbitration tribunals are not bound by the law of the forum simply via a reference to the seat of the arbitration.[18] The choice of the seat of the arbitration is not to be construed as a hypothetic choice of the *lex fori* by the parties. Arbitration tribunals cannot be said to have a forum in the same way as state courts because they are not acting within their capacity as organs of the judicative power, and with regard to Germany, are not subject to Art 20(3) GG. The parties cannot be deemed to regularly mean to choose the law at the seat of the arbitration since this seat is often chosen for reasons of neutrality and convenience rather than for reasons of the applicable law. Arbitration tribunals do not derive their authority from the state legislator but from the parties. Therefore their intentions regarding choice of law, is to be established by reference to the individual case and not to general state legislation at the seat of the arbitration tribunal.

It is therefore the arbitrator's primary duty to establish the choice of law according to the parties' intentions, not necessarily referring to national conflict rules. The arbitrator, de facto, enjoys wide discretion due to the common (international) practice not to subject arbitration awards to the so-called revision au fond, ie, full judicial review as to questions of law.

The decision of the arbitrator to apply a particular law is exclusively subject to judicial review under aspects of enforceability of the award and recourse against it. Even then, however, the decision of the arbitrator will be largely upheld unless it contravenes the *ordre public* or exceeds the authority conferred by the parties. The fact that the 'wrong' law was applied according to conflict rules of the enforcing state does not give rise to a ground for setting aside under any of those two headings, though.[19]

---

17 Compare 187 (1) IPRG and see below. Compare also Solomon, op cit (n 9), 985 col 1 and further references.

18 Compare Solomon, ibid, 986. This is in line with the traditional practice and case law.

19 §1059 ZPO, see BGHZ 96, 40 = NJW 1986, 1436; see Solomon, op cit (n 9), 987 col 1.

### 8.1.3 Case law

The decision which is frequently cited in this context (and others) is BGHZ 96, 40 et seq of 26 September 1985, also published in NJW 1986, 1436 et seq. This is one of the very few judgments rendered by German courts that concerned recourse against arbitration awards. This decision does not expressly decide whether the application of the 'wrong' law would give rise to setting aside of the award. The decision concerned the question whether or not the arbitration tribunal had applied law or equity.[20] The court did not review the decision of the tribunal to apply English law but simply accepted it:

*Ob die übereinstimmenden Meinungsäußerungen der Parteien das Schiedsgericht verpflichteten, englisches Recht anzuwenden, kann letztlich dahinstehen. Denn das Schiedsgericht hat seiner Entscheidung englisches Recht zugrundegelegt.* [21]
(Whether or not the unanimous opinions expressed by the parties[22] obliged the tribunal to apply English law can remain undecided. Because the tribunal did in fact apply English law.)

Obviously the question whether English law was the 'right' (correct) law was not disputed and did not need a definitive answer. The idea of a 'correct law' does, however, appear in the decision in the following way:

*... denn unrichtige Anwendung des (richtigen) materiellen Rechts ist kein Grund für die Aufhebung eines Schiedsspruchs.* [23]
(... because the wrong application of the (correct) substantive law does not provide any reason for the setting aside of an arbitration award.)

The correctness of the law applied to the substance of the dispute depends on the intentions of the parties. It is to be established by giving effect to party autonomy which authorises the decision of the arbitrator. The law at the seat of the tribunal is not the prime reference to decide this question.
The Federal Court does not express a view on the question as to the correct law and how it is to be established in the above quoted decision, but gives guidelines as to an aspect connected with it.

The facts that the parties had (implicitly in the course of the arbitration proceedings and in accordance with the Rules of Arbitration of the ICC[24]) chosen German procedural law, as well as that the seat of the arbitration (obviously) was in Germany,[25] did not lead the Court to infer that German substantive or conflict law had been chosen as governing law by the parties or was to be applied ex offi-

---

[20] This was answered in the affirmative, see NJW 1986, 1437 and see below.
[21] BGH in NJW 1986, 1437.
[22] Responding to an ICC questionnaire which asked for submission of legal opinions as to the applicable law, at least for the recourse procedures.
[23] BGH in NJW 1986, 1437.
[24] BGH in NJW 1986, 1436.
[25] Compare BGH in NJW 1986, 1437.

cio by the tribunal. This view was also not influenced by the fact that because of this choice of procedural rules the award was considered a domestic award and accepted for the recourse procedures of the then §1041 ZPO (*Aufhebungsklage*). At the time of the decision §1051 ZPO did not exist, and the previously governing ZPO did not contain a comparable provision. Since it has to be assumed that the decision of the Federal Court of 26 September 1985 either created or reflected the applicable German law at that time,[26] the official reasons accompanying the draft §1051 ZPO should have stated whether or not it was intended to alter the existing *lex lata* by the new provisions.

Again, the full significance of the wording of §1051 (2) ZPO was most probably not recognised by the drafters.

### 8.1.4 Status quo regarding the application of the UPICC in arbitration proceedings under German law

This legal situation does not provide legal certainty for arbitral tribunals and parties to an international contract to decide on the applicable law other than municipal law. As a result the ZPO does not encourage the application of a-national law absent choice of law in arbitration proceedings.

A specific uncertainty is created by the following view which most of the traditional writers take towards the application of a-national law rules; absent choice of law such a choice by an arbitrator subjects the award to the heading of *ex aequo et bono* decision under §1051(3) ZPO unless rules like the UPICC were to be qualified as 'trade usages'. Trade usages are regularly to be observed, as are contract terms under s 4 of §1051, which is in line with Art 28(4) of the UNCITRAL Model Law and Art 17(2) of the ICC rules. As far as the UPICC are not regarded as 'law' or 'trade usages', however, they could be deemed to have been unduly applied without the express authorisation by the parties to rule *ex aequo* et bono.[27] Arbitration awards based on the UPICC or other a-national terms of reference would then be open to setting aside under §1059(2)(d) ZPO on the ground of tribunal exceeding the contractual or arbitral agreement as to the applicable law.

This is a detrimental outcome for the cause of the integration of the UPICC into domestic legal doctrine and practice under German *lex lata*.

### 8.1.5 Comparing other national legislation relating to choice of law in commercial arbitration

Other national laws as well as international institutional arbitration rules accept a wider discretion of arbitral tribunals as to the applicable law.

French law provides for the famous '*amiable compositeur*' role of the arbitrator in the very scarce provision of Art 1474 of the new Code of Civil Procedure (*Nou-*

---

[26] See also Solomon, op cit (n 9), 988 col 1 for further reference.

[27] See below for further discussion.

*veau Code de Procedure Civile*, NCPC) in force as of 12 May 1981. It provides for the arbitrator to decide 'according to the rules of law unless the parties have vested in him the office to rule as *amiable compositeur*'. This wording obviously leaves room for discussion as to whether the rules of law referred to are necessarily state law or might imply a-national law. It is important to note, that under French procedural law the judge, in the case of an appeal or application for setting aside against the award, decides 'within the limits of the arbitrator' (Art 1485 NCPC), and especially decides as *amiable compositeur* if this 'office' was conferred to the arbitrator by the parties (Art 1483, second phrase). This means that the French state recognises cases in which the state judge is not exclusively guided by formal state legislation, but additionally by certain other rules of law which are recognised by the litigating parties by way of preceding agreements. Appeal procedures and remedies against arbitral awards involving *amiables compositeurs* can only take place if the parties have agreed to it in their arbitration agreement, Art 1482 NCPC. State courts are thereby voluntarily included into the private dispute settlement allowing for a great deal of freedom as to the applicable law governing the substance of the dispute and thereby strengthening party autonomy.

The UNCITRAL Model Law, adopted by UNCITRAL as of 21 June 1985, provides for the application of those 'rules of law' which have been agreed upon by the parties, Art 28(1) first sentence. In the event that no choice has been made, the arbitrator is free to decide on the conflict law which takes him to decide on the governing law, Art 28(2). The same is provided by Art 16 of the 'Vienna [Arbitration] Rules' of the Austrian Chamber of Commerce.

The ICC arbitration rules in force from 1 January 1998, even provide for a completely free choice of law by the arbitrator without arriving at the substantive law via conflict rules. The governing law can be applied directly (*voie directe*), Art 17(2) ICC rules.

The Swiss Chamber of Commerce rules for international arbitration, of 1 January 1989,[28] incorporate a similar provision as the German civil code. Article 4 points to the Swiss conflict of law rules of the IPRG.[29] The IPRG provides in Art 187(1) that the law applicable to the substance of the dispute is 'the law with which the matter is most closely connected'. The choice of this wording ('law') again suggests that state law is meant to apply exclusively.[30] The scope of this wording in relation to the conflict rules applying to contract law has already been

[28] German text printed in H W Labes, and T Lörcher, eds, *Nationales und Internationales Schiedsverfahrensrecht* (1998) 308-322.

[29] *Bundesgesetz über das Internationale Privatrecht,* IPRG, of 1 January 1989; for original text see *Journal des Tribunaux* 1989 I, 98 and 544; or *Receuil des arrets du Tribunal fédéral* 115 [1989] II 97.

[30] Contrary to the view of S Shackleton, 'The Applicable Law in International Arbitration Under the New English Arbitration Act 1996' Arbitration International 13.4 (1997) 375-389, 382 who lists Switzerland together with a number of countries who have adopted more liberal arbitration laws as to the applicable law the Swiss code restricts the choice of law depicting the provision of Art 4(1) first sentence of the 1980 Rome Convention.

explained above and so has the relationship of this provision with the identically worded German provision in §1051 (2) ZPO.[31]

The English Arbitration Act 1996,[32] in force since 31 January 1997, expressly allows for disputes to be resolved under 'provisions other than law';[33] section 46(1)(b) provides: 'The arbitral tribunal shall decide the dispute ... if the parties so agree, in accordance with such other considerations as are agreed by them determined by the tribunal.'

Further to this, section 46 (3), gives the arbitrators absent choice of law discretion as to the applicable conflict rules. There is thus no general and express authorisation under English Law to apply a-national law directly to the substance of a dispute (*voie directe*) in the absence of an express choice of such rules by the parties.

It is disputed by commentators whether this provision promotes the evolution of a modern arbitration law [34] The formulation '... the conflict of law rules which it considers applicable', in s 46(3), as opposed to 'considers appropriate',[35] thereby suggesting that the establishment of the applicable conflict rules ought to follow recognised methods. Section 46(3) of the English Arbitration Act 1996 does not prescribe any further details as to the applicable conflict rules, though. It is not clear from the case law and the comments to date the extent to which this provision is meant to subject the arbitrator to the conflict of laws of the *lex fori* and/or just to the same 'regime' as a state judge would be in his place[36] and thereby aims to guarantee the equivalent outcome. If either of these options were the objective of Parliament it would indeed be if anything, a more elegant solution than the one pursued in the recently reformed continental statutes, where a mere copy of the provisions relating to contract conflicts was imported into arbitration legislation regardless of the different spheres of application.[37]

Section 8.1 identified the status quo of the current law of arbitration with regard to choice of law and the main areas of difficulties within this legislation. The current, even recently reformed German law shows severe deficiencies on the doctrinal side, whereas English arbitration law, although leaving room for interpreta-

---

31 Compare 8.1.2.

32 The magnificent elephant: see V V Veeder, '*La nouvelle loi anglaise sur l'arbitrage 1996: la naissance d'un magnifique éléphant*' Revue de l'Arbitrage 1 (1997) 24.

33 Schedule 2 (4) of Arbitration Act 1996 (Commencement No 1) Order 1996.

34 If modern can be understood as internationalisation and harmonisation of English arbitration law and its 'universal adaptability across legal cultures': compare Shackleton, op cit (n 30), 387 as opposed to fit to supersede and make obsolete any alleged *lex mercatoria*; compare Lord Mustill in Mustill and Boyd, *The Law and Practice of Commercial Arbitration in England* (1989) 81.

35 Compare Shackleton, op cit (n 30), 389.

36 Shackleton, op cit (n 30), 377. Compare also this passage from the 'Report on the Arbitration Bill' Departmental Advisory Committee on Arbitration Law, 1996, 49: 'In such circumstances the tribunal must decide what conflict rules are applicable and use those rules in order to determine the applicable law. It cannot simply make up rules for this purpose.'

37 See above.

tion, seems to rely on traditional views on choice of law whereby state law, determined under general choice of law rules, is the first point of reference absent choice of law. Other national laws leave more room for a wider interpretation and use of a-national contract law to govern international contracts, but these are wrongly referred to in German law as models and points of reference for the current national legislation.

Section 8.1 reviewed the status quo of the current law of arbitration with regard to choice of law and identified the main areas of difficulties within this legislation if the use of uniform contract law is intended. The current, even recently reformed, German law shows severe doctrinal deficiencies, whereas the English arbitration law, although leaving room for interpretation, seems to rely on traditional views on choice of law whereby state law, determined under general choice of law rules, is the first point of reference absent choice of law. Other national laws leave more room for a wider interpretation and use of a-national contract law to govern international contracts, namely the French, but these are wrongly referred to in German law as models and points of reference for the current national legislation.

## 8.2 Challenging awards based on a-national law under domestic arbitration law

The previous section has given account of the current status quo of express choice of law provisions in national arbitration laws and their position in legal doctrine. This section asks more specifically what the current law allows state courts to do with arbitration awards which have been reached relying on a-national uniform contract law (8.2.1). It investigates specific instances in case law where arbitration awards have been challenged or constellations where they might be challenged under domestic English (8.2.2) and German (8.2.3) law, with specific regard to instances of employing the UPICC as governing law.

Enforcement, appeal and recourse procedures under national laws are the second column on which the arbitration award, and with it the underlying (legal) reasoning, rests. Only if the chances of an award employing a-national law to pass the test of transformation into domestic laws are reasonable, can arbitrators refer to those a-national rules of law confidently and legitimately.

### 8.2.1 Scope of judicial supervision in selected arbitration laws

In a number of legal systems the only criterion giving rise to judicial review on questions of law is whether or not the arbitrator or arbitration tribunal exceeded the competence conferred to them by the parties. This principle is incorporated in Art 34(2)(iii) of the UNCITRAL Model Law which many countries worldwide have been striving to incorporate into their domestic arbitration law in the last 18 years – since it was adopted by UNCITRAL in 1985. It now appears in the English (Arbitration Act 1996 s 68(2)(b) and (e)), French (Art 1484 No 3 NCPC), and

German (§1059(2)(d) ZPO), law relating to arbitration. The Swiss IPRG however, only provides for an appeal against the award on the grounds of violation of the ordre public, Art 190(e) IPRG, and not in case the arbitrators exceeded competences such as deciding *ex aequo et bono* absent an express authorisation under Art 187(2) IPRG. Questions arising out of the application of substantive law in arbitration procedures are thus not subject to judicial review at all according to the black letter rules of Swiss procedural law.[38]

## 8.2.2 Judicial review of arbitration awards based on a-national law rules under current English law

This situation is probably most distant from English law as contained in ss 66-71 Arbitration Act 1996. The above mentioned excess of powers as incorporated in s 68(2)(b) and (e), are one of a wide range of grounds to challenge arbitration awards and appeal against them. Besides challenging the award on the grounds of substantive jurisdiction and serious irregularity, 'appeal on point of law', ie, a review on the merits of the award, is still an option under English law after the enactment of the Arbitration Act 1996. This is not the case in Germany, Switzerland, Austria, The Netherlands and a number of other civil law countries.

From the literal wording of the rules in s 69(2)(c)(i) and (ii) and (2)(d) it does not follow that awards based on a-national law such as the UPICC will be considered unlawful without more. A decision by an arbitral tribunal employing the UPICC need not necessarily be 'obviously wrong' (s 69(2)(c)(i)), 'open to serious doubt', or raise concerns of 'general public importance' (s 69(2)(c)(ii)). It will therefore depend on additional factors, such as existing authority and some views in legal literature how this question has to be answered.

### *8.2.2.1 Significance of judicial review for the development of English commercial law*

The use of a-national law in arbitration awards might turn into an opportunity for state courts to apply and revise decisions based on the UPICC and thereby render legally binding opinions as to the legal nature of these provisions and the methods of application. Judging by some words taken from the *Donaldson Report*,[39] this would probably eventually meet the objectives of the political and official organs: Judicial review of arbitral awards is an

> opportunity which it has afforded to the Courts of developing English commercial law in line with the changing needs of the times.[40]

---

[38] Unless, of course, one were to assume that deciding *ex aequo et bono* without express authorisation generally violates the *ordre public.*

[39] The 1978 Commercial Court Committee Report on Arbitration, named after its Chairman, Mr Justice Donaldson.

[40] Ibid, para. 15; quoted in Shackleton, op cit (n 30), 388.

Even though the 'continued production of English law'[41] is a rather ironic remark made by critics of the traditionally overly-strong tendency of English courts to readily review arbitration awards and interfere with arbitration procedures, this mechanism could still lead, on a positive note, to the eventual (evolutionary) acceptance of a-national law in domestic legal systems. Such a process would also be evidence of the much appraised capability of the common law practice to adapt to changing standards of the times, while preserving traditional and proven values, as the above cited quote does not forget to emphasise.

#### *8.2.2.2 Traditional position in English law set forth in the Arbitration Act 1996?*

The tradition of extensive judicial review and intervention in relation to arbitration proceedings has most prominently manifested in *Charnikow* v *Roth Schmidt & Co.*[42] It is only necessary to note that central statements on the acceptance or rejection of a-national rules of law are expected to arise from decisions in the area of arbitration law, whereas in German law such evaluations are almost entirely developed by legal science.[43] In the *Charnikow* decision, Lord Justice Bankes expressed the view that there can be no law created by commercial entities like trade associations (in that case the Refined Sugar Association) or commercial arbitral tribunals:

> … and to secure that the law that is administered by an arbitrator is in substance the law of the land and not some home-made law of the particular arbitrator or the particular association.[44]

His view was supported by Lord Justice Atkin:

> If it [ie, special statutory jurisdiction of the court] did not exist, arbitration clauses … would leave lay arbitrators at liberty to adopt any principles of law they pleased … the result

[41] Shackleton, op cit (n 30), 388, n 60, thereby unwittingly picking up the idea put forward by Mankowski ('*Rechtswahl für Verträge des internationalen Wirtschaftsverkehrs*' RIW 1 (2003) 2-15, 6, col 2) who sees a 'public asset' in the creation of a body of case law within common law jurisdictions and attributes an economic value to it, but with a different value judgment attached to it. This was also seen by Lord Diplock: '…the abolition of the [case stated] procedure in England would "cripple the continued development of commercial law that has made it the favoured choice as proper law of international contracts even where they have no territorial connection with this country"' (A Samuel, 'The 1979 Arbitration Act – Judicial Review of Arbitration Awards on the Merits in England' Journal of International Arbitration 2.4 (1985), 53 and 56 quoted in O Chukwumerije 'Judicial Supervision of Commercial Arbitration: The English Arbitration Act of 1996' Arbitration International 15.2 (1999) 171-191, 187); see also below.

[42] [1922] 2 KB 478.

[43] See below.

[44] Bankes, LJ in *Charnikow* v *Roth Schmidt & Co* [1922] 2 KB 478, 484.

might be that in time codes of law would come to be administered in various trades differing substantially from the English mercantile law.[45]

The objective behind this reasoning was; 'to prevent and redress any injustice on the part of the arbitrator',[46] and thereby indeed contributing to maintaining a high standard of the established and generally welcomed arbitration proceedings in England:

Among commercial men what are commonly called commercial arbitrations are undoubtedly and deservedly popular. That they will continue their present popularity I entertain no doubt, as long as the law retains sufficient hold over them ...[47]

Since so-called *ex aequo et bono* decisions by arbitrators, as incorporated in French law in the form of the 'office' of *amiable compositeur*, has been unknown to English law, the decision in *Charnikow* confirms this position:

To release real and effective control over commercial arbitrations is to allow the arbitrators ... to give ... them a free hand to decide according to law or not to law as he or they think fit, in other words to be outside the law ... At present no individual or association is, so far as I am aware, outside the law except a trade union.'[48]

This decision is usually said to enshrine the traditional attitude of English law[49] towards arbitration, and this attitude is sometimes characterised as 'hostile to legal pluralism',[50] 'historically suspicious of the arbitral process',[51] and as adhering to a 'unitary conception'[52] and a 'statist character'.[53]

It is hence seen to be the basis of a presently existing rejection of the application of 'autonomous' transnational rules from the point of view of English law, which has remained the position throughout the development of arbitration law even under the new Arbitration Act 1996.

Having excluded reference by arbitrators to principles of *lex mercatoria*, ... the 1996 Act retains limited authority for English courts to decide questions of English law that have been decided by an arbitral tribunal where the court is satisfied that the question is one of 'general public importance'. This provision can only be understood from the perspective of

45 Ibid, 488.
46 Ibid, 484.
47 Ibid.
48 Bankes, LJ, ibid, 484.
49 Even officially incorporated into the 1978 Commercial Court Committee Report on Arbitration; compare Shackleton, op cit (n 30), 379, note 13.
50 Shackleton, op cit (n 30), 379.
51 O Chukwumerije, 'Judicial Supervision of Commercial Arbitration: The English Arbitration Act of 1996' Arbitration International 15.2 (1999) 171-191, 171.
52 Shackleton, op cit (n 30), 379.
53 Ibid, 385.

the logic operating in *Czarnikow*: the state reasserts its role as the sole legitimate normative authority for English law.[54]

The critical views of the author of this statement can well serve as a starting point for a discussion of the position of transnational law under the current English law and court practice.

#### 8.2.2.3 Legal situation under the Arbitration Act 1996

The stipulation of transnational rules as the law governing the contract is either clearly rejected by some influential legal writers,[55] or not supported, in that an in-depth discussion and clear distinction of the relevant problems is avoided. The latter attitude is to be found in the DAC Report;[56] along with some other commentators, it does not distinguish the 'other considerations' of s 46(1)(b) from *ex aequo et bono* decisions and thereby assumes that ruling according to *lex mercatoria* or a-national law is the same as a procedure employing the *amiable compositeur*. Just as in the German official report,[57] one gains the impression that the subtleties of the subject matter are not in the awareness of the departments' legal team. Another such instance of insufficient consideration is the article by Chukumerije:

> In this regard it is notable that the Act now clearly permits arbitrating parties to choose the *lex mercatoria* as their governing law or to invest their tribunal with the power to act as *amiable compositeur*.[58]

The former of these alternatives is by no means undisputed and therefore needs further explanation. The question whether the application of a-national rules of law, such as the UPICC, will be considered governing law or implied terms is decisive for their integration into domestic commercial law. The position under English law seems clearly rejective:

> In England, an express choice by the parties of *lex mercatoria* will be given effect, but will not be viewed under the new Arbitration Act as choice of an applicable law and it would appear that any implied choice by the parties of *lex mercatoria* as the applicable law, either alone or in addition to a designated municipal law, cannot be given effect.[59]

This position has been adopted by influential commentators even before the enactment of the 1996 Arbitration Act:

---

[54] Compare Shackleton, op cit (n 30), 375-389.

[55] Eg, by Lord Mustill and the editors of *Dicey and Morris*, as quoted below in this section.

[56] Departmental Advisory Commitee (DAC), Chairman Lord Justice Saville, *Report on the Arbitration Bill*, February 1996, published in abridged version as 'Supplementary Report on the Arbitration Act', Arbitration International 13.3 (1997) 317-330.

[57] See 8.1.2, above.

[58] Chukwumerije, op cit (n 51), 189.

[59] Shackleton, op cit (n 30), 379.

If the transaction is governed by an international agreement or a standard form of rules which require the arbitrator to choose the 'law' which he deems applicable to the substance of the dispute, is he thereby enabled to apply the *lex mercatoria* or general principles of law? ... I suggest that the answer must surely be no. [60]

*Dicey and Morris* also confirm this position for the application of a-national law absent choice of law:

... there is no scope for the arbitrators to apply (in the absence of the agreement of the parties) the *lex mercatoria* or general principles of law. [61]

This is a clear vote. Its quotation by Shackleton,[62] in the specific context of his article again shows, that there is only little appreciation of the distinctive potential instances of application of a-national law rules, perhaps according to their nature, certainly according to conflict of law rules and under judicial review considerations, and subsequently, a different life of such rules within domestic law in these different instances. The distinction between values of trade usages, *ex aequo et bono decisions*, *lex mercatoria*, general principles of law and other a-national law, is therefore essential, especially since the Arbitration Act 1996 aimed to integrate some features of international arbitration practice that had been alien to English law before, and have therefore not been categorised on this level. Measuring the English Arbitration Act according to its 'internationalisation', however, does require a differentiation as to the notions imported from the international (ie, foreign) level. All depends therefore on the treatment of arbitration awards involving a-national rules of law under English arbitration law as regards judicial review and supervision.

#### 8.2.2.4 Case law: Authority following the Channel Tunnel litigation

One example of such an award being brought before English courts was the litigation ensued with the Channel Tunnel project – performed by a consortium of British and French companies.[63] Not only is this litigation an example for the significance of 'neutral' choice of law clauses in commercial contracts, as discussed above in Chapters 7 and 1, but it also demonstrates how British courts have dealt with a-national rules of law and will possibly deal with them in the future.

When the case came before the House of Lords the court was asked to set aside the stay of action in favour of pre-arbitrational proceedings and to decide on the facts of the case. This was considered by the Lords to be an attempt to evade the arbitration agreement in the contract and thus, the stay of action under English law was ultimately upheld and the interim relief or injunction sought by the appellant

---

60 Lord Mustill in Mustill and Boyd, *The Law and Practice of Commercial Arbitration in England* (1989), 96-97.

61 Dicey and Morris, eds, *The Conflict of Laws*, 4th Cum Supp to the 12th edn, 1997, 102.

62 Shackleton, op cit (n 30), 385.

63 *Eurotunnel* v *Balfour Beatty* [1992] 2 Lloyd's Rep 7 (CA); [1993] 1 Lloyd's Rep 291 (HL).

Euro tunnel consortium against the Balfour Beatty Group (contractors), was refused.[64] The considerations that were made involving substantive law, and in particular the general principle of *exceptio non adimpleti contractus* or *l'exception d'inexecution*, were discussed in connection with the question of whether the court should have a power to give a summary judgment because the matter in dispute could not give rise to a dispute due to the absence of an arguable case. This was based by the appellants on an interpretation and application of the Arbitration Act 1975 s 1(1) as well as RSC Order 14. The House of Lords elaborated, however, that the principle of civil law was a recognised standard of trade law and attributed enough legal significance to it that a dispute about the legal effect of this principle was material to giving rise to a dispute, as referred to under the applicable Arbitration Act 1975.[65] This discussion also implied that the choice of law was undisputed and was undoubtedly respected by the Court:

That the doctrine is a part of the international trade law which is made applicable to the contract by cl 68 is common ground, and it is also common ground (at least for the purposes of these proceedings) that the doctrine is capable of being excluded by consent.

The Court also recognised the motivations for including the specific choice of law clause, as well as the arbitration and dispute settlement agreement, and with it forced the parties to stick to their original decision to have contractual disputes settled according to neutral principles of law and outside the regular state jurisdiction:

I have no doubt that the dispute resolution mechanism of cl 67 were the subject of careful thought and negotiation. The parties chose an indeterminate 'law' to govern their substantive rights; an elaborate process for ascertaining those; and a location for that process outside the territories of the participants.[66] This conspicuously neutral, 'a-national' and extra-judicial structure may well have been the right choice for the special needs of the Channel Tunnel venture. But whether it was right or wrong, it is the choice which the parties have made. The appellants now regret that choice. To push their claim for mandatory relief through the mechanisms of cl 67 is too slow and cumbersome to suit their purpose, and they now wish to obtain far reaching relief through the judicial means which they have been scrupulous to exclude. Notwithstanding that the Court can and should in the right case provide reinforcement for the arbitral process by granting interim relief I am quite satisfied that this is not such a case, and that to order an injunction here would be to act contrary both to the general tenor of the construction contract and to the spirit of international arbitration.[67]

I believe that this is a clear and convincing confession of English law to international arbitration which does not need much further explanation.

[64] *Eurotunnel* v *Balfour Beatty* [1993] 1 Lloyd's Rep 291 (HL), 300, 305 and 311.
[65] Ibid, 302 and 303.
[66] Brussels was the stipulated seat of arbitration.
[67] *Eurotunnel* v *Balfour Beatty* [1993] 1 Lloyd's Rep 291 (HL), 311.

#### 8.2.2.5 Scope of appeal on questions of law

Under the Arbitration Act 1996 only questions of English law are subject to judicial supervision; s 82(1): ' "questions of law" means – (a) for a court in England and Wales, a question of the law of England and Wales …'. Instances where these criterions have been considered unfulfilled were cases raising questions on Islamic law, Swiss law and on the Vienna Convention. This indicates that there is a 'negative' definition of sources of law, ie, specifying that they are not English law. This way, the courts do not have to answer the question if certain rules of law are formal law or in any way recognised as forming a legislative basis. Rules of a-national law are thereby not necessarily 'stigmatised' because they are not necessarily positively dismissed as rules of law. There is, therefore, still a chance for an evolutionary development towards recognition of certain rules of law, such as the UPICC, due to their special qualities[68] and the practical experience that has already been gained using the UPICC along with 'general principles of law'.

#### 8.2.2.6 Discussion of the position under English arbitration legislation and the formative role of the courts

Even after the reform brought about by the enactment of the Arbitration Act, 1996, English law certainly provides more scope for judicial supervision and review (on the part of the courts), and for challenging the award (on the part of parties to arbitration proceedings), than other jurisdictions, namely certain continental European ones. This does not necessarily mean a disadvantage for the arbitration proceedings taking place in England, even when viewed particularly under the aspect of employing a-national law rules either with, or without, an express choice by the parties to a dispute.

The traditional attitude taken by English courts had as its objective the correct administration of English law, the protection of English citizens against injustice arising from arbitration proceedings and even the prevention of the growth of areas inaccessible to English law within the English jurisdiction.[69] The same objectives have been pursued by other legal systems, such as the German system. The idea to provide a minimum standard for arbitration proceedings has brought all legislation relating to arbitration into existence.

> The second consideration is the interest of States, in particular the seat of arbitration, in guaranteeing the fairness and impartiality of the procedure. As the binding character of arbitration awards depends on national law, national courts should play a role in securing the integrity of arbitrations conducted within their jurisdiction. Moreover, judicial control that guarantees the integrity of the process is not inconsistent with the legitimate expectation of the parties. [70]

---

[68] See the discussion in the context of the article by Professor Mankowski at 8.2.3.3, below, et seq.

[69] Ie, areas '…where the King's writ does not run': Bankes, LJ in *Charnikow* v *Roth Schmidt & Co* [1922] 2 KB 478 (compare 8.2.2.2, above).

[70] Chukwumerije, op cit (n 51), 183.

This objective is less 'an interest of States' but rather, a responsibility of States. English law has traditionally been particularly concerned with high standards of procedural rules. This concern has found its expression in the case law, especially in the case quoted above, *Czarnikow*.[71] It is questionable, however, whether the attitude behind this line of decisions should give rise to such concerns as raised by Shackleton in his comments on the Arbitration Act 1996,[72] with a view to assessing the chances for an application of a-national rules of law to arbitration proceedings. Comparing this attitude taken by the courts, and the case law developed thereby, to the attitude within the German legal 'environment' leads to the following understanding.

In England, the focus of the discussion is more on the role of the courts as opposed to arbitration tribunals. This is clearly evidenced by the material quoted above which served English commentators to demonstrate the 'static', and 'suspicious', attitude of English law towards arbitration. In my view English courts should not be equalled with 'the state' without more as is possibly done by Shackleton:

> Autonomous sources of legal norms have been generally unwelcome in English arbitration law. They are naturally a challenge to the competence of state systems to control and resolve disputes ... It runs contrary to positivist views which closely associate law with the state and which dominate legal thinking in common law jurisdictions. [73]

Clearly, the competition does not run between the 'state' and the arbitral tribunals but between the (state) courts and those tribunals. To me, Shackleton's sentence should read: 'They are naturally a challenge to the competence of English courts to control and resolve disputes'. The English system is not only the mother and origin of all other 'common law jurisdictions' it also embodies one of the world's most prominent, independent and autonomous court systems. The English court system benefits from historical continuity and uninterrupted identity and is therefore certainly unique in the world. The role of English courts with their individual historical role as King's and Queen's juridical bodies and their unique method of establishing English law, the common law and the law of equity, occasionally referring straight back to decisions rendered in the Middle Ages and taking into account a wealth of experience and commercial practice, rightly invoke for themselves a great deal of authority if it comes to matters of fair trials and just proceedings.[74] The appearance of laymen acting as arbitrators in commercial matters can therefore easily amount to intrusion from the point of view of the courts. The courts in England are independent from the state (ie, Parliament and the ex-

---

[71] Compare 8.2.2.2, above.

[72] Shackleton, op cit (n 30), 375-389.

[73] Shackleton, op cit (n 30), 380-381.

[74] Note the formulation of Chukwumerije, op cit (n 51), 171-172: 'English courts now adopt a position more of partnership than confrontation towards arbitration. This change in attitude has been reflected in successive English arbitration laws which have increasingly enhanced the authority and effectiveness of arbitral tribunals.'

ecutive powers) and cultivate a strong awareness of this fact. Assertion of power in the domain of the law is therefore a natural phenomenon in such an environment, much more so than in a state like Germany where, since the enactment of the first modern and uniform codification of the civil law only one hundred and fifty years ago, the fourth state is now at work.[75] Although German courts are certainly independent too, they do not in the least have the same sense of identity and material formative influence on the development of the law. From a comparative perspective, the aspect of competition between courts and private tribunals is certainly a prominent feature to be kept in mind when evaluating the current situation of arbitration and the evolution of transnational law rules in English law.

The aspect of judicial supervision and review therefore also extends predominantly to the area of procedural matters. The heading of 'procedural irregularity', comprising 'substantive jurisdiction' and 'serious irregularity', is therefore the one conferring the more comprehensive powers of adjudication to the Courts (Arbitration Act 1996 ss 67 and 68).

The general objective of ensuring the minimum standard of procedure is in keeping with most other Western jurisdictions but does not show substantially greater possibilities to involve the courts in arbitration proceedings.

Over the last eighty years, since *Czarnikow*, this involvement has doubtlessly moved away from intervention and supervision towards assistance and co-operation.[76] This was motivated by pragmatic considerations. Clearly, awareness of the value of arbitration was in the courts even before the 1979 Arbitration Act and the resort of businesses to commercial arbitration was respected:

> Among commercial men what are commonly called commercial arbitrations are undoubtedly and deservedly popular. [77]

From this grew the motivation to enhance English arbitration so that more arbitration proceedings would be attracted,[78] and there is certainly a general awareness of the requirements of arbitration in terms of independence from courts.[79]

One of the objectives behind the various reforms of the law relating to arbitration was therefore competitiveness. Internationalisation, harmonisation and the

---

75 Compare 8.3.3.

76 See only Chukwumerije, op cit (n 51), 171: 'This traditional English judicial attitude has significantly changed in recent decades. English courts now adopt a position more of partnership than confrontation towards arbitration.'

77 Bankes, LJ in *Charnikow* v *Roth Schmidt & Co* [1922] 2 KB 478, 484.

78 See Shackleton, op cit (n 30), 381, note 20 quoting from the *Mustill Report*, para 109: English arbitration law be reformed so that it remained 'in the vanguard of the various systems currently enjoying the preference of regular international users'.

79 See, for instance, Chukwumerije, op cit (n 51), 185 quoting from the DAC Report on the 1996 Arbitration Bill: 'The test of substantive injustice is intended to be applied by way of support for the arbitral process, not by way of interference with that process....the test is not what would have happened had the matter been litigated...to apply such a test would be to ignore the fact that the parties have agreed to arbitrate not to litigate.'

curtailing of the judicial supervision was though pragmatically motivated.[80] From this follows the justified expectation that English courts will recognise when the time has arrived to give effect to a choice of a-national law rules within commercial law and arbitration.

The so-called 'unitary conception' of English law[81] is not an obstacle to the further growth of commercial case law, which could in fact one day express a view under English law that there are autonomous rules of law carrying some source of law function which they have acquired at the international level. Again speaking with the DAC Report which, regarding choice of law in arbitration, 'declined to "lay down principles in this highly complex area" in the interest of "flexibility"'.[82]

The idea of 'maintaining a single system of law'[83] does not necessarily generally prevent the acknowledgement 'that, international transactions are distinct from domestic contracts and may be governed by specific substantive rules evolved at the international level'.[84]

Another observation by Shackleton seems to equal the one made from the perspective of German law; the predominance of positivism and unitary conceptions of national law:

> Indeed the essence of much criticism of *lex mercatoria* and other transnational normative structures as distinct bodies of law is the lack of resemblance to state legal systems invariably presented as having superseded other forms of law ... Positivism, moreover, is analytically inadequate to account for non-statist legal phenomena, and might even be specifically constructed not to account for it. *Lex mercatoria*, theories of a-national legal norms and the spontaneous development of international law form the parties' expectations in international practice and transactions are more closely connected to pre-positivist theories of natural law and civil law conceptions of subjective rights which have no directly corresponding category in common law.[85]

A system like the common law seems to be most suited for responding to developments on the international level, compared with the civil law systems which the author refers to above. Due to the tradition of 'restating' the law both by Acts of Parliament and by precedent, resemblances to the natural law theories appear to be more natural than for civil law systems which function through legislation entirely and are thereby prone to positivist traditions.

The tension arising from the alleged parallel existence of national and a-national rules of law in arbitration is rather due to the nature of arbitration and is 'to some extent inevitable in any attempt by the state to regulate a process which

---

80 Compare Chukwumerije, op cit (n 51), 171-191; see also M Kerr, 'Arbitration and the Courts: The UNCITRAL Model Law' ICLQ 34.1 (1985) 1 et seq, who tellingly uses the term 'customer' to describe the role of arbitration law.

81 Shackleton, op cit (n 30), 379.

82 DAC Report quoted in Shackleton, op cit (n 30), 389.

83 Ibid, 386 referring to the 1978 Commercial Court Committee Report on Arbitration, para 14.

84 Shackleton, op cit (n 30), 379.

85 Ibid, 381.

occurs by definition outside the state'.[86] Rather than asserting the state's 'role as the sole legitimate normative authority for English law',[87] the English legislator has taken responsibility to guarantee that 'the integrity of the process is not inconsistent with the legitimate expectation of the parties'.[88] It does not seem adequate to focus solely on 'the state' with regard to the formation of private law rules in a common law jurisdiction relying on precedent:

> Secondly, the limitations placed on the arbitrators' choice of law in section 46 puts the state's interests first and will, in some circumstances result in a violation of the will of the parties.[89]

Indeed, relying entirely on party autonomy, the arbitrator would have to establish the rules governing the contract (or dispute) strictly by reference to the individual case.[90] However, compared to the solution offered by the new German arbitration law in §1051 ZPO,[91] the provision in s 46 opts for the more liberal choice suggested by the UNCITRAL Model law. At least under the scope and in the signatory states of the RC, it cannot be said that:

> What constitutes 'law' or even a 'recognized system of law', differs greatly from country to country … and [that] there is little justification for imposing such anglo-centric legal conceptions on foreign parties arbitrating in England.'[92]

The subtle distinction between 'law' and 'rules of law' is a recognised standard among the European jurisdictions and will certainly be within the expectations of civil law based parties. The identification of 'law' with 'state' and ensuing positivism certainly arises more from the civil law sphere, and especially from the history of the past one hundred and fifty or one hundred and sixty years with the formation of the modern nation states. This is because codification was very closely linked to political movements striving for unification, liberalisation of public life and constitutionalism. This movement was less successful and less interruptive for legal evolution in England than on the continent.[93]

Arbitration is an area where the state allows private dispute resolution and thereby implicitly steps back. The fact that the special self-regulating environment in international trade and the high degree of its development remains unrecognised in recent legislation, might therefore be understood not only as a sign of obliviousness and statist conception, but also as continued reliance on the role of the courts as a motor for adaptation to the requirements of changing times:

---

86 Shackleton, op cit (n 30), 388; see also below and compare Solomon, op cit (n 9), 990.
87 Shackleton, op cit (n 30), 389.
88 Chukwumerije, op cit (n 51), 183: see above.
89 Shackleton, op cit (n 30), 387.
90 See below.
91 See below.
92 Shackleton, op cit (n 30), 387.
93 See Part 2, 5.3, above.

However, where English law is chosen by the parties and the place of arbitration is in England, much will depend on the willingness of English courts to tolerate any latitude exercised boldly by arbitrators in their appreciation of the rules which govern international contractual relations.[94]

### 8.2.2.7 Conclusion

Under the Arbitration Act 1996 parties can opt to choose the UPICC as governing law of the contract, s 46(1)(b). Absent choice of law, however, the arbitrator cannot apply the UPICC as governing law, s 46(3). The use of the UPICC can be subject to appeal proceedings on questions of law, s 69, as well as to challenging the award for serious irregularity, s 68(2)(b) and (e). Out of these rules only ss 46 and 69 can be dispensed with by agreement of the parties (s 4(2) and Schedule 1). Since only questions of English law are subject to s 69 of the Arbitration Act, 1996, it is likely that the courts will disregard questions arising in the course of applying the UPICC:

> Given the restriction on Court intervention where a law other than English law is applied, arbitrators may yet enjoy some freedom from sanction for the application of forms of law unrecognised in England, including *lex mercatoria* or general principles of law.'[95]

There is, however, a possibility that matters of public policy or other aspects falling under the criteria of s 69(1)(c) and (d) could arise in such cases, especially since rules like the UPICC are not recognised sources of law in English case law and legal writing yet. The court practice so far has shown a general recognition and appreciation of the requirements of arbitration proceedings and the interests of international trade, so that legitimate expectations of the parties to arbitration proceedings are likely to be considered. This applies specifically since some notions introduced by the Arbitration Act 1996 have not been recognised in English law, such as the concept of *amiable compositeur*. These notions have been deliberately imported in order to adapt to international practice so that these will be given effect. Subsequently other standards of international law, such as autonomous rules of law, might be considered of a comparable value to the promotion of a competitive English forum for arbitration, trade and commercial legal practice.

The question of whether the treatment of rules, such as the UPICC, as governing law in the technical sense of conflict rules, and thereby as 'law' as opposed to 'rules of law', or whether they will be regarded as implied terms or will have to be incorporated into the contract is open at present. There is not enough authority or analysis on this question in sufficient detail. Again, it will be up to the courts to develop an attitude when the case arises.[96]

---

[94] Shackleton, op cit (n 30), 389.
[95] Ibid, 389.
[96] Compare ibid, 3.

### 8.2.3 Judicial review of commercial arbitration awards under current German law

#### *8.2.3.1 No clear position in legal writings*

In my view the traditional position prevailing in German legal science, as reported so far in this section, is unsuitable for meeting modern developments in international commercial law and practice. It ignores the actual developments and requirements both in international commercial arbitration, drafting practice, and also on the domestic level in state litigation. It suffers from defective foundations, because the positions brought forward are presented in an inconsistent way and represent unfounded prejudices against a-national law. This seems to result from a lack of awareness of the proper nature and objectives of private law. The particular circumstances of the application of *lex mercatoria*, general principles of law, the UPICC or other a-national law are to be reviewed, therefore.

#### *8.2.3.2 Critical voices and well-preserved prejudices*

To illustrate this situation under the German *lex lata* a recent contribution is highlighted in the following analysis.

##### *8.2.3.2.1 The use of CISG in Germany – recommended*

Professor Mankowski advocates the application of the CISG to international contracts in his article on the recommendable (right) choice of law for international commercial contracts. Although in force in Germany from 1 January 1991, CISG is regularly excluded in international contract terms following standard recommendations of lawyers.[97] The reason observed by Mankowski is that German lawyers[98] are afraid to be confronted with issues which they have not been trained in.[99] Further arguments include the fact that there is no precise body of case law or judicial authority to review the meaning of the Articles of the CISG since they are very open textured. Special difficulties are anticipated as arising from the provisions on breach of obligation and fundamental breach of contract (eg, in Art 45 and Art 64(1)(a)), of the CISG, and the alleged fact that the Convention is too buyer friendly as a whole, due to the contribution of developing countries to its making. These prejudices or defences against the use of the CISG are correctly de-

---

[97] P Mankowski, '*Rechtswahl für Verträge des internationalen Wirtschaftsverkehrs*' RIW 1 (2003) 2-15, 8; see also F Ferrari in ZEuP 2002, 737; this was also reported by lawyers on the UNIDROIT conference held in Basel in 1997 on the topic of the UPICC.

[98] Along with Swiss lawyers according to the discussions on the 1997 Basel UNIDROIT conference.

[99] Mankowski, op cit (n 97), 8.

scribed as plainly resulting from the *horror alieni* by Mankowski and others.[100] Mankowski then responds to each of these obviously unfounded arguments. At this point in time, the most important response is that the notion of breach of obligation has been introduced into German domestic contract law in the course of the 2002 reform of the BGB,[101] following the implementation of several recent directives on consumer protection and unfair contract terms.[102]

Beyond these prejudices the advantages of CISG for international trade are seen by Mankowski in the fact that there is a wealth of documentation which makes the CISG accessible and prevents high costs for consulting and research. He praises especially the high standard of electronic databases enabling practitioners to track decisions on CISG worldwide, as well as the fact that much literature is available in all major languages. Mankowski does not forget to emphasise that some of the most influential standard works on the CISG are German.[103]

The benefits of the application of the CISG to international (sales) contracts are to Mankowski the fact that they provide a 'uniform platform', especially for string sales,[104] because the uniformity allows equal access to the rules by all the parties involved. The uniformity also saves costs and the effort to establish the applicable law via conflict rules. The rules of the CISG are flexible; they can be modified[105] and thus adapted to the need of the different branches of international trade who should not unduly insist on using their own standard terms which allegedly uniquely serve their specific needs.[106] Mankowski even suggests the CISG 'could become a true *lex mercatoria* – but codified and with a clear, ascertainable content.'[107]

As to the choice of law aspect of the CISG Mankowski points out that the Convention on its own cannot become the law governing the contract under Art 27(1) EGBGB (*kollisionsrechtliche Verweisung*). Mankowski describes the CISG as a '*Rechtskorpus, aber kein eigenständiges Recht*',[108] a legal corpus, a body of law, but no autonomous law.

Obviously, the CISG is part of German civil law and applies to cases falling under the scope of the Convention, as set out in its Articles 1 to 6. It would therefore apply following a choice of law of German law and likewise in other countries who have adopted CISG. Mankowski, however, mentions expressly that the

---

[100] Ibid; see also H Lübbert in I Schwenzer, *Schuldrecht, Rechtsvergleichung und Rechtsvereinheitlichung im 21. Jh. – Symposium aus Anlaß des 65. Geburtstages von Peter Schlechtriehm* (1999) 8 et seq; compare Magnus in ibid.

[101] Namely §§280, 281 and 323 BGB.

[102] EC Directives 93/13/EEC, 94/47/EC, 97/7/EC and 99/44/EC.

[103] Mankowski, op cit (n 97), 10; Professor Mankowski himself is a commentator on the CISG in Benicke, Ferrari, Mankowski and Reinhart, *UN-Kaufrecht* (1991).

[104] Ibid, 10, col 2.

[105] Under Art 6 CISG.

[106] Mankowski, op cit (n 97), 10, col 1.

[107] Ibid, 10, col 1: '*Die CISG kann, wenn man sie denn endlich akzeptieren würde, eine wahre lex mercatoria werden – aber kodifiziert und mit klarem, feststellbarem Inhalt.*'

[108] Ibid, col 2, ie, the law of a state which exclusively can be the object of a choice of law under Art 27 EGBGB.

CISG would then apply '*unter dem Vorbehalt des intern-rechtlich zwingenden Rechts des eigentlichen Vertragsstatuts*', meaning that the rules of CISG cannot override the mandatory rules of the state whose law it is part of. The formulation '*Sie [CISG] stünde unter dem Vorbehalt*', however, suggests that the CISG needs a specific additional authority or permission to apply within German law which is not the case.[109] It also appears to imply that there are issues that better remain subject to German mandatory rules. Here, as in so many other cases of the mentioning of mandatory rules no specific example is given. Usually, legislation relating to unfair contract terms and to consumer protection is meant by this remark.[110] Suffice it to say at this point, even the so-called '*Indizfunktion*' (indicating function) of §10 AGBG (§308 BGB (2002)) and the application of the rules of §11 Nos 5 and 6 AGBG (§309 No 5 and §306 BGB (2002)), forbidding penalty clauses and lump sum damages,[111] which are unknown to German law are disputed in German legal science as far as international commercial contracts are concerned.[112] Since the CISG, other than the UPICC, does not even contain such controversial rules, the unavoidable mention of 'mandatory rules' all the more appears to be a reflex occurring regularly in the context of international rules of law.[113] It appears indeed to be the reflex triggered by the *horror alieni* and a deep underlying conviction that the (own) domestic law undoubtedly provides the best solutions for any case.[114]

##### *8.2.3.2.2 But not the UPICC*

Having advertised the substantive benefits of the CISG for international contracts as described above, Mankowski does not recommend the UPICC for the sake of these same qualities in the UPICC,[115] despite their obviously being equally suited

---

[109] German domestic contract law was considered to apply in complementation to CISG according to Art 7(2) CISG in the award of 29 December 1998 rendered by the Schiedsgericht Hamburger Freundschaftliche Arbitrage in Hamburg: see RIW vol 5 (1999) 394-396, 395 (II 3).

[110] Compare C-W Canaris, '*Die Stellung der "UNIDROIT Principles" und "Principles of European Contract Law" im System der Rechtsquellen*', 21-28.

[111] A favourite target of controversial discourse.

[112] See H Stoll: '*Rechtliche Inhaltskontrolle bei internationalen Handelsgeschäften*' in *Festschrift für Kegel* (1987) 658 and C-W Canaris, '*Gesamtunwirksamkeit und Teilgültigkeit rechtsgeschäftlicher Regelungen*' in *Fetschrift für Steindorff* (1990) 559.

[113] Why would the German legislator enact a Convention that would lead to clashes with existing mandatory rules?

[114] Compare U Eisenhardt, *Deutsche Rechtsgeschichte* (2004) No 445; Eisenhardt summarises the passionate defence by Heinrich Freiherr von Gagern (1766-1852) of the French *Code Civil* in the local parliament which was in use in the Rhenish lands (Rhenish Law) following the Napoleonic conquest. The citizens of those areas much preferred the qualities of the *Code Civil* to those of the traditional and feudalistic German law which, as Gagern pointed out was foreign anyway (sic!) since it originated from Roman law, the law of previous conquerors. A nice example of law introduced *ratione imperii* and then acquiring support *imperio rationis*.

[115] Mankowski, op cit (n 97), 11, col 1.

to international commercial contracts and providing a scope extending beyond sales contracts. The UPICC even abstain from extending their scope to consumer contracts (which the scope of the CISG includes) so that concerns relating to the protection of weaker parties, commonly raised against the application of international uniform law, have no room.[116] Mankowski just warns of the lack of formal recognition as rules of law and of the costly insecurity arising from this fact.[117] For parties wishing to have the UPICC govern their contract he recommends their incorporation as contractual terms (*materiellrechtliche Verweisung*), even under the regime of arbitration law, which in Germany potentially does allow for the choice of a-national rules of law under §1051(1) ZPO.[118] Under Mankowski's own condition that the UPICC cannot apply unqualified by mandatory domestic law, the UPICC are subject to the rules relating to contractual construction rather than to statutory interpretation.

This result seems unfavourable given that even Mankowski recognises the specific qualities of the UPICC in relation to a choice of *lex mercatoria* or general principles of law:

*Die Principles leisten genau solche Präzisierungen, wie sie der lex mercatoria fehlen, und vermeiden genau jene Gefahren, welche die lex mercatoria aufzuwerfen droht.*'[119]
(The Principles achieve precisely the kind of certainty which lack in the *lex mercatoria* and avoid the dangers that can arise from the *lex mercatoria*.)[120]

One should expect this view to result into a clear recommendation of the UPICC, especially for non-sales contracts.

#### 8.2.3.3 Advocated motivations for choice of law

Despite this, the desire of some international contract negotiators to look for a 'neutral' choice of law is not considered a valid motivation by this (prevailing) view in German legal science.[121] Mankowski points out that only a small percentage of arbitration proceedings before the ICC Court of International Arbitration[122] involved a choice of *lex mercatoria*, general principles of law or trade usages, and none of the cases decided before the Vienna Chamber of Commerce involved the

---

116 Ibid, 11, col 1: Mankowski suggests that the UPICC 'escape' these reproaches ('*entgehen diesen Vorwürfen*') by excluding these sensitive issues of typically weaker parties and thereby elegantly implies the evasion of mandatory rules providing for the protection of weaker parties.

117 Ibid, 12, col 1.

118 Ibid, 12, col 1 and 14, col 1. For a full discussion of the interpretation of §1051 ZPO see Solomon, op cit (n 9), 981-990.

119 Mankowski, op cit (n 97), 14, col 1.

120 Ie, unpredictability, vagueness and the lack of recognition as 'law' by state courts, as described by Mankowski, ibid, 13.

121 See below.

122 Only 0.8% of all cases.

UPICC as governing law or contract terms.[123] He also explains in detail the factors giving rise to the choice of law clauses that are actually included in international commercial contracts. These reasons deserve a more detailed analysis.[124] At this point it can be stated that Mankowski does not consider the actual motivations behind the choice in most cases in which a 'neutral choice' is attempted agreeable. Instead he pursues the 'education' of the negotiators towards the best solution which he deems to be above all the law of a state, especially one which leads to the application of CISG.[125] The justifiable motivations behind such a choice are almost entirely of a monetary nature. This sounds attractive in the context of international commercial contracts and also explains why an elaborated doctrine relating to the integration of transnational substantive contract law is not considered wanted.

#### 8.2.3.4 Stigmatising a-national rules of law regarding choice of law in international contracts for the wrong reasons

It reinforces the prevailing view of German legal scholars that it is positively the requirement of state law, rather than merely that status of formal legislation[126] of a given set of law rules, which makes for its eligibility to be governing law under (any) German conflict rule.

Unfortunately the proponents of this strict opinion overlook the danger of arguing in a circle; the small percentage of cases employing a-national law in arbitration might be due to the detrimental situation in this area of law and this legal situation in turn is not changed due to the lack of a visible interest of the 'users' of the law [127] in such a change.

The monetary interests that Mankowski relies on to recommend certain choices of law are costs generally induced by uncertainty, caution and error, as well as costs for professional services to investigate the exact contents of a foreign law, and the outcome of any dispute under the stipulated law (*Unsicherheitskosten, Rechtsermittlungskosten, Vorsichtskosten, Irrtumskosten*). Another type of monetary interest, especially when benefiting foreign parties, such as the British law profession, provide a reason for Mankowski to advise against a recommendation of a choice of their law, ie, the Common Law,[128] despite his own argument that the chosen law should '... present [itself] ... in a familiar, not exotic language',[129] a criterion which the English language obviously fulfils.

---

[123] Mankowski, op cit (n 97), 11 col 1.

[124] See below. Also, it might be worthwhile looking at the value of cases settled under *lex mercatoria* or similar. It might turn out that the mere number of disputes is less telling than the commercial weight of its subject matter. Again, the Channel Tunnel litigation is a significant example for the role of choice of law in international business.

[125] Mankowski recommends not routinely to exclude the CISG; Mankowski, op cit (n 97), 14.

[126] As suggested by Canaris, op cit (n 110), 5-31: compare above.

[127] See below.

[128] Mankowski, op cit (n 97), 6.

[129] Ibid, 3-4.

#### 8.2.3.5 Protectionist viewpoint

The first such 'undesirable' commercial interest is the profit which the predominantly London based law profession gains out of the vivid marketing effect of the location and ensuing conviction that English law is the 'best' law for transactions in branches like the commodities trade, financial services and carriage of goods by sea. The law profession, according to Mankowski, is inclined to recommend out-of-court dispute settlement in order to avoid sharing the fees.[130] The other commercial factor is explained to be the creation of a body of case law forming a 'public asset' which would then only serve the national interest (of the UK) rather than that of the foreigners who contribute to its creation while bearing risks and costs.[131] The Common Law jurisdictions are said to typically only 'concentrate on the effects on market participants who are resident in their own sphere of application'[132] so that foreign parties do not benefit (commercially) to the same extent.[133] Together with the effects of the stipulation of a Common Law country as the forum, this 'advantage' of the common lawyer 'increases nearly into exclusivity',[134] especially through the growing body of case law. As much as it seems desirable for the chosen law to include a large body of case law for the sake of predictability and perhaps even the prevention of disputes, the number of precedence according to Mankowski, does not necessarily indicate a high quality of the law but rather a large quantity of users; a so-called 'positive *Netzwerkexternaltiät*', positive network externality. This phenomenon[135] simply distorts the fair competition between the legal systems by attracting uncritical users as parts of a general movement.[136] Still, Mankowski postulates that the desirable law should 'be open for the developments, requirements and interests of international commercial relations',[137] it should be 'open, modern and economy oriented'.[138] He appears however, to dislike seeing it work as efficiently as English law and favouring the economic interest of the City of London. It may be left open if this attitude serves the development of an open, modern and competitive German legal system.

---

130 Ibid, 6, col 2.

131 Ibid, 6 and 7.

132 Ibid, 6, col 2. This argument is taken from a work by Hudson, *The Law on Financial Derivatives* (1988) 159 and is obviously ill-placed in this context and is not suitable for generalisation. It just goes to show that branches might actually very much need their own specific choice of law guidelines, contrary to Mankowski's view expressed in his article at 10, col 1.

133 Ibid, also 7.

134 Ibid 7, col 1.

135 Observed and named by Mankowski.

136 Mankowski, op cit (n 97), 7, col 1.

137 Ibid, 3, col 2.

138 Ibid, 5, col 2.

### 8.2.3.6 The actual motivations behind choice of law clauses in international commercial contracts

Also the Swiss law profession gains advantage of the unhappy fact that a 'neutral' legal system is often misconceived by negotiators as being located in a (politically) 'neutral' country.[139] This argument inspires the collection of motivations for the choice of law in contract negotiations, which Mankowski presents in his article, and which frequently form the actual choice of law clauses.

These motivations are taken from empirical records. They are predominantly irrational. Very often negotiations are first completed by the business team and only then discussed among the law departments.[140] Some businessmen like to boast of their dislike of paperwork and legal technicalities. Consequently, choice of law questions are not considered important at all or subject to the wrong assumptions. Such assumptions are the above mentioned misconception of the significance of political neutrality of a country for a choice of its law, ideas about '*Aequidistanz*' (equal distance) of the chosen law from both parties' familiar legal system, either geographically or substantively, and of course part of a kind of 'atavistic power game'.[141]

This latter motivation seems to have a considerable impact on choice of law clauses especially in the context of state party negotiations involving a-national, 'neutral' law.

The economical (rational) reason behind the negotiation of the applicable law is that none of the parties wants to be burdened with the costs that research into the legal background of the transaction will cause,[142] but since these costs can never really be 'calculated', even in one's own familiar legal system, this argument is not driving parties to be as competitive about the question as they actually are. Again, the Channel Tunnel litigation, and ICC case No 7110 are telling examples. In both cases prestige issues were the decisive factor for the choice of 'neutral law'. A project like the Channel Tunnel gave enough reason for all negotiating parties not to concede the application of each other's law. In the ICC case the agent of a sovereign of the Islamic sphere could not afford to submit to the law of a foreign Western country.[143] This is an important and just issue of power ascertaining strategy. Cost efficiency is not the driving force.[144] At least with the latter constellation

---

[139] Ibid, 5 col 2; the well-planned attempt to induce the other party to choose the home legal system of the interested (Swiss or Swedish) party just like a 'Trojan horse' can even be disguised by the wrong meaning of neutrality: ibid, 6 col 1.

[140] Best characterised by H Kronke, *Festschrift für Henrich* (2000) 390 as '*Champagnerstundensyndrom*', champagne-hour syndrome, referring to the businessmen celebrating the deal while the lawyers still 'clean up' next door.

[141] Mankowski, op cit (n 97), 2, col 2.

[142] Ibid, 3.

[143] 'Neutral' choice of law clauses are typical for contracts between agents of Islamic countries and Western businesses or states.

[144] Although in the ensuing arbitration economic interest in fact drove the claimant counsel to fight so hard for the application of the UPICC facing the limitation rules of English law that would otherwise have applied and invalidated their claim.

of a state contract, commercial projects may regularly involve aspects of international relations. Choice of law clauses are therefore not merely to be considered under financial aspects. This applies especially if one sees state sovereignty as a precondition for the existence of 'law' in the positivistic sense. Although it does not seem to fit into the picture of cool and calculating businessmen, these motivations are a matter of fact and cannot be judged by monetary aspects only. The atavistic and irrational component is real and requires room in the legal order.

Domestic arbitration law and conflict rules should therefore consider these interests within the international business world to resort to general principles of law or similar a-national choices of law.

#### 8.2.3.7 Giving effect to choice of law clauses under the scope of the Rome Convention

The legislator of the ZPO did strive to make arbitration in Germany more attractive.[145] This was to be achieved by adopting the suggested rules of the UNCITRAL Model Law. The liberty contained in Art 28(2) of the Model Law as to the applicable conflict rules absent choice of law was not imported into the ZPO though, but the arbitrator can only apply the law of a state under German law absent choice of law and is also bound by the standard prescribed in §1051(2) ZPO. This was done because the legislator saw himself bound by the RC; the official Parliamentary notes and the report of the reform commission[146] do mention a connection between the Rome Convention and the rules of the new §1051 ZPO. Solomon puts the question more precisely: Is the German legislator obliged under the Rome Convention to enact corresponding conflict rules for arbitration proceedings?[147] Solomon states that this question has not yet been discussed[148] and contends that such an obligation does not exist.[149] Because the legislator does not enforce the conflict rules contained in §1051 ZPO by way of sanctioning non-compliance, the arbitrator is de facto not obliged to comply with the conflict rules of the forum. The RC does not extend to arbitration law because this matter is generally outside the scope of state legislation:

*Mit §1051 ZPO-E bzw. seinem Gegenstück Art 28 ModellG wird nach alledem versucht, eine Frage zu regeln, die gesetzlicher Regelung im Grunde nicht zugänglich ist.*
(By §1051 of the draft ZPO and its counterpart Art 28 of UNCITRAL Model Law, it is after all attempted to regulate a question which is basically not open to legislative regulation.) [150]

---

[145] Solomon, op cit (n 9), 981 and 989; see also *BT-Drucksache* 13/1572, 52 which contains the official reasons for the reform.

[146] Kommission zur Neuordnung des Schiedverfahrensrecht, *Bericht mit einem Diskussionsentwurf zur Neufassung des Zehn ten Buchs der ZPO*, edited by Bundesministerium der Justiz (1994) 166 et seq.

[147] Solomon, op cit (n 9), 988, col 1.

[148] Ibid, 988, col 2.

[149] Ibid, 988-989.

[150] Ibid, 990.

In Solomon's opinion the legislator is free to issue different rules for arbitration than for state litigation. He subsequently reminds that certainly such differences would surprise given that the legislator seeks to find the best solution from his point of view:

*Schreibt er nun für Schiedsgerichte eine andere, insbesondere eine flexiblere Lösung vor, so stellt sich die Frage, warum er diese nicht auch für die staatlichen Gerichte für angemessen hält.*
(If he now prescribes a different, and especially a more flexible solution for arbitration tribunals, the question arises why he does not consider this appropriate also for state courts.)

This different treatment can be justified, according to Solomon, by the role of party autonomy in arbitration. State legislation and litigation require not only the interest of the parties but also other interests and considerations to be taken into account. The prevalence of party autonomy, however, makes §1051 ZPO 'the legislative interpretation of the typical intentions of the parties' regarding choice of law.[151]

#### 8.2.3.8 Conclusion

This section, 8.2, reviewed the current legislation relating to the recourse against arbitration awards in English and German law and its use and interpretation. It identified weaknesses in both the wording of the legislation and its application which could convincingly be rectified thereby allowing transnational uniform law and especially the UPICC to be used as governing law in arbitration proceedings.

What then is the best solution for choice of law rules in arbitration and in state litigation?

## 8.3 The desirable standard in the law of arbitration: Discussion

Following the previous two sections of Chapter 8 in which have set out and reviewed the current status of the *lex lata*, this section asks what the necessary consequences from these findings are. It investigates possible solutions to the problems and obstacles caused by traditional doctrine and current legislation in arbitration law in respect of the smooth application of specialised uniform commercial contract law on an international level. It analyses doctrinal ways of supporting more modern and favourable attitudes – in courts, legislation and doctrine – towards the application of uniform contract law and thereby examines possibilities for the development of a modern doctrine and methodology of international contract law.

[151] Ibid, 989, col 1.

The best solution is one which is based on the correct understanding of the objective to be promoted and achieved through the rules.

### 8.3.1 The nature and objective of arbitration

Solomon correctly characterises arbitration proceedings as a manner of dispute resolution which is allowed by the state, possibly desired, but not managed or supervised (‘*verantwortet*’) by the state.[152] Arbitration seems to be desired as far as the legislator expresses his wish to create an attractive forum for arbitration.[153] This implies that positive effects are expected to result from the activities of private dispute resolution, for example, the economic growth within some branches of trade and legal services. On the part of the litigants, however, the attractiveness of arbitration is the aspect of confidentiality and greater flexibility compared to state litigation. Considerations relating to costs and speed of proceedings are less convincing, given that arbitration procedures are not necessarily ‘cheap’ and fast. The interest of the business world is well described by Mankowski:[154]

*Zum einen versuchen Wirtschaftskreise, sich aus der Regulierung des staatlichen Rechts zu lösen und sich gleichsam ihr eigenes Recht zu schaffen [sic!]. Die Befürworter der lex mercatoria ist insoweit eine verklausulierende Chiffre für den Willen zur Selbstregulierung in den betreffenden Wirtschaftskreisen ... Dem können ... ein gewisser Wunsch nach Entrechtlichung und Entformalisierung des grenzüberschreitenden Handelsverkehrs zu Grunde liegen.*
(On the one hand business circles are trying to free themselves from the regulation of state law and quasi create their own law [sic!]. The support of the *lex mercatoria* is insofar an encrypting code for the will of self governance in the respective business circles ... At the basis of this could lie ... a certain desire for de-legalisation and de- formalisation of cross-border trade.)

Contrary to Mankowski’s underlying view that this driving force within international business circles is unfavourable, it is legitimate and actually gets support from most of the national laws relating to arbitration. The observation of this process shows that state law does not provide the appropriate environment for the specific needs of international trade dispute settlement. The deficiencies are to be found in the lack of recognition of the fundamental difference between domestic and international commercial contracts regarding the subject matter on the part of national legislators. The other deficiency is the fact that the original source of contract law (party autonomy and the freedom of contract) is not recognised by many practitioners within the domestic legal services. State legislators allow arbitration proceedings by offering state proceedings to help with the enforcement of awards. The high compliance rate of arbitration shows the success of this policy. It proves

[152] Ibid, 988-989.
[153] Compare Mankowski, op cit (n 97), 13, col 1.
[154] Mankowski, op cit (n 97), 13, col 1.

the point that de-regulation and self-governance are what is needed in international (and in domestic) commercial dispute settlement.

### 8.3.2 Regulating contract law in the state

It is a misconception that contract law is a natural area of state legislation in terms of exercising a policing role among litigating parties. Contract law is one area of private law which is less subject to the requirements of a social order in modern society. This is often forgotten. Berger, for instance, does point out that the state does not precede 'the law', but fails to distinguish contract law from 'the law'.[155] Berger wants to remind us that it has always been common ground; that there are in fact general principles of law or natural justice which are independent of the existence of a sovereign and state and its territory. Therefore, it is also inappropriate to raise concerns against the creation of a quasi-independent law within business circles.[156] This phenomenon is nothing but the consequence of the exercise of freedom of contract and party autonomy which modern western states guarantee. The modern business world and the economies of western countries are founded on party autonomy. It is one of the basic civil liberties. Contract law, therefore plays an ambiguous role within the state legislation.

### 8.3.3 Historic argument: Forming identity

Once more it shows that appropriate answers to modern questions of law cannot be given without recourse to the roots of the present day state and its law. These roots are to be found in legal history and theory. The idea of a patronising state legislation in the area of contract law has been alien to the European type of nation state. Concepts taken from modern welfare legislation and from consumer protection interventions headed by the EU organs are not to be mistaken as originating from traditional general contract law itself. The situation of Germany invites cutting off the ties linking the present to the past, ie, the true origins of the present contract law as it is embodied in the civil code, even after the recent reform. The German state has so little continuity that relatively recent, ie, post-war developments in contract law including contracts for employment and services and sales as far as consumer rights are concerned, might suggest that a protective and patronising attitude of the state is natural to apply to contracts and state adjudication. However, the protective element is rooted in the natural role of the state as a social order from which authority is derived to operate the criminal justice system, as well as the whole realm of social legislation and administration. In the course of the growth of this aspect of state activity, in the Federal Republic of 1949, a jungle of 'public law' rules have been created, many of which lead to a sometimes un-

[155] K P Berger, *The Creeping Codification of the* Lex Mercatoria (1999) at 103.
[156] As Mankowski does, as quoted above.

healthy marriage of market economy and state regulation. Examples are the health systems [157] and labour law.

Discontinuity in German history might have made it difficult for lawyers to look back at a time 'four states' ago, in the first half of the nineteenth century when the first codifications were created and fought for.[158] Codification in the civil (ie, private) law was strongly opposed to due to the predominance of local usages and 'common law'. The contract law which was then eventually drafted over a period of about fifty years by scientists was based on common principles of a long tradition of German '*Partikularrechte*' and the Roman law in the form of *ius commune*.[159] It was not directly adapted to the hierarchic structures of the feudalistic society, but restated ancient and fundamental principles of European (Roman) and Germanic law. Examples for typical legislation in civil matters of a bygone age are rather to be found in the family law and the inheritance rules of those days (eg, relating to divorce and illegitimate children). The conflict of laws remained largely unregulated and was subject to practice and judge-made law.

This practice of recourse to 'general principles' and usages was the prevailing and well tested practice for many centuries, while codification and ensuing positivism has been prevailing for only the last one hundred and fifty years. This reminiscence should be enough to make a strong point that general principles of law are ascertainable and manageable. The arbitral tribunal in ICC case No 7110 at least showed considerable proficiency in doing so. A list of recognised principles has been published by Lord Mustill and K P Berger[160] and their existence as terms of reference is undisputed among practitioners.

Dealing with general principles and a-national law, however, means accepting a paradox for the state legislator. The pre-Kaiserreich-Germany, the 'Holy Roman Empire of the German Nation' contained a large number of local laws which were tied together by an inconsistent confession to the *ius commune*, the surviving Roman Law. This universal presence of 'common law', Roman or Germanic, was common to all individual German states that each had their local particular legal system. 'Diversity in unity' was a reality to this extent. No sovereign, however,

---

[157] For an interesting insight, see M Löwisch, ed, *Wettbewerb, Kollektivverträge und Konfliktlösung in der Reform des Gesundheitswesens* (1999). This volume presents the papers delivered and the discussions on a symposium on the law and relevant aspects relating to the reform of the health system in Germany.

[158] See Part 2, at 5.3 above for details on the first enactment of the BGB. Many of the protagonists of the drafting process of the BGB were MPs and there were vivid discussions in public about its provisions and concepts.

[159] Compare Part 1, 2.2.2.1.2, above.

[160] K P Berger, *Internationale Wirtschaftsschiedsgerichtsbarkeit – Verfahrens- und materiallrechtliche Grundprobleme im Spiegel moderner Schiedsgesetze und Schiedspraxis* (1992) at 374-375; M J Mustill, 'The New *Lex Mercatoria* – The First Twenty-five Years" Arbitration International (1988) 86. See also K P Berger, *The Creeping Codification of the Lex Mercatoria* (1999) and W J H Wiggers, *International Commercial Law – Source Materials* (2001) and R Goode, *Transnational Commercial Law: International Instruments and Commentary* (2004) for an overview of all relevant source materials of *lex maercatoria*.

had the ambition to regulate contract law. There were restrictions to free trade and exchange of goods through customs and taxes, but these are essentially different from contract law. This insight is reflected by the exclusion of contract law from the competences of the EU. Because of a lack of relevance of common contract rules for the common market, the drafting of a European Civil Code has been taken off the agenda of the common legal policies.

Contract law within a territorial nation state is thus national law but not essentially a state matter of regulation. Nevertheless, the contract law is only in force within the boundaries of that state and addresses its inhabitants.[161] Regarding the content of contract law, it is obvious that it aims at balancing material, economic interests,[162] rather than imposing behavioural standards. This essentially corresponds to the nature of commercial relationships. The prime reference is the law of damages. Damages are traditionally measured and awarded in money and only recently are immaterial losses, emotional suffering, etc, recognised as giving rise to a claim. The moral and social aspect is dealt with under the criminal law and other legislation.[163]

The latter aspects typically serve the long term community life of any human society. Contracts, however, concern only temporary relationships which are not necessarily determined by geographical circumstances.[164] This special aspect has always made commercial law require different treatment when compared to domestic private law.[165] Travelling and leaving the protection of the home territory has always been characteristic for international trade.[166] Traders however, did not set out to settle in other territories as citizens or subjects of that other sovereign, but entered into legal relationships limited by very specific objectives; exchange of goods, services and currency.

Self-governance in international trade is a reality and a necessity even today and has a long tradition. Modern legal systems are to be measured by the flexibility and openness with which they meet these requirements. Protectionist anxiety[167] instead of dynamic competitiveness does not seem a helpful attitude in this context. Preventing the liberal choice of applicable law rules by an arbitrator is therefore not a desirable objective in a modern code for civil procedure.

---

[161] Forming the paradox of contract law, compare Part 1, 1.1.3.1, above.

[162] Germanic law even recognised this technique to remedy physical injury and murder: the higher the victim's social position the more the murderer or his family had to pay in damages: see K Kroeschell, *Deutsche Rechtsgeschichte I*, Vol 8 (1985) 43 et seq.

[163] Leading to loss of rights or claims or offices.

[164] Especially since the internet has emerged as a market place.

[165] See below.

[166] See, eg, the world of German medieval merchants in England and Russia forming the Hanseatic League; compare U Ziegler, *Die Hanse – Aufstieg, Blütezeit und Niedergang der ersten europäischen Wirtschaftsgemeinschaft* (1996).

[167] As raised by Mankowski, op cit (n 97), 6, col 2; see also above.

### 8.3.4 Recommended adjustment of legislation and analytical foundations

Along with Solomon it should therefore be recommended to cancel §1051 ZPO or replace it with an open rule allowing for an arbitrator's discretion as to the applicable law absent choice of law, including so called *lex mercatoria* and general principles of law as governing law in arbitration proceedings. The minimum standard should be the rule suggested in Art 28(2) UNCITRAL Model Law which allows a free choice of the conflict rules. For the purposes and within the scope of arbitration, there can be no doubt that general principles, the UPICC and other a-national law codifications are considered law by their 'users'. They are recognised standards which provide a suitable basis for arbitral adjudication.

It is therefore necessary to make it clear that deciding an arbitration case according to general principles, the *lex mercatoria* or the UPICC, does not equal an *ex aequo et bono* decision and thus does not per se overstep the limits set by the parties in their arbitration agreement.[168] In cases where these rules are referred to in the conflict of law clauses of an international contract it must be possible for the arbitrator to apply such rules as the governing law of the contract, as it was done in ICC case No 7110. This means that national law does not dominate the legal reasoning, but serves as a default set of rules merely to complement the international substantive law where gaps arise. The technique to do this is demonstrated in Chapter 4 of this study and should serve as an example of how to develop a modern methodology of applying uniform substantive contract law.

#### *8.3.4.1 Equity decisions distinct from application of a-national rules of law*

In cases where there is no choice of law clause, the parties' intentions are to be investigated by the arbitrator and a-national law can be applied if this seems appropriate. State contracts are a strong indicator that national law was meant to be disregarded (negative choice law) by the parties. It seems an appropriate assumption to deem this a standard default choice of law in a range of typical constellations, for instance those involving specific branches or a degree of complexity of the contracts under consideration.[169]

The application of a-national law is not a case of deciding *ex aequo et bono*. This latter way of deciding is another, separate form of arbitral procedure. *Ex aequo et bono* decisions are characterised by focusing even more on the individual case and thereby deliberately disregarding any general legal norms. It is the classic role of the arbitrator as umpire.[170] The focus is on the decision, not on the reason-

---

[168] Ie, if it does not contain an express authorisation to act as *amiable compositeur*.

[169] See below for further discussion of defining cases of application of a-national law and compare Chapter 7.

[170] Note in this context that French law conceives of the *amiable compositeur* as an 'office' and thereby marks the difference between this and the standard arbitration process, see Art 1474. NCPC and below.

ing or the grounds for this decision. It is a misunderstanding to classify any discretionary argumentation and decision by an arbitration tribunal as acting as *amiable compositeur*, as Mankowski does:

*Zweitens wäre eine Wahl der lex mercatoria ein echter Sprung ins Dunkle. Was würde man damit eigentlich wählen? ... Daß ein Schiedsgericht ad hoc eine ihm geeignet erscheinende Rechtsregel bildet und diese Regel dann als Rechtssatz deklariert, ist jedenfalls nicht auszuschließen ... Dieses wird noch erhöht durch Anreize für den Schiedsrichter, die lex mercatoria als angebliche Grundlage anzuführen, sich in Wahrheit aber als amiable compositeur selbst den Dispens von Rechtsnormen zu erteilen, ohne daß dazu eine Ermächtigung durch die Parteien bestünde.* [171]
(Secondly a choice of the *lex mercatoria* would be a real leap into the dark. What would one choose with it? ... It cannot be prevented that an arbitration tribunal forms ad hoc a rule of law which they deem appropriate and then declares this a legal norm [*Rechtssatz*, formal law] ... This is reinforced by incentives for the arbitrator to declare the *lex mercatoria* a basis [for this] while actually granting himself leave from applying any rule of law and act as *amiable compositeur* without authority of the parties.)

This view does not correctly reflect the mechanisms of arbitration proceedings. As long as an arbitrator demonstrates that he (or she) intends to form his decision according to any rules of law, the arbitrator is not acting *ex aequo et bono*, irrespective of the quality of the legal norms or rules of law applied, or the method of application.

#### 8.3.4.2 Reassuring position in case law

This position has been confirmed by the German Federal Court (Bundesgerichtshof) in a decision of 26 September 1985.[172] In that case an arbitration tribunal decided a case according to English law absent an express choice of law under German conflict rules. These conflict rules had been made applicable via a choice of the parties to decide the case according to the German procedural rules relating to arbitration. It was contested as to whether the arbitration tribunal had decided the case according to English law, or rather, acted as *amiable compositeur* thereby exceeding its powers conferred by the parties. The court held:

*Aus dem Schiedsspruch ist aber hinreichend deutlich zu entnehmen, daß das Schiedsgericht nach Rechtsgrundsätzen und nicht nach Billigkeit entscheiden wollte.* [173]
(The award makes it sufficiently clear, however, that the arbitration tribunal wanted to decide according to principles of law [sic!] and not according to equity.)
From this it follows that a decision *ex aequo et bono* must be the recognisable intention of the arbitrator and cannot be derived from the quality of the applied rules of law alone.

[171] Mankowski, op cit (n 97), 13-14.
[172] BGHZ 96, 40 = NJW (1986) 1436 et seq
[173] BGH NJW (1986) 1437.

### 8.3.5 Status quo under German law: Conclusion

Regarding the recognition of a-national law, in particular the UPICC and general principles of law, the situation under German domestic arbitration law is simply undecided. There are no court decisions clarifying the position unequivocally and distinguishing the notions of equity from the application of a-national rules of law. There is no in-depth discussion in legal science. The matter is not in the centre of interest. Therefore a position has to be developed within German legal theory based on a modern conception of contract law.

### 8.3.6 Comment and suggestion for a doctrine of international commercial contract within the German legal system

Legal theory in Germany should develop a concept of international commercial contract. By defining the notion of international commercial contract, a-national law can become the law governing the contract in certain instances where domestic law does not cover the underlying questions or, where it draws exclusively on objectives which are typical for domestic constellations, but not for international commercial relationships. This can be achieved by drawing on existing definitions contained in the CISG and in the UNCITRAL Model law.

After all, on the domestic level of adjudication in commercial matters, German law already provides an existing infrastructure for such developments; district courts (*Landgericht*), are staffed with expert judges who are laymen,[174] to sit trials in so called 'chambers for commercial matters' (*Kammern für Handelssachen*).[175] These are specialised panels of judges (chambers) who apply their special knowledge of commercial issues to decide the case appropriately.[176] This special competence is voluntary and applies on request of the claimant, §96 GVG. Disregarding this competence does not give rise to appeal.[177]

The definition of commercial matters in §95 GVG includes claims against '*Kaufleute*', meaning 'merchants', as well as matters arising out of cheques and bankers drafts and matters involving competition law, stock exchange and the transformation of enterprises (*Umwandlungsgesetz*).

This definition of commercial matters based on the term '*Kaufmann*' (merchant or trader) is a peculiarity of German law that is decisive within the discussion of a-national commercial law. German law bases a whole commercial code (HGB) on its definition of merchant which draws on the person of the trader, the merchant himself and the nature of his business, rather than on the nature of the transaction.

---

[174] So-called '*Handelsrichter*', commercial judges are appointed by the chamber of commerce under §108 GVG for a period of four years.

[175] §93 GVG (text in H Thomas and H Putzo, *Zivilprozeßordnung* (2003) 1705 et seq).

[176] Compare §§93-114 GVG.

[177] See Thomas and Putzo, op cit (n 173), No 1, §93 GVG.

This justifies[178] the operation of a so-called '*Sonderprivatrecht der Kaufleute*', a special civil law for merchants in Germany (along with Austria and Switzerland). This situation plainly invites the development of a specific legal environment for international commercial matters.

The fact that the RC makes the law of a state the law governing the contract absent choice of law, does not mean that any law by definition presupposes a state legislator. In order to develop a theoretical foundation for a 'new *lex mercatoria*', ie, an appropriate body of law rules to govern international commercial contracts, it is necessary to consider attributing a source of law function to the UPICC and other a-national law including general principles of law which are the 'common laws' of the merchant community. The traditional catalogue of sources of law as set out by Canaris[179] needs to be supplemented by another value incorporated by the UPICC.[180]

Perhaps this could be called a source of law *sui generis* and apply as *lex specialis* for international merchants as '*Sonderprivatrecht der internationalen Kaufleute*'.

## 8.4 Summary: Autonomous source of law function of a-national rules of law

It follows from the discussion so far, particularly in the preceding section, that it is not correct to deny the UPICC, the *lex mercatoria*, or general principles of law, the quality of law. There is enough evidence to suggest that these form a recognised legal basis, at least for arbitral decisions and are handled with sufficient certainty by arbitral tribunals. Predictability should not be the criterion, but persuasion, ie, the convincing deduction of individual solutions from the uniform international substantive contract law rules upon appropriate legal reasoning.

---

178 Ie, under Art 3(1) GG, the right to equality under the constitution. It is accepted that the special circumstances applicable to merchants, such as their special knowledge and experience justify their subjection to different rules of private law, incorporated in the HGB, the commercial code. Classic examples are rules relating to offer and acceptance and contractual rights relating to defective goods.

179 See 6.2 et seq, above; Canaris, op cit (n 110), 5-31.

180 Note in this context the remark made by Professor Peter Mankowski, op cit (n 97), 13 who states that jointly discovering the *lex mercatoria* is highly attractive intellectually. This may certainly be understood as describing his impression that over-ambitious academics use the research in this field to promote themselves and to this end pursue openly a marketing strategy for the benefit of both the *lex mercatoria* and themselves. This resentment is based on a misinterpretation of a genuine attitude towards the promotion of a potentially emerging novel international legal methodology. This methodology will have to give new answers to some important questions of international commercial law. Compare F Blasé, 'Leaving the Shadow for the Test of Practice – on the Future of the Principles of European Contract Law' The Vindobona Journal of International Commercial Law and Arbitration 3.1 (1999) 3-14, 13.

It is not necessary, though, to attribute qualities to the *lex mercatoria* which turn it into a 'legal system',[181] or decide ultimately the relationship between the *lex mercatoria* and the UPICC.[182]

In my view the term *lex mercatoria* is not meant to describe a precise set of legal rules but rather describes a whole set of phenomena. Lex is not only the substantive but also the procedural rules including usages and practice. It is a general and unspecific descriptive term. This does not diminish the value and position of the UPICC. They doubtlessly have the same qualities as the CISG and should be recognised as legal rules to apply to contracts falling within their scope. The specific circumstances, which are set up by the international trading community formed by the businesses and the bodies of self-governance of certain branches, such as the trade associations based in London or elsewhere, and international arbitration institutions such as the ICC, LCIA, German arbitration institutions, the Vienna and Zurich Chambers of Commerce, etc; do provide enough authority to confer the quality of source of law legitimately to the UPICC and general principles of law.

## 8.5 Conclusion

Chapter 8 has demonstrated how arbitration awards based on a-national contract law are dealt with in national legal systems. It shows that they are in fact normally upheld and hardly ever overturned, despite the lack of express provisions in virtually all European national arbitration laws and the strong criticism expressed towards the use of a-national law in the conflict of laws doctrine.[183] The high degree of diligence in reaching arbitration decisions and their acceptance by parties is strong evidence of the legitimacy of the use of a-national uniform contract law, such as the UPICC, as law governing the contract. An important condition for this, however, is the development of a notion of international commercial contract which has been neglected so far in legal science. A clear definition of this notion could provide the basis for the application of the UPICC as lex specialis. This method has a strong doctrinal foundation in German law with its specific infrastructure of law merchant in both contract law and procedural law. It also seems a possibility under English law given the importance assigned to commercial matters and arguments by the courts in the British legal tradition.

A need for the use of transnational law such as the UPICC is clearly indicated by the experience of contract negotiating and arbitration proceedings, showing that irrational and atavistic motivations dominate choice of law decisions, rather than purely economical factors such as foreseeable results. This observation sup-

[181] As Berger does: op cit (n 154).

[182] Do they constitute the *lex mercatoria* or are they an *aliud* (Mankowski, op cit (n 97), 14).

[183] Compare Chapter 7.

ports the arguments set out in Chapters 2, 6, and 7 regarding the need for uniform contract law.

# 9 Conclusion

The study has identified three obstacles to the easy application of transnational uniform contract law in national legal systems and has examined ways of overcoming these using the examples of English and German contract law.

1. The first of these obstacles is to be found in current legal theory of contract law (Part 1). The prevailing view in both countries maintains the theory of unity of law and state and does not see the necessity and potential of unity of law. Unity, or uniformity of laws is often understood as providing uniformity of results upon its application and is also understood to be derived from, or presupposed to, a legislative power flowing from a centralised political force (such as the European Union or the United Nations through their commissions) weakening the sovereignty of nation states. Therefore the term unity or uniformity is often replaced by that of harmonisation, meaning the same, but being disguised in this form, appearing as a pleasant metaphor.

Part 1 proved (in Chapters 1 and 2) that both issues can be resolved by reviewing these traditional positions and by considering more specialised research results, many of which are already part of established modern contract doctrine.

The theory of unity of law and state cannot claim universal acceptance and is not necessarily to be followed in a modern doctrine of international contract law (Chapter 1). A review of the status and nature of the concept of contract law in general shows that the arguments regarding legitimacy of transnational law rules, which are normally used against the use of transnational uniform law, are unfounded. A pluralistic concept of legislative power in contract law is an accepted contemporary standard, while the doctrine of unity of law and state can be shown to be derived from the era of feudalism, and subsequently an outdated and unduly limiting understanding of nation state and national law, which links questions of territoriality and state sovereignty with that of legislation. This is not appropriate in the area of private law, especially contract law. Chapter 1 proved that modern pluralistic democracies have to review the underlying concepts of modern contract law. It established that due to the openness of contract doctrine, there is room for developing it in such a way as to accommodate uniform contract law, such as the UPICC, as a legitimate form of contract law.

Chapter 2 defined uniform contract law as providing uniformity of sources covering areas where the need for it is present. This need promotes and maintains the standard and the degree of such uniformity, not a central political power. Fears of loss of sovereignty are therefore unfounded with regard to uniform contract law or its origin. The evolution of this law is driven by its protagonists such as arbitrators, merchants, lawyers and the state courts. Chapter 2 confirmed that there is no supervisory instance in state courts needed to provide justification and identity to transnational uniform law. Chapter 2 explained that uniform law derives its justification from the need for uniformity of contract law in international trade, not from values like predictability and uniformity of results.

Both chapters provide an example of a modern methodology of international contract law by carrying out reviews of existing concepts, which are often used uncritically, thereby creating barriers against modern developments in international trade law and wrongly assuming adverse effects and difficulties in existing domestic contract law.

These are the findings of Part 1 of the thesis relating to general contract doctrine.

2. Part 2 of the thesis (Chapters 3, 4 and 5) identified the second barrier against applying uniform law in domestic legal systems; the method of application by lawyers is guided by unhelpful habits of thought leading to a shortfall of the potential of transnational contract law.

Objections against the drafting of individual rules of transnational law and thereby the quality of this law are often based on an inconsequent method of application as well as a preconceived understanding of doctrinal concepts. Chapter 4 identified an instance of such an application method and explained how it can lead to unfounded results; the user does not employ the same technique that he or she would use in their own domestic legal system without realising this, or explaining why. The user also does not apply an autonomous interpretation technique but conceives of rules of the UPICC as isolated stand alone rules. Generally, concepts are often superficially understood and efforts are not made to integrate them into domestic law. As an example, Chapters 4 and 5 could prove that the concept of specific performance is not a general obstacle to integrating UPICC into English law, and that the individual rule regulating payment obligations in the UPICC (Art 7.2.1) does not lead to an overly rigid right to performance if appropriately applied.

Chapters 4 and 5 carried out an exemplary application of this rule in English and German law and showed ways in which this rule could be used in both legal systems by applying established methods of interpretation and application of national law. Different aspects in both systems have been identified as providing the solution; under English law acceptance by the courts is the most important condition, and a favourable environment for such an acceptance is assumed (Chapter 4). Under German law, UPICC rules can be applied to international commercial contracts under the doctrine of lex specialis regulating specialised issues and superseding the national contract rule. The UPICC are also a valuable model for law reform of the existing law of construction contracts (Chapter 5).

Part 2 of the thesis has proven that individual rules of uniform contract law such as the UPICC can be successfully applied within a context of national contract law.

The method of applying UPICC carried out in Part 2 of the study was an extended autonomous interpretation; it included recapitulating relevant historic developments and reconsidering concepts in the light of European legal history. This was an important element of a novel methodology of international contract law.

3. The last part (Part 3) of the study examined the third obstacle to the application of the UPICC: their treatment in the conflict of laws. The conservative attitude in prevailing legal doctrine and legislation hinders application because it creates insecurity as to whether decisions obtained by relying on transnational uniform law will be upheld and be enforceable.

Other than Part 2, this part does not deal with the substantive law aspects of the UPICC such as the content and quality of its rules, but rather, with the procedural and conflict law aspects of its use.

There are two important factors forming the status of the UPICC in the conflict of laws; the question of whether UPICC can be stipulated by international contractors as the law governing the contract to the exclusion of national laws implying its source of law function and the role of such uniform law in dispute resolution, namely in arbitration.

Part Three has proven that the UPICC are a source of law *sui generis* (Chapters 6 and 7).

The UPICC are regarded as sources of law in modern contract doctrine, and many scholars have presented solutions for their integration into current legal doctrine. None of those are being agreed with by the prevailing views in either English or German legal doctrine, and they have not resulted in express legislation.

Chapter 6 recapitulated the relevant doctrines and opinions brought forward in connection with UPICC as *lex contractus*. It especially highlighted flaws in current modern legislation regulating the conflict of laws and arbitration law. This is forming a barrier against the use of UPICC by creating insecurity. There are numerous examples of inconsistent legislation and contract doctrine in England and Germany, and also in other European countries.

Chapter 7 explained suggestions in legal science of how integration of uniform law into domestic conflict of laws could be achieved. It demonstrated the ways in which the UPICC are dealt with in arbitration and revealed how established methods of using international uniform law in the conflict of laws can be successfully employed. It highlighted common errors in the use of such law, namely the habit of wrongly understanding these methods as conflict rules (eg, the theory of gaps and the complementary use of domestic law). It is important to use the autonomous method of interpretation consequently and reconsider the theory of gaps. If traditional ideas about the general superiority of national contract law are dropped, these established methods of applying uniform law can be successfully carried out. They then respect the international character of the norms and their subject matter, international commercial contracts.

Chapter 8 particularly, demonstrated that the traditional positions contain contradictions and are based on irrational preconceptions (such as the *horror alieni* and certain forms of protectionism in the legal profession) so that they may not be upheld for much longer in a modern world of global trade. Chapter 8 also confirmed the motivations of international contractors in choice of law negotiations, providing further evidence of the need for uniform contract law.

Although arbitration case law cannot offer or replace a consistent scholarly doctrine of source of law for transnational uniform contract law, it provides evidence of its source of law function (Chapter 7). It is up to legal science and the state courts to develop a consistent theory of uniform contract law. The willingness to do so can be derived from English and German case law since arbitration awards based on uniform law are generally upheld (Chapter 8). However, neither legislation nor doctrine expressly acknowledge the source of law function, and thereby deny the possibility of choosing UPICC as the law governing the contract for international commercial contracts. A novel doctrine and method of uniform international contract law, therefore primarily has to work out a definition of international commercial contract and move away from static concepts of contract doctrine assigning unqualified priority to national contract law, which is naturally not designed for international dealings.

4. The study introduced a novel doctrine of international contract law based on an autonomous method of application of rules of transnational uniform contract law, such as the UPICC, extended by reviewing and recapitulating relevant concepts and doctrines in general contract law, including their historic origins. Under this doctrine the UPICC have a source of law function *sui generis* and can be chosen as governing law of international commercial contracts. They apply as *lex specialis* in relation to domestic contract law, with the effect that the national contract law is thereby generally excluded but will apply as a complementary law where the uniform law leaves gaps. The gaps arise on the level of substantive uniform law and do not amount to further choice of law effects like a conflict of law rule. Uniform law rules as they are provided by the UPICC, provide better and easier solutions for international contract disputes due to the uniformity of sources, the neutral status and the scholarly high level of specialised drafting technique, forming one important aspect of their source of law quality, the persuasive force (Part 2 and Chapters 6 and 7).

This method also has to be applied to international conventions such as CISG and other Model Laws, and also to international Treaties affecting private law, such as Double Taxation Treaties and certain EU legislation.

# Bibliography


*Aktuelle Wirtschaftsgesetze 2002* Beck'sche Textausgaben (Munich: C H Beck, 2002) 55

*BGB – Bürgerliches Gesetzbuch mit zugehörigen Gesetzen und EG - Richtlinien* 105th edn Beck'sche Textausgaben (Munich: C H Beck, 1999)

*BGB – Bürgerliches Gesetzbuch* annual edn, Beck-Texte im dtv (Munich: Deutscher Taschenbuchverlag)

Bundestags-Drucksache (BT-Drucks) 13/5374, published by Deutscher Bundestag

*Code Civil Textes, jurisprudence, annotations*, 2000 edn (Paris: Dalloz, 2000)

*Code Civil Textes, jurisprudence, annotations*, 2005 edn (Paris: Dalloz, 2005)

*Kommission zur Neuordnung des Schiedsverfahrensrechts: Bericht mit einem Diskussionsentwurf zur Neufassung des Zehnten Buchs der ZPO* (Bundesministerium der Justiz, 1994)

*Neues Schuldrecht: Genegnüberstellung BGB neu-alt mit Nebemgesetzen* 1st edn (Munich: Deutscher Taschenbuch Verlag, 2002)

*Report on the Arbitration Bill* Departmental Advisory Committee on Arbitration Law, 1996

*Vergabe- und Vertragsordnung für Bauleistungen* 23rd edn, Beck-Texte im dtv (Munich: Deutscher Taschenbuchverlag, 2006)

Arrowsmith, Sue, 'Public Procurement: An Appraisal of the UNCITRAL Model Law as a Global Standard' ICLQ 53 (2004), 17

Atiyah, P S, *An Introduction to the Law of Contract* 5th edn (Oxford: 1995)

Bar, Christian von, *Internationales Privatrecht* 1st edn (Munich: C H Beck, 1991) 2 Besondere Lehren

Bar, Christian von, and Mankowski, Peter, *Internationales Privatrecht* 2nd edn (Munich: CH Beck, 2003) 1 Allgemeine Lehren

Basedow, Jürgen, 'The UNIDROIT Principles of International Commercial Contracts and German Law' (Bristol: International Academy of Comparative Law, 1998)

Basedow, Jürgen, 'German National Report on the UNIDROIT Principles of International Commercial Contracts', in Bonell, Michael Joachim (ed), *A New Approach to International Commercial Contracts* (The Hague / Boston / London: Kluwer Law International, 1999) 125

Basedow, Jürgen(ed), *Europäische Vertragsrechtsvereinheitlichung und deutsches Recht* (Tübingen: Mohr, 2000)

Baur, Jürgen F, and Stürner, Rolf, *Lehrbuch des Sachenrechts* 17th edn (Munich: C H Beck, 1999)

Berger, Klaus Peter, *Internationale Wirtschaftsschiedsgerichtsbarkeit – Verfahrens- und materiallrechtliche Grundprobleme im Spiegel moderner Schiedsgesetze und Schiedspraxis* Recht des internationalen Wirtschaftsverkehrs, Horn, Norbert et al (eds) (Berlin, New York: W de Gruyter, 1992) 10

Berger, Klaus Peter, *The Creeping Codification of the* Lex Mercatoria (The Hague / London / Boston: Kluwer Law International, 1999)

Bernstein, Herbert, and Zweigert, Konrad, eds, *Festschrift für Konrad Zweigert* (Tübingen: Mohr, 1981) XIV, 941

Binder, Peter, *International Commercial Arbitration in UNCITRAL Model Law Jurisdictions* 1st edn (London: Sweet & Maxwell, 2000)

Bishop, William, 'The Choice of Remedy for Breach of Contract', The Journal of Legal Studies 14 (1985) 299

Blase, Friedrich, 'Leaving the Shadow for the Test of Practice – on the Future of the Principles of European Contract Law', The Vindobona Journal of International Commercial Law and Arbitration 31 (1999) 3

Boele-Woelki, Katharina, 'Principles and Private International Law', Uniform Law Review 4 (1996) 652

Boggiano, Antonio, *International standard contracts: the price of fairness*, (Dordrecht / Boston / London: Kluwer, 1990)

Bonell, Michael Joachim, *Harmonisation of Private Law Rules between civil and common law jurisdictions* (Montreal: 1990)

Bonell, Michael Joachim, '*Das UNIDROIT-Projekt für die Ausarbeitung von Regeln für internationale Handelsverträge*', Rabels Zeitschrift für ausländisches und internationales Privatrecht 56 (1992) 274

Bonell, Michael Joachim, 'The UNIDROIT Principles of International commercial Contracts and CISG – Alternatives or Complementary Instruments?' (Faculty of Law, University of Toronto: Workshop, 1995) 62

Bonell, Michael Joachim, 'The UNIDROIT Principles of International Contracts and CISG – Alternatives or Complementary Instruments?', Uniform Law Review 1 (1996) 26

Bonell, Michael Joachim, 'The UNIDROIT Principles in Practice: The Experience of the First Two Years' Uniform Law Review 1 (1997) 34

Bonell, Michael Joachim, 'The UNIDROIT Principles: First Practical Experiences', European Journal of Law Reform 13 (1999) 193

Bonell, Michael Joachim (ed), *A New Approach to International Commercial Contracts* (The Hague: Kluwer Law International, 1999) 456

Bonell, Michael Joachim, 'General Report' in Bonell, Michael Joachim (ed), *A New Approach to International Commercial Contracts* (The Hague: Kluwer Law International, 1999) 1

Bonell, Michael Joachim, 'UNIDROIT Principles 2004 – The New Edition of the Principles of International Commercial Contracts adopted by the Institute for the Unification of Private Law' Uniform Law Review 1 (2004) 5

Bridge, Michael, 'Does Anglo-Canadian contract law need a doctrine of good faith ?', Canadian Business Law Journal 94 (1984) 385

Bridge, Michael, 'The 1973 Mississippi Floods: "*Force Majeure*" and Export Prohibition', in McKendrick, E (ed) *Force Majeure and Frustration* (London: Lloyds of London, 1991) 287

Bridge, Michael, 'International Private Commodity Sales', Canadian Business Law Journal 19 (1991) 485

Bridge, Michael, 'Good Faith in Commercial Contracts', in Brownsword, Roger, Hird, Norma J, and Howells, Geraint (eds), *Good faith in Contract – Concept and Context* (Aldershot / Vermont: Ashgate, 1999) 139

Brinckmann, Hans, 'Juristische Fachsprache als Wissenschaftssprache?', in Ladnar, Ulrike, and Plottnitz, Cornelia von (eds), *Fachsprache der Justiz* (Frankfurt am Main, etc: Diesterweg, 1977) 70

Brownsword, Roger, Hird, Norma J, and Howells, Geraint (eds), *Good faith in Contract – Concept and Context* (Aldershot / Vermont: Ashgate, 1999)

Brox, Hans, *Allgemeiner Teil des Bürgerlichen Gesetzbuchs*, 29th edn Academia Iuris (Cologne / Berlin / Bonn / Munich: Carl Heymanns, 2005)

Buchholz, Stephan, '*Zur Rechtsvereinheitlichung in Deutschland in der zweiten Hälfte des 19 Jahrhunderts*' ('Observations on the Unification of Law in Germany during the Nineteenth Century; summary'), Rabels Zeitschrift für ausländisches und internationales Privatrecht 50 (1986) 77

Bundestag, Deutscher, *Entwurf eines Gesetzes zur Modernisierung des Schuldrechts*, Drucksache 14/6040 (Berlinn: Deutscher Bundestag, 14 Wahlperiode, 14 May 2001)

Busse, Dietrich, *Juristische Semantik: Grundfragen der juristischen Interpretationstheorie in sprachwissenschaftlicher Sicht*, Schriften zur Rechtstheorie (Berlin: Duncker & Humblot, 1993) 157

Caemmerer, von, Schlechtriem, and Huber, in Schlechtriem, Peter (ed) *Kommentar zum Einheitlichen UN-Kaufrecht*, 2nd edn, (Munich: C H Beck, 1995)

Canaris, Claus-Wilhelm, '*Konsens und Verfahren als Grundelemente der Rechtsordnung – Gedanken vor dem Hintergrund der "Eumeniden" des Aischylos*', Juristische Schulung 7 (1996) 573

Canaris, Claus-Wilhelm, '*Die Stellung der "UNIDROIT Principles" und* "Principles of European Contract Law" *im System der Rechtsquellen*', in Basedow, Juergen (ed) *Europaeische Vertragsrechtsvereinheitlichung und deutsches Recht* Archiv fuer die civilistische Praxis / Rabels Zeitschrift (Tuebingen: Mohr, 2000) 5

Chitty (ed) and Harris, *Chitty on Contracts – General Principles*, 27th edn (London: 1994) I

Chukwumerije, Okezie, 'Judicial Supervision of Commercial Arbitration: The English Arbitration Act of 1996', Arbitration International 152 (1999) 171

Collier, J G, *Conflict of laws*, 1st edn, Cambridge Studies in International and Comparative Law (Cambridge: Cambridge University Press, 1987)

Collier, J G, *Conflict of laws*, 3rd edn, Cambridge Studies in International and Comparative Law (Cambridge: Cambridge University Press, 2001)

Corbin, Arthur Linton, *Corbin on Contracts* (St Paul, Minn: 1951) 4

Corbin, Arthur Linton, *Corbin on Contracts* (St Paul, Minn: 1963) 1

Craig, W L, Park, W W, and Paulsson, J, *International Chamber of Commerce Arbitration*, 2nd edn (New York / Paris: Oceana Pub / ICC, 1990)

Cremades, Bernardo M, 'The Impact of International Arbitration on the Development of Business Law', American Journal of Comparative Law 31 (1983) 526

Dagtoglou, P D, 'The English Judge and European Community Law', Cambridge Law Journal 371 (1978) 76

David, Rene, 'International Unification of Private Law', in David, R, Graveson, R, and Egawa, H (eds) *International Encyclopedia of Comparative Law* (Tübingen: Mohr, 1984) II, Ch 5

Dawson, 'Specific Performance in France and Germany', Michigan Law Review 57 (1959) 495

Dicey and Morris (eds), *The Conflict of Laws* (London: Sweet & Maxwell, 1997)

Dreier, Ralf, '*Was ist Gerechtigkeit*', Juristische Schulung 7 (1996) 581

Drobnig, Ulrich, '*Ein Vertragsrecht für Europa*', in *Festschrift für Ernst Steindorf* (1990) 1141

Drobnig, Ulrich, 'The UNIDROIT Principles in the Conflict of Laws', Uniform Law Review 2/3 (1998) 385

Eisenhardt, Ulrich, *Deutsche Rechtsgeschichte*, Grundrisse des Rechts (Munich: C H Beck, 1984)

Eisenhardt, Ulrich, *Deutsche Rechtsgeschichte*, 4th edn Grundrisse des Rechts (Munich: C H Beck, 2004)

Fauvarque-Cosson, Bénédicte, 'Comparative Law and Conflict of Laws: Allies or Enemies? New Perspectives on an Old Couple', Am J Com L 49 (2001) 407

Fawcett, J J, 'Evasion of law and mandatory rules in private international law', Cambridge Law Journal 491 (1990) 44

Fawcett, James, 'The interrelationships of jurisdiction and choice of law in private international law', Current Legal Problems 44 (1991) 39

Fentiman, Richard, *Foreign Law in English Courts*, Oxford Monographs in Private International Law (Oxford: Oxford University Press, 1998)

Ferrari, Franco, 'Defining the sphere of application of the 1994 "UNIDROIT principles of international commercial contracts"', Tulane Law Review 69 (1995) 1225

Ferrari, Franco, '*Das Verhältnis zwischen den Unidroit-Grundsätzen und den allgemeinen Grundsätzen internationaler Einheitsprivatrechtskonventionen*', Juristenzeitung 1 (1998) 9

Fitzgerald, Brian F, 'An Emerging Liberal Theory of International Law and the Non-Enforcement of Foreign Public Laws', Australian Yearbook of International Law 16 (1995) 311

Fox, Eleanor, 'Harmonization of Law and Procedures in a Globalized world', Antitrust Law Journal 60 (1992) 593

Frege, Gottlob, *Conceptual Notation and related articles* (Oxford: Clarendon Press, 1972)

Garro, Alejandro M, 'The gap-filling role of the UNIDROIT principles in international sales law: some comments on the interplay between the principles and the CISG', Tulane Law Review 69 (1995) 1149

Gera, Benjamin, 'Uniformity in Commercial Law: is the UCC exportable?', Loyola of LA Law Review 29 (1996) 1035

Glenn, H Patrick, 'Unification of Law, Harmonisation of Law and Private International Law' in *Liber Memorialis Francois Laurent* (1989) 783

Glenn, H Patrick, 'Reception and Reconciliation of Law', in Sack, P, Wellman, C P and Yaski, M (eds), *Monismus oder Pluralismus der Rechtskulturen? Anthropologische und ethnologische Grundlagen traditioneller und moderner Rechtssysteme* (Rechtstheorie: Beiheft No XIII, 1990)

Glenn, H Patrick, 'Harmonisation of law, foreign law and private international law' European Review of Private International Law 1 (1993) 47

Glenn, H Patrick, 'Codification of Private International Law in Quebec' Rabels Zeitschrift für ausländisches und internationales Privatrecht 60 (1996) 231

Goode, Sir Roy, *Commercial Law*, 2nd edn (London: Penguin, 1995)

Goode, Sir Roy, *Commercial Law*, 3rd edn (London: Penguin, 2004)

Goode, Sir Roy, 'Usage and its Reception in Transnational Commercial Law', International and Comparative Law Quarterly 46 (1997) 1

Goode, Sir Roy, Kronke, Herbert, and McKendrick, Ewan, *Transnational Commercial Law: International Instruments and Commentary* (Oxford: Oxford University Press, 2004)

Goode, Sir Roy, *Commercial Law*, 3rd edn (London: Penguin, 2004)

Gottwald, Peter, and Henrich, Dieter, eds, *Festschrift für Dieter Henrich* (Bielefeld: Gieseking, 2000)

Graff, Gerald, '*Keep off the grass, Drop Dead,* and other Indeterminacies: A Response to Sanford Levinson' in Levinson, Sanford, and Mailloux, Steven (eds), *Interpreting Law and Literature: a Hermeneutic Reader* (Evanston, Il: Northwestern University Press, 1988) 175

Grimme, Rainer, *Die Erfüllung beim Werkvertrag*, Schriften zum Bürgerlichen Recht (Berlin: Duncker & Humblodt, 1987) 105

Grundmann, Stefan, and Stuyck, Jules (eds), *An Academic Green Paper on European Contract Law* (The Hague / London / NewYork: Kluwer Law International, 2002) 2

Haight, Charles S, 'Babel Afloat: Some Reflections on Uniformity in Maritime Law' Journal of Maritime Law and Commerce 28.2 (1997) 189

Hanbury, Harold G, and Maudsley, Ronald H, *Modern Equity*, 13th edn (Martin, Jill E, ed) (London: Stevens & Sons, 1989)

Hartley, Trevor C, 'The European Court, Judicial Objectivity and the Constitution of the European Union', Law Quarterly Review 112 (1996) 95

Hartley, Trevor C, *The Transposition and Interpretation of EC Directives: The British Viewpoint* (Graz, Austria: 1997)

Hattenhauer, Hans, and Buschmann, Arno, *Textbuch zur Privatrechtsgeschichte der Neuzeit*, 1st edn (Munich: C H Beck, 1967)

Hay, Peter, '*Zur extraterritorialen Anwendung US-amerikanischen Rechts*', *Rabels Zeitschrift für ausländisches und internationales Privatrecht* 60 (1996) 303

Hayder, Roberto, '*Privatrechtsvereinheitlichung durch die Europäische Gemeinschaft – Kommentar zum Vortrag von Hans Claudius Taschner*', in Müller-

Graff, Peter-Christian (ed) *Gemeinsames Privatrecht in der Europäischen Gemeinschaft*, Schriftenreihe des Arbeitskreises Europäische Integration (Baden-Baden: Nomos, 1993) 33, 167

Heck, Philipp, *Gesetzesauslegung und Interessenjurisprudenz* (Tuebingen: Mohr, 1914)

Heck, Philipp, *Begriffsbildung und Interessenjurisprudenz* (Tuebingen: Mohr, 1932)

Herber, Rolf, and Czerwenka, Beate, *Internationales Kaufrecht, Kommentar*, (Munich: C H Beck, 1991)

Herings, P Jean-Jacques, and Kanning, Arnald J, *Unifying Commercial Laws of Nation-States: Coordination of Legal Systems and Economic Growth*, Research Memoranda (internet: http://13712022236/ww-edocs/loader/fileasp?id=647: METEOR (Maastricht Research School of Economics of Technology and Organization) 2002) 027

Hill, Richard, 'A Businessman's view of the UPICC', Journal of International Arbitration (1996) 163

Hillman, 'Court Adjustment of Long-Term Contracts: an analysis under modern contract law', Duke Law Journal 14-17 (1987)

Holtzmann, Howard M, and Neuhaus, Joseph E, *A Guide to the UNCITRAL Model Law on International Commercial Arbitration: Legislative History and Commentary*, (Deventer / Boston: Kluwer Law and Taxation, 1989)

Honnold, John (ed), *Unification of the Law Governing International Sales of Goods: The Comparison and possible Harmonisation of National and Regional Unifications* (Paris: 1966)

Honnold, John O, *Uniform Law for International Sales under the 1980 United Nations Convention* 3rd edn (Philadelphia: Kluwer, 1999)

Horn, Norbert, 'The Lawful German Revolution: Privatization and Market Economy in a Re-Unification', American Journal of Comparative Law 39 (1991) 725

Hunter, Robert, 'Arbitration in Germany – A Common Law Perspective', Schieds V Z – German Arbitration Journal 4 (2003) 155

Hübner, Heinrich, *Allgemeiner Teil des Bürgerlichen Gesetzbuches*, 2nd edn (Berlin, New York: de Gruyter, 1996)

Hyland, Ken, 'Scientific Claims and Community Values: Articulation in an Academic Culture' Language & Communication – an interdisciplinary journal 17 (1997) 13

ICC, ed, *Exchange Rate Risks in International Contracts* (Paris: ICC Publishing SA, 1987) Publication No 440/3

Jackson, Bernard S, *Semiotics and legal theory* (London: Routledge & Kegan Paul, 1985)

Jackson, Bernard S, *Making Sense in Law* Legal Semiotics Monographs (Liverpool: Deborah Charles Publications, 1995) 4

Jackson, Bernard S, *Making Sense in Jurisprudence*, Legal Semiotics Monographs (Liverpool: Deborah Charles Publications, 1996) 5

Jauernig, Othmar, and Schlechtriem, Peter, *Bürgerliches Gesetzbuch* 7th edn (Munich: 1994)

Jauernig, Othmar, *Bürgerliches Gesetzbuch*, 11th edn (Munich: C H Beck, 2004)

Jayme, Erik, and Hausmann, Rainer (eds), *Internationales Privat-und Verfahrensrecht* (Munich: C H Beck, 1998)

Jayme, Erik, and Hausmann, Rainer (eds), *Internationales Privat-und Verfahrensrecht* (Munich: C H Beck, 2002)

Jayme, Erik, and Hausmann, Rainer (eds), *Internationales Privat-und Verfahrensrecht* (Munich: C H Beck, 2004)

Jefferson, Michael, 'Comparing the proper law and the law applicable' Student Law Review 9, sum (1993) 16

Joussen, Peter, *Der Industrieanlagen-Vertrag* (Heidelberg: Verlagsgesellschaft Recht und Wirtschaft GmbH, 1981)

Justiz, Bundesministerium der, *Einführung in den Entwurf der Bundesregierung und der Koalitionsfraktionen für ein Gesetz zur Modernisierung des Schuldrechts, BR-Drs 338-01, BT-Drs 14-6040*, 15 June 2001 edn (Berlin: Bundesministerium für Justiz, 15 June 2001) 39

Kastely, Amy H, 'The Right to Require Performance in International Sales: Towards an International Interpretation of the Vienna Convention', Washington Law Review 63 (1988) 607

Keenan, Dennis, *Smith & Keenan's English Law*, 14th edn (London: Pearson Longman, 2004)

Kegel, Gerhard, *Internationales Privatrecht*, 6th edn (Munich: C H Beck, 1987)

Kegel, Gerhard, and Schurig, Klaus, *Internationales Privatrecht*, 8th edn, Juristische Kurzlehrbücher (Munich: C H Beck, 2000)

Kegel, Gerhard, and Schurig, Klaus, *Internationales Privatrecht*, 9th edn, (Munich: C H Beck, 2004)

Kerr, Michael, 'Arbitration and the Courts: The UNCITRAL Model Law', ICLQ 341 (1985) 1

Kirchner, Christian, '*Europäisches Vertragsrecht*', in Weyers, Hans-Leo (ed), *Europäisches Vertragsrecht* Arbeiten zur Rechtsvergleichung (Baden-Baden: Nomos, 1997) 182, 103

Kohler, Jürgen, '*Rechtssetzung im demokratischen Rechtsstaat und Rechtswissenschaft – Anmerkungen zu Stil und Bedeutung neuerer Gesetzgebung*', *Kritische Vierteljahresschrift für Gesetzgebung und Rechtswissenschaft - Krit V* 4 (2002) 369

Kötz, Hein, '*Rechtsvereinheitlichung – Nutzen, Kosten, Methoden Ziele*' ('Unification of Law – Costs, Benefits, Methods and Aims; summary'), Rabels *Zeitschrift für ausländisches und internationales Privatrecht* 50 (1986) 1

Kötz, Hein, 'Taking Civil Codes Less Seriously', Modern Law Review 50 (1987) 1

Kramer, E, *Europäische Privatrechtsvereinheitlichung* (1988)

Kramer, E, *Die Gültigkeit der Verträge nach den Unidroit – Principles* (Basel: Uni Basel, Juristische Fakultät, 1997)

Kramer, Ernst, 'Contractual Validity according to the UNIDROIT Principles', European Journal of Law Reform 13 (1998/1999) 269

Kramer, Ernst, '*Die Gültigkeit der Verträge nach den Unidroit – Principles*', *Zeitschrift für Europäisches Privatrecht* 2 (1999) 209

Kramm, Manfred, *Rechtsnorm und semantische Eindeutigkeit* doctoral thesis. Erlangen-Nürnberg, 1970.

Kroeschell, Karl, *Deutsche Rechtsgeschichte I*, 7th edn WV Studium (Opladen: Westdeutscher Verlag, 1985) 8

Kropholler, Jan, *Internationales Privatrecht*, 4th edn (Tübingen: Mohr Siebeck, 2001)

Kuß, Horst, *Verdingungsordnung für Bauleistungen (VOB), Teile A und B mit Erläuterungen*, 2nd edn (Munich: C H Beck, 1997)

Labes, Hubertus W, and Lörcher, Torsten, eds, 'Nationales und Internationales Schiedsverfahrensrecht', (Munich: CH Beck, 1998)

Ladnar, Ulrike, and Plottnitz, Cornelia von, eds, *Fachsprache der Justiz* (Frankfurt am Main, etc: Diesterweg, 1977)

Lando, Ole, 'Principles of European Contract Law An Alternative or a Precursor of European Legislation', *Rabels Zeitschrift für ausländisches und internationales Privatrecht* 56 (1992) 261

Lando, Ole, 'Is codification needed in Europe? Principles of European Contract Law and the relation to Dutch Law', European Review of Private Law 11-2 (1993) 157

Lando, Ole, '*Die Regeln des europäischen Vertragsrechts*', in Müller-Graff, Peter-Christian (ed) *Gemeinsames Privatrecht in der Europäischen Gemeinschaft* (Baden-Baden: Nomos, 1993)

Lando, Ole, 'Assessing the UNIDROIT Principles in the Harmonization of Arbitration Law', Tulane Journal of International and Comparative Law 3 (1994) pp 129

Lando, Ole, '*Homo judicans*', Uniform Law Review 2/3 (1998) 535

Langer, Stefan, *Grundlagen einer internationalen Wirtschaftsverfassung*, Municher Universitätsschriften, ed Canaris, Lerche, and Roxin (Munich: C H Beck, 1995) 109, 308

Larenz, Karl, *Lehrbuch des Schuldrechts Erster Band: Allgemeiner Teil*, 13th edn (Munich: C H Beck, 1982)

Larenz, Karl, *Allgemeiner Teil des Deutschen Bürgerlichen Rechts*, 6th edn (Munich: C H Beck, 1983)

Larenz, Karl, *Methodenlehre der Rechtswissenschaft*, 2nd edn, in Albach (ed) *Enzyklopädie der Rechts- und Staatswissenschaft* (Berlin, etc: Springer, 1991)

Larenz, Karl, and Wolf, Manfred, *Allgemeiner Teil des Deutschen Bürgerlichen Rechts*, 9th edn (Munich: C H Beck, 2004)

Leebron, David W, 'Lying down with Procrustes: an analysis of harmonisation claims' (Faculty of Law, University of Toronto: Workshop, 1995) 1

Levinson, Sanford, and Mailloux, Steven (eds), *Interpreting Law and Literature: a Hermeneutic Reader* (Evanston, Il: Northwestern University Press, 1988)

Levinson, Sanford, 'Law as Literature', in Levinson, Sanford, and Mailloux, Steven (eds), *Interpreting Law and Literature: a Hermeneutic Reader* (Evanston, Il: Northwestern University Press, 1988) 155

Liebs, Detlef, *Römisches Recht*, 5th edn, UTB für Wissenschaft (Göttingen: Vandenhoeck & Ruprecht, 1999) 465

Lionnet, Klaus, 'Should the procedural law applicable to arbitration be denationalised or unified? The answer of the Uncitral Model Law', Journal of International Arbitration (1991) 5

Lookofsky, Joseph M, 'Loose ends and contortions in International Sales: Problems in the Harmonisation of private law rules', The American Journal of Comparative Law 29 (1991) 403

Lookofsky, Joseph M, 'Danish National Report on the UNIDROIT Principles of International Commercial Contracts', in Bonell, Michael Joachim (ed), *A New Approach to International Commercial Contracts* (The Hague / Boston / London: Kluwer Law International, 1999) 71

Löwisch, Manfred (ed), *Wettbewerb, Kollektivverträge und Konfliktlösung in der Reform des Gesundheitswesens* (Baden-Baden: Nomos, 1999)

Ly, Filip de, 'Dutch National Report', in Bonell, Michael Joachim (ed), *A New Approach to International Commercial Contracts* (The Hague / Boston / London: Kluwer Law International, 1999) 203

Macneil, Ian R, *The New Social Contract: An Inquiry into Modern Contractual Relations* (New Haven, Conn: Yale University Press, 1980)

Maier, Harold G, 'Interest Balancing and Extraterritorial Jurisdiction', American Journal of Comparative Law 31 (1983) 579

Mankowski, Peter, '*Rechtswahl für Verträge des internationalen Wirtschaftsverkehrs*', RIW 1 (2003) 2

Martiny, Dieter, '*Europäisches Internationales Vertragsrecht – Erosion der Römischen Konvention?*', *Zeitschrift für Europäisches Privatrecht* 1 (1997) 107

Mattei, Ugo, 'Why the Wind changed', American Journal of Comparative Law 42 (1994) 195

Mattei, Ugo, and Bussani, Mauro, 'In Search of the common core of European Private Law', European Review of Private Law 2 (1995) 485

May, Anthony, *Keating on Building Contracts*, 6th edn (London: Sweet & Maxwell, 1995)

McClean, J D, 'The contribution of the Hague Conference to the development of Private International Law in common law countries', *Recueil des Cours* II (1992) 275

Mellinkoff, David, *The Language of the Law* (Boston/Toronto: Little, Brown and Company, 1963).

Merschformann, Ulrike, *Die objektive Bestimmung des Vertragsstatuts beim internationalen Warenkauf* Nomos Universitätsschriften (Baden-Baden: Nomos, 1991) 65

Mertens, Hans-Joachim, '*Lex Mercatoria*: A Self-Applying System beyond National Law', in Teubner, Gunther (ed), *Global Law without a state*, 4 vols, (Brookfield: Dartmouth, 1996) 4, 31

Musielak, Hans-Joachim, and Kegel, Gerhard (eds), *Festschrift für Gerhard Kegel* (Stuttgart, etc: Kohlhammer, 1987) 662

Mustill, Michael John, 'The New *Lex Mercatoria* – The First Twenty-five Years', Arbitration International (1988) 86

Mustill, Sir Michael J, and Boyd, Stewart C, *The Law and Practice of Commercial Arbitration in England*, 2nd edn (London: Butterworths, 1989)

Mustill, Lord, and Boyd, Stewart C, *Commercial Arbitration 2001 – Companion Volume to the Second Edition* (London: Butterworths, 2001)

Müller-Graff, Peter-Christian, '*Privatrecht und europäisches Gemeinschaftsrecht*', in Müller-Graff, Peter-Christian (ed), *Gemeinsames Privatrecht in der Europäischen Gemeinschaft* (Baden-Baden: Nomos, 1993)

Neufang, Paul, '*Erfüllungszwang als* "remedy" *bei Nichterfüllung*', *Schriftenreihe der Gesellschaft für Rechtsvergleichung* (Baden-Baden: Nomos Verlagsgesellschaft, 1998) 186

Nicklisch, Fritz, '*Empfiehlt sich eine Neukonzeption des Werkvertragsrechts? - unter besonderer Berücksichtigung komplexer Langzeitverträge*', Juristenzeitung 39 (1984) 757

North, Peter, 'Problems of codification in a common law country', Rabels Zeitschrift 46 (1982) 94

North, Peter, 'Private International Law: Change or Decay?', International and Comparative Law Quarterly 50 (2001) 477

Oles, Douglas, 'Remedies for Nonpayment in Four Standard Construction Contracts', *The Construction Lawyer* (1996) 20

Olsen, Lena, 'The choice of the aggrieved party – An analysis of the remedies in the Principles of the European Contract Law', European Review of Private Law 1 (1999) 21

Palandt and Heinrichs, *Bürgerliches Gesetzbuch*, 57th edn, Beck'sche Kurzkommentare (Munich: C H Beck, 1998)

Palandt and Heinrichs, *Bürgerliches Gesetzbuch*, 60th edn, Beck'sche Kurzkommentare (Munich: C H Beck, 2001)

Palandt and Heinrichs, *Bürgerliches Gesetzbuch*, 65th edn, Beck'sche Kurzkommentare (Munich: C H Beck, 2006)

Palandt and Heldrich, *Bürgerliches Gesetzbuch*, 57th edn, Beck'sche Kurzkommentare (Munich: C H Beck, 1998)

Palandt and Heldrich, *Bürgerliches Gesetzbuch*, 65th edn, Beck'sche Kurzkommentare (Munich: C H Beck, 2006)

Palandt and Sprau, *Bürgerliches Gesetzbuch*, 57th edn, Beck'sche Kurzkommentare (Munich: C H Beck, 1998)

Palandt and Sprau, *Bürgerliches Gesetzbuch*, 65th edn, Beck'sche Kurzkommentare (Munich: C H Beck, 2006)

Parra-Aranguren, Gonzalo, 'Conflict of law aspects of the UNIDROIT principles of international commercial contracts', Tulane Law Review 69 (1995) 1239

Paulsen, 'An Historical Overview of the Development of Uniformity in International Maritime Law' Tulane Law Review 57 (1983) 1065

Pèdamon, Michel, '*Le Centenaire du BGB*', *Zeitschrift für Europäisches Privatrecht* 1 (1997) 1

Peters, Frank, '*Die Stornierung von Verträgen*', *Juristenzeitung* (1996) 73

Petöfi, Podlech, and Savigny, v, (eds), *Fachsprache – Umgangssprache* (Kronberg/Ts: Scriptor, 1975) 4

Pike, Andrew, *Engineering tenders, sales, and contracts: standard forms and procedures* (London and New York: Sweet & Maxwell, 1982)

Pirrung, J, *Internationales Privat-und Verfahrensrecht nach dem Inkrafttreten der Neuregelung des IPR Texte, Materialien, Hinweise* (1987)

Planiol, Marcel, and Ripert, Georges, *Traité Pratique de Droit Civil Français*, 2nd edn (Paris: Librairie Générale de Droit et de Jurisprudence Picho, 1954) 7 Obligations : 2 partie

Podlech, Adalbert, 'Die juristische Fachsprache und die Umgangssprache' in-Petöfi, Podlech, and Savigny, v, (eds), *Fachsprache – Umgangssprache* (Kronberg/Ts: Scriptor, 1975) 4

Podlech, Albert, 'Die juristische Fachsprache und die Umgangssprache' in Koch, Hans-Joachim (ed), *Juristische Methodenlehre und analytische Philosophie* 1st edn (Kronberg/Ts: Athenäum, 1976)

Quinn, Anthony P, 'The Rome Convention on Contracts – its relevance to arbitration', Arbitration and Dispute Resolution Law Journal 2 (1994) 101

Rivkin, David W, 'Enforceability of Arbitral Awards Based on *Lex Mercatoria*', Arbitration International 91 (1993) 67

Robé, Jean-Philippe, 'Mulitinational Enterprises: The Constitution of a Pluralistic Legal Order', in Teubner, Gunther (ed), *Global Law without a state*, 4 vols, (Brookfield: Dartmouth, 1996) 4, 45

Rose, Alan D, 'The Challenges for Uniform Law in the 21st Century', Uniform Law Review 1 (1996) 9

Rosett, Arthur, 'Unification, Harmonisation, Restatement, Codification and Reform in International Commercial Law' American Journal of Comparative Law 40 (1992) 683

Sacco, Rodolfo, 'Legal Formants: A dynamic approach to comparative law (instalment I of II)', American Journal of Comparative Law 29 (1991) 343

Sacco, Rodolfo, 'Legal Formants: a dynamic approach to comparative law: Instalment II of II', American Journal of Comparative Law 39 (1991) 1

Samuel, A, 'The 1979 Arbitration Act – Judicial Review of Arbitration Awards on the Merits in England', Journal of International Arbitration (1985) 24

Savigny, Carl Friedrich von, *System des heutigen römischen Rechts* (Berlin: Veit, 1840) 1

Savigny, Eike v, 'Inwiefern ist die Umgangssprache grundlegend für die Fachsprache?' in Petöfi, Podlech, and Savigny, v, (eds), *Fachsprache – Umgangssprache* (Kronberg/Ts: Scriptor, 1975) 4

Saville, Chairman Lord Justice, *Report on the Arbitration Bill* Departmental Advisory Commitee (DAC), 1996

Saville, Lord Justice, 'Supplementary Report on the Arbitration Act', Arbitration International 133 (1997) 317

Saxer, Urs W, *Die Zukunft des Nationalstaates, Basler Schriften zur Europäischen Integration*, ed Basel, Europa-Institut an der Universität (Basel: Europa-Institut an der Universität Basel, 1994) 6

Scherrer, *Zur Frage der internationalen Vereinheitlichung des Privatrechts* (Basel: 1939)

Schlechtriem, Peter, 'Termination and Adjustment of Contracts', European Journal of Law Reform 13 (1998/1999) 305

Schmidt, Karsten, *Das HGB und die Gegenwartsaufgaben des Handelsrechts* (1983)

Schmidt, Karsten, *Geldrecht: Geld, Zins und Währung im deutschen Recht*, 12th edn (Berlin: Schweitzer de Gruyter, 1983) XXXIII 563

Schmidt, John M, 'The invalidity of certain choice of law clauses under German Law', Journal of Banking Law (May 1995) 308

Schmidt, Burkhard, '*Zur unberechtigten Kündigung aus wichtigem Grunde beim Werkvertrag*', Neue Juristische Wochenschrift 20 (1995) 1313

Schnell, J, '*Über die Zuständigkeit zum Erlaß von gesetzlichen Vorschriften über die räumliche Herrschaft der Rechtsnormen*', *Niemeyers Zeitschrift für internationales Recht* (1895) 337

Schubert, Werner, '*Die ersten deutschen Übersetzungen des Code Civil/Code Napoléon* (1804-1814)', in Eckert, Jörn, and Hattenhauer, Hans (eds), *Sprache – Recht – Geschichte* (Heidelberg: 1991), 133

Schwenzer, Ingeborg, *Erfüllung und Schadensersatz nach den Unidroit – Prinzipien* (Basel: 1997)

Schwenzer, Ingeborg, 'Specific Performance and Damages According to the 1994 UNIDROIT Principles of International Commercial Contracts', European Journal of Law Reform 1 (1998/1999) 289

Shackleton, Stewart, 'The Applicable Law in International Arbitration Under the New English Arbitration Act 1996', Arbitration International 134 (1997) 375

Shackleton, Stewart, 'Challenging Arbitration Awards – Part III: Appeals on Questions of Law', New Law Journal (6 December 2002) 1834

Shapira, Giora, 'UNCITRAL and its work – harmonisation and unification of international trade law', New Zealand Law Journal (1992) 309

Shaw, Malcolm N, 'The Heritage of States: the Principle of *Uti Possidetis Juris* Today', The British Yearbook of International Law 67 (1996) 75

Solomon, Dennis, '*Das vom Schiedsgericht in der Sache anzuwendende Recht nach dem Entwurf eines Gesetzes zur Neuregelung des Schiedsverfahrensrechts*', RIW 12 (1997) 981

Spellenberg, Ulrich, 'Einleitung', in Rebmann, Kurt (ed), *Münchener Kommentar zum Bürgerlichen Gesetzbuch* (3rd and 4th edns, München: C H Beck, 2003) 1

Steindorff, Ernst, '*Grenzen der EG – Kompetenzen*', *Zeitschrift für das gesamte Handelsrecht und Wirtschaftsrecht, Beiheft Heft* (1990) 65

Stoll, Heinrich, '*Die Lehre von den Leistungsstörungen*', in Ellscheid, Gunther (ed), *Interessenjurisprudenz*, Wege der Forschung (Darmstadt: Wissenschaftliche Buchgesellschaft, 1974) 345, 153

Stolleis, Michael (ed), *Juristen – Ein biographisches Lexikon von der Antike bis zum 20Jh* (Munich: C H Beck, 1995)

Stürner, Rolf, 'Der hundertste Geburtstag des BGB – nationale Kodifikation im Greisenalter?', Juristenzeitung 15/16 (1996) 741

Teichmann, Arndt, '*Empfiehlt sich eine Neukonzeption des Werkvertragsrechts?*', Verhandlungen des 55 Deutschen Juristentages Hamburg 1994 1 Gutachten A (1984), pages A

Teubner, Gunther (ed), *Global Law without a state,* 4 vols (Brookfield: Dartmouth, 1996) 4

Teubner, Gunther, '"Global *Bukowina*": Legal Pluralism in the World Society', in Teubner, Gunther (ed), *Global Law without a state,* 4 vols (Brookfield: Dartmouth, 1996) 4, 3

Teubner, Gunther, 'Legal Irritants: Good Faith in British Law', Modern Law Review 61 (1998) 11

Thomas, Heinz, and Putzo, Hans, *Zivilprozeßordnung*, 25th edn (Munich: C H Beck, 2003)

Treitel, G H, *Doctrine and Discretion in the Law of Contract* (Oxford: Clarendon Press, 1981)

Treitel, G H, *The Law of Contract*, 8th edn (London: 1991)

Treitel, G H, *Frustration and Force majeure* (London: Sweet & Maxwell Ltd, 1994)

UNIDROIT, *Principles of International Commercial Contracts* (Rome: International Institute for the Unification of Private Law (Unidroit), 1994)

Usher, John A, 'Community Law and Private Law', in Müller-Graff, Peter-Christian (ed), *Gemeinsames Privatrecht in der Europäischen Gemeinschaft, Schriftenreihe des Arbeitskreises Europäische Integration* (Baden-Baden: Nomos, 1993) 33, 171

Veeder, VV, '*La nouvelle loi anglaise sur l'arbitrage 1996: la naissance d'un magnifique éléphant*', *Revue de l'Arbitrage* 1 (1997) 124

Veytia, Hernany, 'The requirement of justice and equity in contracts', Tulane Law Review 69 (1995) 1191

Vischer, Frank, 'General Course on Private International Law', *Receuil des Cours* (19)

Vischer, Frank, *Die Relevanz der UNIDROIT Principles für die richterliche und schiedsrichterliche Beurteilung von Streitigkeiten aus internationalen Verträgen* (Basel: Europa Institut Basel, 1997)

Vischer, Frank, 'The Relevance of the UNIDROIT Principles for Judges and Arbitrators in Disputes Arising out of International Contracts', European Journal of Law Reform 13 (1999) 203

Vorpeil, Klaus, '*Neuere Entwicklungen im englischen Handels-und Wirtschaftsrecht*', *Recht der Internationalen Wirtschaft* 3 (1997) 242

Watson, Alan, *Legal Transplants* (1974)

Weinrich, Harald, 'Sprache und Wissenschaft' in Kretzenbacher, Heinz L., and Weinrich, Harald (eds), *Linguistik der Wissenschaftssprache – Forschungsberichte* (Berlin: de Gruyter, 1994) 10

Weyers, Hans-Leo, '*Welche Ergänzungen und Fortentwicklungen sind im Werkvertragsrecht im Hinblick auf die technischen, wirtschaftlichen und juristischen Weiterentwicklungen der Rechtswirklichkeit geboten?*', in Justiz, Bundesminister der (ed), *Gutachten und Vorschläge zur Überarbeitung des Schuldrechts* (Cologne: 1981) II, 1115

Weyers, Hans-Leo (ed), *Europäisches Vertragsrecht* (Baden-Baden: Nomos, 1997) 182

Wichard, Johannes Christian, '*Die Anwendung der UNIDROIT – Prinzipien für internationale Handelsverträge durch Schiedsgerichte und nationale Gerichte*', *Rabels Zeitschrift für ausländisches und internationales Privatrecht* 60 (1996), 269

Wiegand, W, 'The reception of American Law in Europe', American Journal of Comparative Law (1991) 229

Wiegand, Christian, 'Brussels and arbitration prospects – 'pros' and 'cons' of unification of the national procedural laws and arbitration schemes within the European Community', Arbitration 612 (1995) 125

Wiggers, Willem J H, *International Commercial Law – Source Materials* (The Hague: Kluwer Law International, 2001)

Wilhemsson, Thomas, 'The Design of an Optional (Re)Statement of Contract Law – Real Life Instead of Dead Concepts', in Grundmann, Stefan, and Stuyck, Jules (eds), *An Academic Green Paper on European Contract Law*, 2 vols Private Law in European Context Series (The Hague / London / New York: Kluwer Law International, 2002) 2

Williston, Samuel, *Williston on Contracts – A Treatise on the Law of Contracts*, 3d edn (Mount Kisko, NY: 1968) 11

Windscheid, Bernhard, '*Die Lehre von der Voraussetzung*', AcP 78 (1892) 1

Winship, Peter, 'Unification of Law in the United States: an Updated Sketch', Uniform Law Review 6 (1996) 633

Yorio, Edward, *Contract Enforcement, Specific Performance and Injunctions*, (Boston / Toronto / London: 1989)

Ziegler, Uwe, *Die Hanse – Aufstieg, Blütezeit und Niedergang der ersten europäischen Wirtschaftsgemeinschaft*, 1st edn (Bern, Munich, Vienna: Scherz, 1996)

Zimmermann, Reinhard, 'Savigny's Legacy: Legal History, Comparative Law and the Emergence of a European Legal Science', LQR 112 (1996) 576

Zweigert, Konrad (ed), *Europäische Zusammenarbeit im Rechtswesen* (Tübingen: 1955)

Zweigert, Konrad, and Kötz, Hein, *An Introduction to Comparative Law*, 3rd edn (Oxford: Clarendon Press, 1998)